Leadership Perspectives

How To Study the Bible For Leadership Insights

by Dr. J. Robert Clinton
Barnabas Publishers

ISBN   978-1-932814-35-4

© 1993 Dr. J. Robert Clinton

These Handbooks are available from,

Dr. J. Robert Clinton
Barnabas Publishers
2175 N. Holliston Ave
Altadena, CA
91001

INTRODUCTION

The Bible says much about leadership. But who has studied it from a leadership focus? Since the Bible was not written to explain leadership, how do you study it for leadership concepts? The Bible and Leadership Series answers this question.

Before you can study the Bible for leadership you need to know something about *what you are looking for* and *how to find it*. HANDBOOK I, LEADERS, LEADERSHIP, AND THE BIBLE --AN OVERVIEW gives the framework for that. Part I of that handbook gives basic definitions for leader, leadership, a leadership act, an integrating framework for leadership issues, influence means, leadership values, leadership behaviors--task, relationship, and inspiration--and a host of other leadership ideas. In addition, it identifies some Philosophical Leadership Models--Harvest, Shepherd, Stewardship, Intercessor. Part II gives help in how to use these concepts and many more to actually study the Bible. It describes the seven sources of leadership information in the Bible. It gives step by step procedures for studying each of these sources for leadership observations. And it gives samples of studies of each of the source types of leadership literature. It goes even further and shows you how to analyze these observations for leadership lessons and values. It helps you identify levels of applications for your findings: absolutes, guidelines, and suggestions. And hopefully this handbook will not only equip you with the overview framework you need for studying about leadership in the Bible, it will also motivate you to want to do so.

The largest single source of leadership literature in the Bible is biographical. There is much information on Bible leaders from every leadership era in the Bible. From the *Patriarchal Age* there is Job, Abraham, Isaac, Jacob, and Joseph. From the *Pre-Kingdom Era* there is Moses, Miriam, Aaron, Joshua, Caleb and a whole group of Judges including Barak and Deborah, Gideon, Jephthah, Samson and the last judge, Samuel. From the *Kingdom Era* come Saul, David, and Solomon and many more kings as well as numerous prophets. From the *Post-Kingdom Era* come Ezekiel, Daniel, Ezra, Nehemiah, Haggai, Zechariah, and Zerubbabel just to name a few. And then in the *New Testament Pre-Church Era* there is Jesus, John the Baptist and others. And finally there is the *New Testament Church Leadership Era* which contains Peter, John, Barnabas, Phillip, Paul, Luke, Timothy, Titus, Philemon and many others. Since this is the largest single source of leadership information and we are exhorted by the leadership mandate in the New Testament[1] to study them, you would probably expect that much has been done in this area. And it has. There are detailed guidelines on what to look for. I have done more than 700 case studies on leaders--Biblical, Historical, and Contemporary. From these studies has arisen a conceptual framework for observing how God develops leaders over a lifetime. This handbook will give an overview of that framework. And then, too, this handbook will also give numerous examples of findings from the study of important leaders. You will especially be interested in those who finished well and why, as well as those who did not finish well, and why. **HANDBOOK II THEY LIVED BY FAITH** gives some findings which will challenge your own life and get you excited about being a leader in a long line of leaders God has used. And hopefully this handbook will not only equip you with the overview framework for studying Bible leaders, it will also motivate you to do so. And soon you will have an important data base of leadership lessons from your favorite Bible heroes or heroines that you can use effectively in your ministry.

HANDBOOK III. THE BIG PICTURE--LEADERSHIP AND THE BIBLE AS A WHOLE, MACRO STUDIES looks at each book in the Bible as a whole for its contribution to leadership lessons. It first evaluates the book hermeneutically to assess its theme, structure, and purposes. It then goes on to point out the contribution of the book to the Redemptive Drama as well as the leadership era to which it belongs. It lists leadership lessons from the book and gives suggestions for further study. Finally, it begins to analyze common lessons across the Bible books. It is a handbook which synthesizes across the Bible with its many incidents of leadership source materials. You will get excited about learning and teaching the Bible from a macro standpoint--the broader perspective.

---

[1] Hebrews 13:7,8 exhort us to study leaders and identify what made their leadership effective and pleasing to God. Next we can expect Jesus to work those same kinds of values and enablement in our own lives. In leadership emergence theory this is called the leadership mandate.

Table of Contents

Page	Topic
3	Introduction
4	Table of Contents
7	Preface
15	**PART I. Basic Leadership Concepts**
15	**Chapter 1 Basic Definitions**
16	Integrative Framework--Tree Diagram of 3 Leadership Elements
17	Table of Components of Leadership Elements
18	Feedback on Three Elements of Leadership

<u>Core Concepts--Leadership Basal Elements</u>

Page	Topic
19	Leadership Act
20	Feedback
21	Leader
22	Feedback
23	Commentary on Leader
25	Leadership
26	Feedback
27	Leadership Functions
29	Feedback
30	Commentary on Leadership Functions
31	Leadership Continua
32	Example: 5 Types of Church Leaders
34	Feedback
36	Commentary on 5 Types of Leaders
38	Followership
40	10 Commandments of Followership

<u>Core Concepts--Leadership Influence Means</u>

Page	Topic
41	Individual Influence Means--Leadership Styles
42	Leadership Style Continuum
43	Leadership Style--Clinton Definition
44	Variations of Leadership Style Definitions
45	4 Major Factors Affecting Your Leadership Style
46	10 Pauline Leadership Styles

Page	Topic
54	Adapted Tree Diagram for Influence, Power, Authority
55	Power Definitions: Power Base and Authority
56	Power Forms
58	Spiritual Authority
59	10 Commandments of Spiritual Authority
60	6 Characteristics and Limits of Spiritual Authority
61	Feedback on Authority/Power Definitions

Core Concepts--Leadership Value Bases

62	Leadership Value
63	Specificity Continuum
64	Value Certainty Continuum
65	Commentary on Leadership Values
66	Examples: Pauline Leadership Values Abstracted
68	For Further Study

Table of Contents continued

Page	Topic

Chapter 2 Models and Miscellaneous Concepts

Philosophical Leadership Models

Page	Topic
70	5 Biblical Leadership Models
71	Stewardship Model
73	Feedback
74	Servant Leader Model
76	Feedback
77	Shepherd Leader Model
79	Feedback
80	Harvest Model
82	Feedback
83	Leader As Intercessor Model
85	Feedback

Miscellaneous Leadership Concepts

Page	Topic
86	5 Kinds of Finishes
89	6 Characteristics of Those Finishing Well
90	Pivotal Points
91	3 Categories of Pivotal Points
92	6 Observations on Pivotal Points
93	6 Barriers To Finishing Well
94	5 Enhancements To Finishing Well
95	Commentary: Enhancements
99	Feedback on Finishing Well and Related Concepts
100	Leadership Transition Concepts
103	Leadership Transitions in the Bible
104	10 Steps in Moses/ Joshua Transition
107	Commentary: On Moses/ Joshua Transition
108	Regime Turnover
111	Feedback
112	7 Major Leadership Lessons
113	Feedback
114	Brokenness
116	Commentary on Brokenness
117	The Ultimate Contribution
118	12 Prime Types of Ultimate Contribution
122	Commentary on Ultimate Contribution
124	Feedback

Table of Contents continued

Page	Topic
125	Paradigm Shifts
126	Commentary on Paradigm Shifts
127	10 Biblical Examples of Paradigm Shifts
129	3 Categories of Paradigm Shifts
130	Commentary On Kinds of Paradigm Shifts
131	Feedback
132	Future Perfect
133	5 stages Leading to the Future Perfect Paradigm
134	Feedback

<u>Ethnotheological Perspectives For Viewing Bible</u>

135	5 Ethnotheological Models
136	Model 1. The Bible-As-Yardstick
137	Model 2. Bible Allowing a Range of Variation
138	Range of Variation
139	Range Variants
140	Model 3. The Bible-As-Tether Model
141	Model 4. The Bible-as-Inspired-Casebook
142	Starting Point Plus Process Model

<u>Miscellaneous Models</u>

143	Movement
144	Feedback
145	5 Factors for a Successful Movement
146	Feedback
147	Sower's 5 Stage Bridging Model
148	Feedback
149	For Further Study

Chapter 3 Leadership Emergence Theory

151	Introduction
152	Article--Overview of Life Long Development
159	Table 1. 12 Common Process Items
162	Spiritual Formation
163	Ministerial Formation
164	Strategic Formation
165	Feedback
166	The Ministry Time-Line and Formations
167	Integrity Check
168	Feedback
169	Obedience Check
170	Feedback
171	Word Check
172	Feedback
173	Commentary: Early Character Shaping Process Items
176	Giftedness Discovery
177	Feedback
179	Giftedness Time-Line/ Example
180	Commentary on Giftedness Development
182	Ministry Conflict Process Item
183	Feedback
185	Destiny Pattern
187	Negative and Positive Testing Patterns
188	Feedback
189	Foundational Ministry Pattern
190	For Further Study

PART II. Studying The Bible For Leadership Lessons

Page	Topic
	Chapter 4 The Bible and Leadership
191	Review
	<u>Leadership in the Bible</u>
192	Time-Line of Biblical Leaders/ Essential Characteristics/ Macro-Lesson Labels
193	Time-Line of Biblical Leaders/ details
	<u>Leadership Source Materials in the Bible</u>
194	Overview--7 Kinds of Source Materials
195	1. Biographical
196	Biblical Leaders To Study
197	12 Steps For Studying Bible Leaders
201	Presentation Format--Findings on Bible Leaders
203	Typical Example--Gideon
210	Abbreviated Presentation Format
211	2. Leadership Act--Defined
212	How To Study A Leadership Act
213	Old Testament Example: Samuel's Final Leadership Act
222	3. Contextual Leadership Passage
223	New Testament Example
228	4. Parabolic Leadership Literature
229	How To Study Parabolic Literature Leadership
230	Parabolic Study Sheets
232	Example Parable--Matthew 25:14-30
236	5. Indirect
238	6. Books as a Whole
239	Example: Jude
242	7. How To Study Across Books in the Bible
243	Listing of Source Materials Identified Thus Far
248	Further Study

Table of Contents continued

Page	Topic
	Chapter 5 Principles of Truth--How To Get Them
249	Review
250	Some Presuppositions
253	Applicational Continuum
254	Applicational Levels of Truth
255	Commentary On Application of Truth
256	7 Kinds of Sources of Truth
258	Principles
259	The Certainty Continuum
260	Certainty Continuum Definitions
261	6 Assumptions Underlying Derivation of Principles
263	Background For Applicability Screen for Bible Passages
264	Certainty Screen for Bible Passages
265	Applicability Screen: Factors/ Appropriate Levels
266	4 Suggestions on Getting The Actual Principle
267	Example of Using Applicability Screen for A Leadership Act
269	Applicability Screen: Non-Biblical Sources of Truth
271	Examples from Biographical Studies
272	Examples from Contextual Leadership Passages
273	Examples from Parabolic
274	Examples from Indirect--Proverbs
275	Examples from Book as a Whole--Macro-Lessons, 2 Timothy
278	Examples from Across Books, The Bible As A Whole-- Macro-Lessons
280	For Further Study
281	**Chapter 6 Where To Now?**
289	Appendix A. List of Process Items
295	Appendix B. List of Patterns
299	Appendix C. List of Macro-Lessons
303	Bibliography

(This page deliberately left blank.)

Preface

Christian leaders need to know their Bibles and to center their lives and ministry around its teaching. But few know the Bible well. Still fewer have studied the Bible seriously with a view to learning what it can teach about leadership.

My own studies of the Bible concerning leadership have led me to identify the following approaches or kinds of Bible literature (genre) which prove useful for leadership information. Recognizing the different sources of leadership information is a first step. Getting tools to study each type is a second. The Handbook series of which this Handbook is one, gives these tools and some findings from each of these kinds of Bible genre.

1. Biographical: Joseph, Moses, Joshua, Caleb, Jephthah, etc.
2. Historical Leadership Acts: Samuel's final leadership act 1 Samuel 12.
3. Actual leadership contexts: e.g. 1 Peter 5:1-5
4. Parabolic leadership literature: e.g. Stewardship parables
5. Indirect--passages dealing with Christian character or behavior which also apply to Christian leadership as well (many of the Proverbs fall into this category; Sermon on the Mount, etc.)
6. Study of Bible books as a whole: placing them in their context-- hermeneutically and in terms of leadership development.
7. The Study across Books for common themes and lessons on leadership.

Part I of the Handbook gives the frameworks which have stimulated me to see leadership concepts in the Scriptures. My last 12 years of research have led me to study secular leadership theory. My grounded theory research on leader's lives led me to study Biblical characters as well as contemporary and historical. All of this research has led me see the Bible with new eyes. And of course when studying the Bible information from the Bible has confirmed my secular theory or clarified it or informed it or corrected it. So there has been a synergistic effect. Secular theory has helped me see more in the Bible and the Bible has helped me see more about leadership theory.

Paul's promise has taken on new meaning to me.

All Scripture is inspired by God and is profitable for doctrine, reproof, correction, instruction in righteousness that the person of God might be fully equipped. 2 Timothy 3:16,17

A major goal for me is to finish well and to help other leaders to finish well. The Bible, if central to our lives and ministry, can inform our leadership. We can avoid barriers that have caused others to fall. We can pick up on enhancements that have helped leaders persevere. All it takes is some know how and a commitment. I can help give you the know how through the three handbooks of the Bible and Leadership Series. But only you can provide the commitment. How about it? Is finishing well important to you? Are you willing to commit yourself to studying the Bible for leadership insights?

CHAPTER 1. GETTING LEADERSHIP EYES

Introduction When I first studied church growth theory with Dr. C. Peter Wagner he stressed our need for *church growth eyes*. He wanted us to see what was happening in our church situations through church growth perspectives. We needed to learn church growth language and use those labels to describe what we saw. We did too. We talked about transfer, conversion and biological growth. We knew the difference between expansion and extension growth. We learned how to compute decadal church growth rates of all kinds. E1, E2, and E3 became familiar. We saw target groups in terms of the resistance/ receptivity axis. Because we had labels to describe what we saw, we actually saw more. Knowing church growth theory with its many unique neologisms created an anticipation for what we would see.

And that's what you need--leadership concepts that will help stimulate you to see leadership issues in the Scriptures. When you go to the Scriptures you should expect to identify different types of leaders. You'll see leadership acts. You identify various leadership styles in those acts. You'll draw out values, lessons, and principles. You will always be conscious of leadership source materials. In short, you will, **IF YOU GET LEADERSHIP EYES**. Chapter 1 will help put those leadership glasses on.

This chapter introduces you to the definitions and concepts for stimulating discovery of leadership ideas in the Bible. The *integrating framework* includes the leadership basal elements (leaders, followers, and situations), leadership influence means (individual influence, corporate influence), and leadership value bases (cultural and theological)..

Basic definitions flowing from this leadership framework follow in an information mapped form. That format puts information into *blocks integrated around a focus*, called a *map*. Read as little or as much of a given *map* as needed to learn the major concept (map title). Usually two or three pages are dedicated to one map which focuses on one definition. Feedback sections force a learning response. Commentaries follow and suggest implications, importance, related reflections and further study.

TREE DIAGRAM OF 3 LEADERSHIP ELEMENTS

introduction   Leadership anywhere in the world is concerned with some basic common issues. These can be grouped and organized under three major categories. The *first category* concerns the basal elements of leadership which occur wherever leadership exists: the leader, the followers, and the situational context affecting both leader and followers. The *second category* involves the ways and means whereby a leader actually influences the followers. This second category includes the leader behavior and means/resources. The *third category*, leadership value bases, is often implicit and not expressed openly. It refers to the underlying purpose, motivation, ethics and philosophy governing the leadership basal elements and the leadership influence means. These 3 major categories are relatively generic and can be used as a framework for leadership analysis in various cultures. Sub-categories under these major categories are less cross-culturally valid directly but most likely have dynamic equivalent forms/functions in various cultures.

THE STUDY OF LEADERSHIP
involves

LEADERSHIP BASAL ELEMENTS including	LEADERSHIP INFLUENCE MEANS such as	LEADERSHIP VALUE BASES including
• LEADER • FOLLOWERS • SITUATION	• INDIVIDUAL MEANS • CORPORATE MEANS	• CULTURAL • THEOLOGICAL

TABLE OF COMPONENTS OF LEADERSHIP ELEMENTS

introduction — The table below shows the detailed factors used to delineate or study the major elements of leadership. It is these factors which integrate what leadership is about. They suggest issues to look for when studying Biblical material.

BASAL ELEMENT	COMPONENT	EXPLANATION
LEADER	leader life history	Biographical studies/ lessons learned, values,
	leader traits	Identity of traits which signal leadership in a given cultural situation with its specific followership
FOLLOWER	followership	Leader-follower relations follower history follower maturity
SITUATION	immediate context	local pressures affecting leader/ follower dynamics
	macro-context	larger regional/ national or international factors affecting leadership dynamics

INFLUENCE MEANS	COMPONENT	EXPLANATION
INDIVIDUAL MEANS	leadership style	task oriented style relationship oriented style inspirational style
CORPORATE MEANS	organizational	culture structures power dynamics
	cultural	group orientation power

VALUE BASES	COMPONENT	EXPLANATION
CULTURAL	standards	ethics evaluation motivation
THEOLOGICAL	standards	Biblical values ultimate purpose

FEEDBACK ON 3 ELEMENTS OF LEADERSHIP

1. If the leadership basal elements answers the "what" of leadership, that is, *What are the essential elements of leadership?* and leadership influence means answers the "how" of leadership, that is, *How do leaders accomplish leadership?* Then what question(s) do the leadership value bases answer?

2. The balanced analytical framework can be used to analyze any specific leadership act (or a series of them). Each of the major items or sub-categories can be used as a screen through which to view the leadership act. Suggested exercises include analysis of the last public act of Samuel's leadership and/or the Jerusalem counsel deliberations of Acts 15 from the standpoint of Barnabas' leadership.

ANSWERS----------

1. The "leadership value bases" answers the "why" of leadership. Why does leadership exist? And what are the standards by which leadership is judged?
2. I'll leave this exercise to you. But if you have access to the Fuller School of World Mission campus then these two acts and many others have been evaluated using this framework and are worth one's reading in order to see these concepts fleshed out in terms of specific situations.

LEADERSHIP ACT   synonym: group influence

introduction   A leadership act occurs when a given person influences a group, in terms of behavioral acts or perception, so that the group acts or thinks differently as a group than before the instance of influence. Such an act can be evaluated in terms of the three major leadership categories: 1) leadership basal elements, 2) leadership influence means and 3) leadership value bases. It should be noted that any given act of leadership may have several persons of the group involved in bringing about the influence. While the process may be complex and difficult to assess, nevertheless, leadership can be seen to happen and be composed essentially of **influencer, group, influence means**, and **resulting change of direction** by the group--the four major parts of a leadership act.

definition   A leadership act is the specific instance at a given point in time of the leadership influence process between a given influencer (person said to be influencing) and follower(s) (person or persons being influenced) in which the followers are influenced toward some goal.

example   Barnabas, Acts 9:26-30; Acts 11:22-24; Acts 11:25-26

example   Agabus, Acts 11:27-28

example   leaders, whole church: Acts 11:29-30

example   Paul, Barnabas, apostles and elders in Jerusalem, Peter, James: Acts 15:1-21

comment   One can differentiate between a momentary instance of leadership which I call a leadership act, as defined above, and leadership as an ongoing process which I call leadership. The momentary leadership act recognizes the reciprocal nature of leadership (that is, the impact of gifts that all have) for any group in a given situation. The repeated persistence of leadership acts by a given person indicates the permanence of a leader in and specifies leadership.

comment   A major difference in one who influences momentarily in a group and one who persistently influences over time is the emergence of vision and sense of responsibility for seeing that vision fulfilled.

FEEDBACK EXERCISES ON LEADERSHIP ACT

1. Examine the leadership act given in Acts 9:26-30. Identify the four major parts of the leadership act.

    a. leader--

    b. followers--

    c. influence means-

    d. the influence goal (resulting change)--

2. For the leadership act in Acts 9:26-30, was the leader successful? If not, why not? If so, why do you think the leader was successful?

3. Describe a recent leadership act you have observed in connection with some ministry you are involved in. Describe,

    a. leader--

    b. followers--

    c. influence means--

    d. results--

ANSWERS----------
1. a. leader--Barnabas b. followers--apostles in Jerusalem, unnamed but most likely including Peter, James, John et al. c. influence means--persuasion backed by credibility. d. the goal was to have Saul recognized as a legitimate Christian and to have him accepted by the apostles.
2. In my opinion, yes. Verse 28 describing Saul's staying in Jerusalem and his ministry there indicates that Barnabas was successful.
3. Your choice. In doing this exercise you will probably note that leadership acts in life are generally much more complex than the biblical example given above (that one was probably complex but we only have a selected summary of it). For one thing, there is usually multiple influence going on in the group. That is, it may not be easy to identify only one leader. For another thing influence goals are not always straightforward or understood by leaders and followers. Sometimes there are differing groups of followers within the same leadership act.

LEADER

introduction	One who persists in leadership acts is a leader. Such an influencer is said to demonstrate leadership. From a study of many leaders in both the Old and New Testaments the following perspectives synthesize a biblical leader.

definition	A <u>leader</u>, as defined from a study of Biblical leadership, and for whom we are interested in tracing leadership development is a person,
	    1) with God-given *capacity* AND
	    2) with God-given *responsibility*
	  WHO IS INFLUENCING
	    3) a *specific group* of God's people
	    4) toward *God's purposes* for the group.

Biblical	Joseph, Moses, Joshua, Jephthah, Samuel, David, Daniel, Paul, Peter, Barnabas, Timothy, Titus
historical	William Carey, J. Hudson Taylor, Cameron Townsend, Charles Simeon, Henrietta Mears, Phineas Bresee, Simon Kimbangi, Livingston Sohn, John Sung, Samuel Mills
central ethic	The central ethic of Biblical leadership is, **INFLUENCING TOWARD GOD'S PURPOSES**. That is, the prime function of leadership is the influencing of groups so as to accomplish God's purposes involving the group. This requires *vision*. This *external direction* is what distinguishes a Christian leader from a secular leader.
comment	The "God-given capacity" denotes giftedness capacity (spiritual gift or natural talent or acquired skill). This capacity is part of the influence means. It also connotes leadership character, as well as potential that to be developed.
comment	The "God-given responsibility" denotes two major ideas: 1) a downward sense of responsibility (a burden from God) to influence others for God. 2) an upward sense of responsibility (accountability to God) for the people being influenced.
comment	Leadership is concerned with the persistent specific influence of a group. It is these followers for which the leader will be responsible and will discern God's purposes.

FEEDBACK ON LEADER

1. Give Biblical evidence for the four points in the definition of leader.

2. Choose any leader mentioned in the examples (or any other--your choice) and illustrate how each of the points in the leadership definition is fulfilled.

3. Explain how you personally interpret the concept of "God-given capacity" to influence?

ANSWERS----------

1. You probably have other answers than those I've hastily jotted down. Concept 1: see Ephesians 4:7-11, and passages on spiritual gifts of ruling, administration, apostleship, and pastoring. Concept 2: see Acts 20:28, Hebrews 13:17. Concept 3: see Acts 20:28, I Peter 5:2. Concept 4: see Acts 20:17-38. The whole passage is Paul's example of this very concept; his letters to churches illustrate this.

2. Maranville (1982) studied Samuel Mills. He was gifted to foster mission organizations. He had an amazing ability to organize, administer, and motivate others to take over the organizations. His influenced mission activity in the United States in the early 1800s. He demonstrated the spiritual gifts of apostleship, administration and faith. Mills' whole lifetime effort seems to indicate that God gave him a national responsibility to motivate North American Christians toward involvement in missions. The groups of people for whom he was responsible (indirectly) were those people already involved in churches but not in missions--which was the majority of Christians in North America. In terms of God's purposes, time and time again Mills saw the need for an organization or a movement which would recruit and activate God's people into missions' involvement. He was able to sense God's timing in events and happenings and develop plans and organizations based on what he saw.

3. I interpret the phrase "God-given capacity to influence" to mean that the person is born with natural abilities for leadership as well as potential to acquire skills that will enable influence. Spiritual gifts important for influencing have also been imparted. Spiritual leadership gifts (that is, those gifts related to influencing) to include what I call the word gifts. Primary word gifts include: teaching, prophecy, exhortation, Secondary word gifts include: apostleship, evangelism and pastoring (and ruling). Tertiary word gifts include word of wisdom and word of knowledge and faith.

COMMENTARY ON LEADER

position or influence
: Frequently missionaries and nationals and particularly women coming to the School of World Mission identify a leader as a person having a formal position of leadership. Notice that the focus of this definition is not on status or position but on functionality. That is, a leader is one who influences others. It is true that there are leaders who are influencing people toward God's purposes who may not have formal positions. It is also true that there are people holding formal positions who are not really functioning as leaders. One can exercise leadership even in situations where structures prohibit them from having formal positions.

women in leadership
: Frequently, women do not think of themselves as leaders. This can occur primarily for two reasons. One, some Christian leaders have convictions against women in leadership and teach against it. Some women who have sat under this kind of teaching find it difficult to freely see themselves as leaders. Two, many women come from male dominated cultures in which formal leadership structures are open only to males. My own conviction allows for women who are gifted and developed by God for leadership to lead; the same for men. My definition of a leader can apply broadly to those who hold my conviction or not--since it is an influence based definition, not a formal/positional one. Sometimes women who study leadership emergence theory go through a paradigm shift[1] in which they move from viewing themselves as not being leaders to being leaders. The real problem, once one admits that God has gifted one to lead, is how to exercise that leadership in terms of the cultural structures and roles available.

ordination and leadership
: My own convictions have led me to believe that ordination is not required in order to exercise leadership. It may be important for civil or government recognition or other purposes. Ordination requirements vary greatly from group to group and are largely traditionally based. See Warkenton

---

[1] A paradigm shift is a radical change in one's mental perspectives. In this case, the women students perceive that their past experience has indeed been filled with repetitive incidents of influence even if they have not held formal positions. An analysis of their giftedness confirms that they are gifted for leadership.

COMMENTARY ON LEADER continued

(1982) on this. What this often means is that women are excluded from ordination due to male biased tradition. I advise sometimes for ordination, or sometimes against it, depending on the situation of a given leader. Regardless of gender, ordination usually encourages a problem of dichotomy between clergy and laity and thus discourages lay leadership.

elements of emergence

Though potential leaders are born, effective leaders are made as a result of, 1) opportunity, 2) training and 3) experience. These three components do not automatically guarantee that one will rise to become a great leader. But without them it is not likely that one will realize maximum potential.

essential difference of leaders and followers

Both leaders and followers actually influence in church and para-church situations. When Christians use their gifts with others, these impact so as to influence. In small groups, the sharing of both leaders and followers will influence. There is a mutuality of leadership. Sometimes followers exert influence spontaneously to a group. Le Peau (1983) stresses that anyone can lead. He describes paths along which anyone can develop as a leader. My understanding of leaders and leadership disagrees somewhat with his approach. I do allow for anyone to lead (that is, exert influence) in the sense of a leadership act. But I strongly assert that this is different from on-going leadership. When I think of a leader I am thinking of permanency, a continuing on-going influence that can build toward accomplishment of vision (a la Ephesians 4:7ff, Christ's gifts to the church for leadership). I am talking about people who have a sense, inherent or instilled, of responsibility to carry out some aspect of God's work and to give an account to God for others. This sense of vertical accountability differentiates *casual leadership* from permanent *on-going leadership*. Those who do not have this sense of accountability are basically followers.

calling and leadership

Leaders need a strong sense of destiny. A call is one indication of that but not the only one. Even without a supernatural call the stewardship model can provide a pseudo-call to those who follow its implications. The model, itself, is enough to give one a sense of destiny toward leadership. If God has given capacity then inherent in it is the destiny to use it.

LEADERSHIP

introduction	Leadership is essentially the ongoing persistence of leadership acts by one person. One who consistently exerts influence over a group is said to manifest leadership. Leadership is then seen to be an ongoing process involving several complex items. This definition flows from a research project in which I studied the development of leadership theory from 1841 till 1986.
definition	<u>Leadership</u> is a dynamic process over an extended period of time in various situations in which a leader utilizing leadership resources, and by specific leadership behaviors, influences followers, toward accomplishment of aims mutually beneficial for leaders and followers.
example	Barnabas' leadership: Acts 4:32-36; 9:26-30; 11:22-24; 11:25-26; 15:1-21. Here Barnabas is seen to exercise influence in various situations over a long period of time. He used various resource means to accomplish this influence.
example	Paul's leadership (a few leadership acts cited): Acts 11:25,26; 13:9-12; 13:13-43; 13:44-48; 14:21-23; 20:17-38.
comment	The major items in the leadership process include: 1. It is a dynamic process over an extended period of time. 2. It is exercised in various situations. 3. It is identified with a leader, one who persists in exercising influence. 4. It involves the use of leadership resources which include various power bases for influencing. 5. It is seen overtly in leadership behaviors which contribute to the influence process. 6. Its nature is seen as motivating followers so that the group responds differently than would be the case otherwise. 7. It is seen as purposeful (directive). It moves followers, toward accomplishment of aims originating with the leader, the followers, or some combination of both. 8. Ideally, it results in mutual benefit for the leader, the followers, and the situation of which they are a part.
comment	Point eight is an ideal not always seen in secular leadership.

FEEDBACK ON LEADERSHIP

1. I have stated in the examples that Barnabas exercised leadership. See leadership acts: Acts 4:32-36, 9:26-30, 11:22-24, 11:25-26, 15:1-21. Do you agree? Quickly scan the biblical passages. How many of the major items of the leadership process are seen in these leadership acts examined as a whole? Check the leadership elements which you feel can be seen.
   ___ a. It is a dynamic process over an extended period of time.
   ___ b. It is exercised in various situations.
   ___ c. It is identified with a leader persisting in exercising influence.
   ___ d. It involves the use of leadership resources and various power bases.
   ___ e. It is seen overtly in leadership behaviors that influence.
   ___ f. Its nature is seen as changing the followers thoughts and/or behavior so that the groups respond differently than otherwise.
   ___ g. It is seen as purposeful (directive).
   ___ h. It results in mutual benefit.

2. Take any two of the leadership elements you checked above and explain them. That is, show what you saw in scripture that prompted you to select the leadership element as being present.

3. If you were to examine an autocratic leader, Hitler, in terms of his leadership acts which of the following leadership elements most likely would not be demonstrated.
   ___ a. His leadership was demonstrated in various situations.
   ___ b. He used various power bases for influencing.
   ___ c. One tremendously effective overt behaviors was public oratory.
   ___ d. His leadership was purposeful (directive) and affected the thoughts and activity of followers, toward accomplishment of his own aims.
   ___ e. It resulted in mutual benefit for the leader, the followers, and the macro context.

ANSWERS----------
1. I checked all of them. "g" is least easiest to demonstrate.
2. I'll explain what I saw concerning (e) and (h). Barnabas used persuasive oratory to convince apostles to accept Saul in Acts 9:26-30. He used modeling as well as oratory to influence behavior in Acts 11:22-24. Barnabas' influence resulted in Paul being accepted as a Christian leader which significantly altered the course of history. His ministry at Antioch provided the base for cross-cultural missionary effort which began the worldwide expansion of the Gospel.
3. e. My opinion of course.

LEADERSHIP FUNCTIONS

introduction	High level Christian leaders perform many leadership functions. In addition to direct ministry functions based on giftedness there are those additional functions that characterize leaders simply because they are people responsible for others. The inspirational functions are part of this added responsibility. The Ohio State model showed that most leadership functions can be grouped under two major functions: consideration functions; initiation of structure functions. In addition to these there are the inspirational functions which flow from word gifted leadership. Note that direct ministry functions flowing from giftedness of the leader, can occur in any of the major categories.
description	<u>Leadership functions</u> describe general activities that leaders must do and/or be responsible for in their influence responsibilities with followers.
comment	The Ohio State Leadership Research paradigm (1948-Ohio State 1967) reduced the many observed functions of secular leadership by factor analysis to two major generic categories: consideration and initiation of structure.
comment	*Consideration* is the Ohio State term which groups all of those activities which a leader does to affirm followers, to provide an atmosphere congenial to accomplishing work, to give emotional and spiritual support for followers so that they can mature, in short, to act relationally with followers in order to enable them to develop and be effective in their contribution to the organization.
comment	*Initiation of structure* is the Ohio State term which groups all of those activities which a leader does to accomplish the task or vision for which the structure exists. Task behaviors involve clarifying goals, setting up structures to help reach them, holding people accountable, disciplining where necessary and in short, to act responsibly to accomplish goals.
comment	Christian leadership is *externally directed*. That is, goals result from vision from God. Such leadership must move followers toward recognition of, acceptance of and participation in bringing about that God-given vision.

LEADERSHIP FUNCTIONS continued

<u>Consideration Functions</u> (toward relationship behaviors)

Christian leaders,
1. must be involved in selection, development and release of emerging leaders.
2. are called upon to solve crises involving relationships between people.
3. will be called upon for decision making focusing on people.
4. must do routine problem solving related to people issues.
5. will coordinate with subordinates, peers, and superiors.
6. must facilitate leadership transition; their own and others.
7. must do direct ministry relating to people (extent depends on giftedness).

<u>Initiation of Structure Functions</u> (task behaviors)

Christian leaders,
1. must provide structures which facilitate accomplishment of vision.
2. will be involved in crisis resolution related to structural issues.
3. must make decisions involving structures.
4. will do routine problem solving concerning structural issues.
5. will adjust structures where necessary to facilitate leadership transitions.
6. must do direct ministry relating to maintaining and changing structures (extent depends on giftedness).

<u>Inspirational Functions</u> (motivating toward vision)

Christian leaders,
1. must motivate followers toward vision.
2. must encourage perseverance and faith of followers.
3. are responsible for the corporate integrity of the structures and organizations of which they are a part.
4. are responsible for developing and maintaining the welfare of the corporate culture of the organization.
5. (especially higher level) are responsible for promoting the public image of the organization.
6. (especially higher level) are responsible for the financial welfare of the organization.
7. are responsible for direct ministry along lines of giftedness which relate to inspirational functions.
8. must model (knowing, being, and doing) so as to inspire followers toward the reality of God's intervention in lives.
9. have corporate accountability to God for the organizations or structures in which they operate.

FEEDBACK ON LEADERSHIP FUNCTIONS

1. The two Ohio State behavioral functions of consideration and initiation of structure are commonly referred to by me as relational behavior and task behavior. The Ohio State findings indicated that the two were independent of each other. A given leader could operate freely in both functional areas. Fiedler (1967) and others generally disagreed and posited that leaders usually are "bent" toward one or the other as dominant in their leadership. What has been your experience? Are leaders in your culture generally task oriented or relationally oriented or some combination? Explain.

2. Give here the name of a leader that you have known who is highly task oriented. Give also an example of a task which has driven this leader.
    a. leader--   b. cultural origin--
    c. culture ministering in-- d. illustration of task--

3. Give here the name of a leader that you have known who is relationally oriented. Give an example of relational behavior from that leader's ministry.
    a. leader--   b. cultural origin--
    c. culture ministering in-- d. illustration of relational behavior--

4. Give here the name of a leader that you have known who operates well in the inspirational functions. Give a specific inspirational function.
    a. leader--   b. cultural origin--
    c. culture ministering in-- d. illustration of inspirational function--

5. Do this exercise after you have studied the 5 Types of Leaders. Consider the total list of functions under the three categories. Beside each function place each type of leader (A,B,C,D,E) if you think that type of leader is heavily responsible for that leadership function.

ANSWERS----------
1. In my culture I have experienced a mix of both although task behavior seems to be more valued and espoused by leadership in general. In the West Indies I found the reverse was more generally true. In either case leaders were not usually both task and relational--one usually dominated to the detriment of the other.
2. your choice. 3. your choice. 4. your choice.
5. The point of this exercise is to see that Types A and B are dominantly involved in direct ministry functions. Type C is usually involved in both depending on the size of organization involved in. Type D and Type E will be concerned more with indirect functions.

COMMENTARY ON LEADERSHIP FUNCTIONS

essentials — There are common activities and unique activities for the three categories of leadership functions. A single list helps pinpoint the essential activities of Christian leaders.

1. Utilize giftedness for direct ministry to those in their sphere of influence.
2. Solve crises.
3. Make decisions.
4. Do routine problem solving.
5. Coordinate people, goals, and structures.
6. Select and develop leaders.
7. Facilitate leadership transition at all levels.
8. Facilitate structures to accomplish vision.
9. Motivate followers toward vision. This usually involves changing what is, and providing/ promoting a sense of progress.
10. Must encourage perseverance and faith of followers. This usually involves maintaining what is and creating a sense of stability. This is usually in dynamic tension with activity 9.
11. Accept responsibility for corporate functions of integrity, culture, finances, and accountability.
12. Must model so as to inspire followers toward the reality of God's intervention in lives and history.

direct versus indirect — Direct ministry involves ministry which produces growth such as evangelism (quantitative growth) or teaching (qualitative growth). Use of word gifts (apostleship, prophesy, evangelism, pastoring, teaching, exhortation) are identified primarily as direct ministry. Indirect ministry involves activities which enable direct ministry to happen. Most of the activities on the condensed list above involve both direct and indirect ministry. But the larger majority are dominantly indirect. As leaders advance in sphere of influence they increasingly are involved in more indirect ministry. They must embrace it as primary because of their understanding of capacity entrusted them. The enabling of others to do direct ministry is the thrust of indirect ministry. This means creating and keeping organizations healthy. On the typology continuum the move from Type B to C involves a shift toward indirect ministry. The shift from C to D is a major shift toward indirect ministry. Processing which develops a leader for these shifts focuses on the first two elements of the leader definition--capacity and responsibility.

LEADERSHIP CONTINUA: 5 TYPES OF LEADERS

introduction It is helpful to differentiate leaders in terms of some criteria. Several can be constructed. One typical example is the following which looks at Christian leadership in a church or denomination. It could be modified to fit parachurch leaders. The primary criterion involves sphere of influence. This spread of leaders along a continuum is helps identify differences in sub-categories of the three basic leadership categories--leadership basal elements, leadership influence means, and leadership value bases--which frequently vary depending on the sphere of influence of the leader. Important characteristics highlighted in this spread include financial base and direct versus indirect ministry.

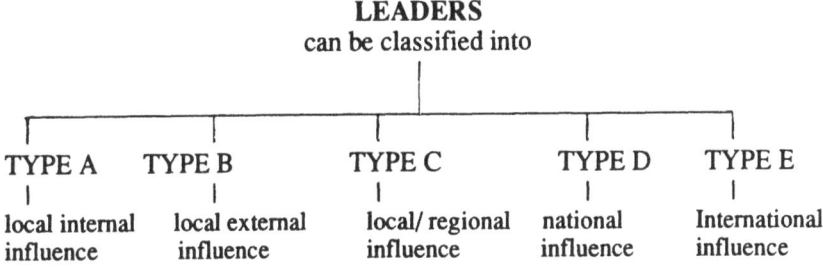

WHICH IS FURTHER DELIMITED LAY/CLERGY CONTINUUM

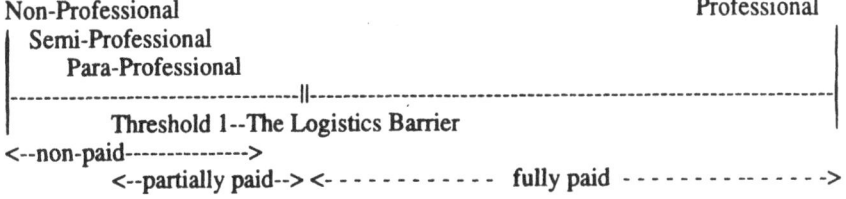

AND IS FURTHER DELIMITED BY THE MINISTRY FOCUS CONTINUUM

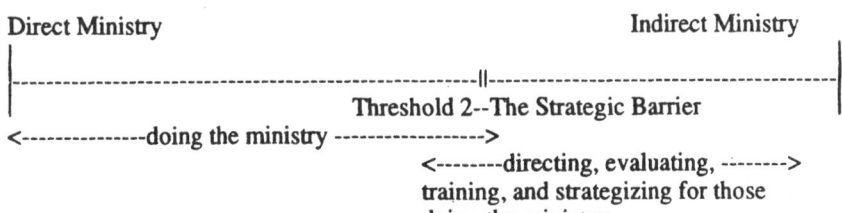

EXAMPLES OF 5 TYPES OF LEADERS

introduction	Below are given examples of the five types of leaders.
examples Type A	Sunday School workers in local church, home group leaders, youth workers.
comment	Type A leaders primarily work with small groups within a local church. Their basic ministry thrust is edification and service within the local body. They are para-professional Christians in that they see their main contribution in life as ministry to the church. Their vocation supports this purpose.
examples Type B	visitation workers, bi-vocational pastor, part-time evangelist, part-time pastor, pastor shared between two small congregations, evangelist/church planting paid worker
comment	Type B leaders can work both within the local church and beyond it. Their basic ministry thrust goes beyond edification to evangelism and other outreach ministries beyond the confines of the local church. The sphere of influence is beyond small groups but usually limited to small churches. They are para-professional Christian workers in that they see their main contribution in life as ministry to the church. Their vocation supports this purpose.
example Type C	full-time paid pastor, youth worker, evangelist, other staff workers in a larger local church.
comment	Type C leaders usually are senior pastors of large churches or those on staff who have large spheres of influence. Usually Type C leaders will have external influence upon other churches or pastors of churches. These are professional Christian workers who are paid to do Christian ministry. Usually these workers will meet ordination requirements and will be recognized by the government as ministers with legal status as such.
examples Type D	Heads of small mission organizations working in a region or country, denominational workers with regional or national influence, national evangelists, teachers in seminaries or other training institutes training full-time Christian workers, national strategists, authors of training materials and books

EXAMPLES OF 5 TYPES OF LEADERS continued

which are used nationally across denominations and in seminaries and institutes, theologians of national influence

comment Type D leaders primarily give direction to Type A, B, and C leadership in a region or a country. They are people who influence Christianity throughout a region or nation. They set trends in terms of evangelistic strategies, training strategies, methodology, evaluation, organizational cooperation, contextualization of theology, and the founding of new organizations. They are usually people who are known widely by Type C leaders.

examples Heads of international organizations, Christian statesmen who travel internationally and influence several nations, prominent theologians, trainers who are training Type D leadership (multi-country), prominent authors of Christian materials which set trends or support wide-spread movements, charismatic leaders who begin movements and organizations which expand worldwide or at least across many nations

comment Often Type E leaders will control large resources of people, finances, and facilities. They will have very broad personal networks with other international leaders and national leaders. They will often be on boards of very influential organizations.

comment It should be explicitly stated here that there is no inherent value attached to any of the types. That is, a Type E leader is not better than a Type A leader. All of the various types are needed in the church. More types A and B are needed than say Type E. The type of leader we become depends on capacity that God has given and God's development of us toward roles which use that capacity. To be gifted for Type B leadership and to aspire for Type D is a mismanagement of stewardship. So too, to be gifted for Type E and yet remain at Type C. None of the types are better than any other. All are needed. We need to operate along the continuum so as to responsibly exercise stewardship of our giftedness and God's development of our leadership.

FEEDBACK ON TYPES OF LEADERS

1. The essential difference between a Type A leader and a Type C leader are (check the one correct answer):
   ___ a. a Type A leader is a full time Christian worker while a Type C worker is usually a bi-vocational worker.
   ___ b. a Type A worker is usually not paid and works with groups primarily within the local church while a Type C worker is paid and works with people both in and out of the church.
   ___ c. neither (a) nor (b)
   ___ d. both (a) and (b)

2. The essential difference between Types A, B, C and Types D, E is (choose any answers which are correct):

   ___ a. Types D, E have a different ministry focus; indirect as opposed to direct.
   ___ b. Types D, E are fully supported while Types A, B, C are not.
   ___ c. Types D, E usually have formal training to do indirect ministry functions while Types A, B, C usually have non-formal and informal training to do direct ministry.

3. Give here an example of each of the Types of leaders and a qualifying phrase showing their ministry focus to show that you understand the basic types.

Type	Name	Descriptive Phrase
A		
B		
C		
D		
E		

ANSWERS----------

See next page.

FEEDBACK ON TYPES OF LEADERS continued

ANSWERS----------

1. b.
2. a.
3.

Type	Name	Descriptive Phrase
A	Althea Penner	Participates in and leads worship for an adult Sunday School class in a large mega church. Has exhortive gift; occupation is nursing.
B	Mike Plessett	Leadership responsibilities in Adult Sunday School Class and other church activities in large mega church. Involved in social and evangelistic ministries outside the church as well. His vocation is a financial investor.
C	Reese Mayo	Pastor in a recent church plant, a full time Christian worker supported by the church.
D	John Tanner	Denominational executive with the Queensland Baptist (Australia); also heads a mission organization for church planting and is on several other mission boards.
E	C. Peter Wagner	Professor of Church Growth at Fuller Theological Seminary; trains type D leaders; has written many books used as texts all around the world; has international ministry in conferences, seminars, and workshops; has influence with several internationally influential organizations. Now head of Global Harvest and organization international in scope.

COMMENTARY ON TYPES OF LEADERS

use	Plots of current leadership in a denomination or country along the continuum might indicate the health or sickness of a church. Such a plot, correlated with age of leaders may prove helpful in anticipating future needs for selection and development of leaders. Elliston (1989:190) has suggested an ideal profile based on size and numbers of churches.
problem	One problem which the continuum helps visualize is often associated with a pre-service transitional training pattern.[2] Leaders often skip Type A and Type B leadership and are trained formally to enter at the level of Type C. Normally, healthy development for a leader involves experiencing each of the previous types before moving to a new type. Skipping any type makes one vulnerable in overseeing leaders of that type. This same kind of problem exists for those who are trained formally at Type C and enter at Type D (say in a Bible College or seminary which is training Type C or B people). Without experiencing Type C functions it is difficult for one to adequately train others for it.
projection tendency	There is a tendency to pressure good Type A and B leaders to *go full time*. The idea being that full time Christian leaders are more dedicated to God than lay leaders. Agnes Sanford (1983: 71,72, 146,147) points out the fallacy of this in two excellent examples describing lay people, their giftedness and their accomplishment for God.
problems	The two thresholds present special problems. Crossing the logistics barrier, threshold 1, involves a major status change for leaders. Laity perceive full time Christian workers differently than lay leaders. Movement across the threshold means that people will view them differently (perhaps have higher expectations of them) even though their roles may not change. And there is the basic problem of how to finance full time Christian work. Type C leaders are usually unprepared to cross threshold 2, the strategic barrier, for two

---

[2]Pre-Service training refers to people who go straight through high school, college and seminary without having any full time Christian work experience. They graduate from seminary with a minimum of actual ministry experience.

COMMENTARY ON TYPES OF LEADERS continued

reasons. Responsibilities that Type D and E leaders perform dominantly require indirect ministry functions, something most Type C leaders were not trained for. So problem 1 in crossing threshold 2 means that most leaders are not prepared to handle the ministry activities of that level and will grope for a period of time as these activities are learned experientially (mainly via negative processing). A second problem of crossing the strategic barrier is that most leaders think tactically and not strategically. That is, they have been rewarded psychologically (affirmation, feeling of competency) for doing direct ministry which involves their gifts. Now they must do indirect ministry (problem solving, crises resolution, structural planning, strategizing, etc.) which does not reward one in the same way as direct ministry. Two things can help overcome the psychological loss perceived by leaders crossing the strategic barrier. One, they can from time to time do forays back into direct ministry which bring satisfaction that was experienced previously. Two, they can learn to see that what is being accomplished has broader potential and more far reaching results than their former direct ministry which had to be sacrificed in accepting Type D ministry. This is strategic thinking and an application of the servant leadership model at a higher capacity level.

why
distinguish

Types of leaders are distinguished not to imply that bigger is better but to indicate that leadership basal elements, leadership influence means, and leadership value bases will vary noticeably with the different types. Types D and E are much more concerned with leadership means/resource items of organizational structure, culture, dynamics, and power. They are multi-style leaders. They are more concerned with leadership value bases and will have heavy accountability to God in these areas. They are concerned with macro-contextual factors. Because leadership functions vary greatly along the continuum, different training is needed for each type. Informal/non-formal training focusing on skills for direct ministry is needed for Types A/B and should usually be in-service. All three modes (informal, non-formal, and formal) are needed to provide skills and perspectives for Types C, D, and E. In-service and interrupted in-service should dominate for Types C, D, and E.

FOLLOWERSHIP

introduction — Leaders, followers, and situations comprise the leadership basal elements. Where ever leadership is going on around the world these three elements can be observed and analyzed. Followership describes the set of issues dealing with the follower basal element.

definition — **Followership** refers to the collective relationship between a leader and those people under that leader's sphere of influence, which has at its base the voluntary acceptance of leadership by the followers and is measured by group characteristics such as:

- **loyalty** to leadership,
- **obedience** to God's vision through the leadership,
- **service** to carry out details of the leader's vision,
- **discipline** imposed upon followers not willing to be loyal, obedient, available for service or to those rebelling against God's will and direction for their lives,
- **sacrifice** displaying their willingness to give of what they have for the carrying out of God's vision,
- quality of **relationships** of followers with each other.

example — Paul points out (from a leadership focus) an essential of followership when he describes his prerequisites for exercising discipline. "Once we are sure of your obedience, we shall not shrink from dealing with those who refuse to obey." II Corinthians 10:6

categories: local — Followership in a local church situation will usually be differentiated into three levels depending on intensity of the church followership measures given above: group 1--an inner core who followership can be depended upon and will carry the bulk of the ministry; group 2--followers that have some initial commitment to the ministry and have potential to be developed into the inner core; group 3--fringe followers--some of whom can be developed toward group 2 and some of whom will fall away.

FOLLOWERSHIP continued

categories: parachurch
: Followership in a parachurch situation will usually be differentiated into three levels also: group 1--an inner core followership made up of those who are the decision makers and those having close access to them; group 2--the workers who carry out the ministry in the field situation; group 3--the support staff who administratively back up the workers.

relating leadership and followership
: Leadership primarily involves the efforts of leaders to motivate followers toward God's purposes for the group. Secondarily, leadership involves the development of followership, that is, for church followership moving group 1 followers into leadership, moving group 2 toward group 1 and group 3 toward group 2 and recruiting outsiders into all three groups. For parachurch leadership development involves the enlargement of group 1, recruitment for group 2, and administrative affirmation for group 3.

major
: Some problems involved in followership include: leadership backlash, jealousy/ambition among rising leaders; release/ hindrances to people as they develop; centralization/ decentralization cycle; perseverance; rebellion.

10 COMMANDMENTS OF FOLLOWERSHIP

Label	Principle
1. LOYALTY	Leadership in voluntary organizations can not be effectively exercised without followership loyalty.
2. DISCIPLINE	Leadership can not apply adequate discipline without a firm base of loyal committed followers.
3. BACKLASH	Even in successful leadership a leader must expect follower backlash due to unforeseen ramifications after the success.
4. SPIRITUAL AUTHORITY	Leaders who dominantly rely upon spiritual authority as the major power base will usually have good followership.
5. VOLUNTEERS	In most Christian organizations leaders must rely upon followership which is dominantly volunteer in nature; this directly effects power bases which can be used.
6. BALANCE	A dynamic tension must exist between centralization (which allows for direction in leadership but can weaken development of followership) and decentralization (which can allow development of followership but may lack the strong direction that is needed).
7. CORE	A wise leader recognizes that there are differing levels of commitment among followership and expects differing responses to efforts to mobilize and develop followers.
8. GOAL	Leadership must give hope to followership.
9. BIRTH	Good followership results in birth of good leaders.
10. RECIPROCAL LIVING	Good followership manifests itself in interrelationships reflecting the reciprocal commands.[3]

---

[3] Reciprocal commands refer to the one another commands in Scripture which describe how Christians should relate to one another. See Harville's **Reciprocal Living**.

INFLUENCE MEANS

introduction	Influence Means refers to the second major category of leadership elements. While the first, leadership basal elements focus on the *what of* leadership, this category focuses on the *how* of leadership. Leaders influence followers individually and in groups. There is the personal influence of the leader but there is also the pressure found in groups or organizations.
definition	<u>Influence means</u> refers to the individual ways that leaders influence followers, usually referred to as leadership styles, and the ways that power, in groups or organizations, is used by leaders to influence followers.
comment	A leader may use a highly directive style of influencing followers such as an apostolic style.
comment	A leader may use a highly non-directive style of influencing such as consensus.
comment	Organizations have power inherently built into the structures and positions. There is both formal, that recognized and delineated on charts and that which is informal, very real but not down on paper.
comment	A given culture may have a strong group focus rather than an individualistic focus. There is much power in the tradition and lore. Leaders from these cultures will use this as well as their own individualistic influence.
comment	In the Bible there is little formal organizational structures (except for perhaps palace and district structures associated with the kingdom era). Therefore, there is not much emphasis on organizational power theory, such as given by Mintzberg, in this manual. The majority of concepts concerning influence means will focus on leadership style theory--an individualistic approach that especially fits leadership which is not organizationally focused.

LEADERSHIP STYLE CONTINUUM

introduction   At the heart of leadership style theory is the way the leader operates toward followers in all that he/she does. These behaviors are usually located upon a continuum which characterizes 4 basic positions.

HIGHLY DIRECTIVE	DIRECTIVE	NON-DIRECTIVE	HIGHLY NON-DIRECTIVE
	----------------------------	----------------------	---	

KEY WORD:

COMMANDING	MOTIVATING	PARTICIPATING	DELEGATING

Decision Making--Controlling Authority

1. leader made decisions	1. leader made decisions 2. leader may dialogue 3. Leader may explain	1. follower-leader decisions 2. leader shares ideas/ facilitates 3. follower-made decisions with guidance and encouragement	1. follower-made decisions 2. follower responsible for decision 3. follower may keep leader informed

Implementing Decisions--Controlling Authority

1. leader gives specific instructions 2. leader closely supervises carrying out of instructions 3. leader feels necessity for personally controlling	1. leader demands feedback 2. leader intervenes frequently to insure results 3. leader feels responsible for implementing 4. leader has need for controlling	1. leader monitors 2. leader gives guidance only when needed 3. follower gives frequent feedback 4. follower feels responsible for implementing results	1. leader observes 2. leader intervenes only for corrective feedback 3. follower feels responsible for implementing and results

LEADERSHIP STYLE

introduction	Assuming that a leader is acting under authority from God in exercising his/her ministry among a group of people, how does that leader exert influence among those for which he/she is accountable? Leadership style refers to that *how*.
definition	<u>Leadership style</u> refers to the individual behaviors a leader utilizes to function in his/her leadership role in order to influence followers. This individual expression includes his/her • methodology for handling crises, • methodology for problem solving, • methodology for decision making, • relationships to peers and followers, • persuasion techniques for exerting shades of influence on others.
comment	Leadership style includes categories such as how the leader: • *motivates or relates to* followers, • *is perceived* by followers in the leader's role, • *solves* group problems, • attempts to bring about *obedience* among followers, • *resolves* differences.
example	One style sometimes seen in the New Testament is obligation persuasion. Paul demonstrates this technique with Philemon. This leadership style carries the force of imperative--a direct command--but falls short of an imperative style in that the decision to obey is still open. It relies upon past experiential relationship for its force.
example	Jesus demonstrates the command/demand or apostolic style among his close-in followers. As their loyalty deepened, his command/demand increases. John 21:15ff is an example of this apostolic (command/demand) leadership style.
example	Paul exemplifies the nurse leadership style in 1 Thessalonians 2:7 in his treatment of those young believers. It represents *gentleness* and *sacrificial* service because of an attitude of loving care toward those being served. It recognizes that a leader gives up rights in order not to impede the nurture of those following him/her.

VARIATIONS OF LEADERSHIP STYLE DEFINITIONS

introduction	Leadership style has many shaded meanings. The below listed definitions help expand our understanding of styles.
definition (simplified)	<u>Leadership style bent</u> is the tendency to use a certain leadership style due to personality and cultural conditioning.
comment	Fiedler[4] asserts that personality is strongly determinant in how a leader uses a leadership style. Some people are more highly directive due to personality. Some are highly non-directive. Some cultures like western cultures which are highly individualistic tend to press a leader toward task behaviors. Other cultures, more group oriented, tend to press a leader toward relationship behaviors.
definition	The <u>dominant leadership style</u> of a leader is that • highly directive or • directive or • non-directive or • highly non-directive consistent behavior pattern that underlies specific overt behavior acts of influence pervading the majority of leadership functions in which that leader exerts influence.
comment	Though it is possible to be both task oriented (toward highly directive behaviors) and relationship oriented (toward less highly directive behaviors) most leaders are one or the other. Hersey and Blanchard[5] identify a double profile for most leaders with a dominant place on the continuum and a secondary one.

---

[4] See Fiedler's two major works for further study--his 1967 book, **A Theory of Leadership Effectiveness**. New York: McGraw-Hill and his co-edited 1977 work with Chemers and Mahar, **Improving Leadership Effectiveness: The Leader Match Concept**.

[5] See Hersey's smaller book, **The Situational Leader**, New York: Warner Books or the more in-depth treatment with Blanchard, **Management of Organizational Behavior--Utilizing Human Resources**. Ask for latest edition.

4 MAJOR FACTORS AFFECTING YOUR LEADERSHIP STYLE

introduction   In my booklet on leadership style[6] I point out that leadership style is conditioned by several factors.

4 Major Factors

1. **Leadership Personality Bent** (task, relational)

   This factor is in line with Fiedler's personality determinant factor though I am more open to multi-style, like Hersey and Blanchard, than is Fiedler.

2. **Leader Function** (what you are doing: crisis, unimportant, structure, etc.)

   The situation or kind of influence warranted can change radically the normal approach that a leader would or could use. For example, crisis speeds up the introduction of change by a leader. So too it may allow him/her to move more heavily toward the highly directive side of the continuum. The speed with which decisions are needed is a key in this.

3. **Follower Maturity**

   The follower maturity certainly affects how a leader influences. He/she has more options with mature followers. Immature followers usually will need more directive styles from a leader.

4. **Leader-follower Relationship**

   The more intimate is a relationship between a leader and group or even individual followers the more a whole range of behaviors can be used. Followers will respond to different behaviors from leaders they love and trust knowing that he/she will use the most appropriate style for the situation.

---

[6]See my 1986 **Coming To Some Conclusions on Leadership Style** available through Barnabas Publishers.

10 PAULINE LEADERSHIP STYLES

introduction	Paul uses different styles depending on the situation and maturity level of followers. While the styles cannot be defined in detail the thrust of its underlying means can.

3 HIGHLY DIRECTIVE STYLES

introduction	The highly directive Pauline styles include the apostolic, confrontation, and Father-Initiator. All assume a prior track record which allows forceful persuasion and pressure.

1. Apostolic

definition	The <u>apostolic leadership style</u> is a method of influence in which the leader • assumes the role of delegated authority over those for whom he/she is responsible, • receives revelation from God concerning decisions, and • commands obedience based on role of delegated authority and revelation concerning God's will.
example	See 1 Thessalonians 5:12,13, 1 Timothy 5:17 (Hebrews 13:17). In 1 Thessalonians 2:6 Paul while choosing not to do so, does assert this Apostolic style as his right.
comment	This top-down, command/demand approach is considered the most highly directive leadership style.

--------- x ---------

2. Confrontation

definition	The <u>confrontation leadership style</u> is an approach to problem solving • which brings the problem out in the open with all parties concerned, • which analyzes the problem in light of revelational truth, • and which brings force to bear upon the parties to accept recommended solutions.
examples	The Corinthian letters especially 1 Corinthians exudes this style. Jude also uses this style. Paul does in the Philippian church--Euodia and Synteche.

10 PAULINE LEADERSHIP STYLES

3 HIGHLY DIRECTIVE STYLES continued

comment	For many leaders, problems, particularly those involving troublesome people and those carrying heavy emotional ramifications, are usually avoided. The basic rationale seems to be, 'This is a tough problem; if I try to do anything about it I'm going to incur wrath, maybe have my character maligned, lose some of my friends and be drained emotionally. Perhaps if I just ignore it, it will go away by itself. "And for some problems perhaps this is a good philosophy, as time does give opportunity for a clearer perspective, for healing, and for indirect conflict to occur. But for most problems, leaders must confront the problem and parties involved directly. At least this seems to be the approaches exemplified in Jude, John, Peter, and Paul in their Scriptural writings.

--------- x ---------

3. Father-Initiator

definition	The <u>father-initiator</u> leadership style is a related style to the apostolic style which uses the fact of the leader having founded the work as a lever for getting acceptance of influence.
example	In 1 Corinthians 4:14,15 Paul writes, "I write this to you, not because I want to make you feel ashamed, but to instruct you as my dear children. For even if you have ten thousand guardians in your Christian life, you have only one father. For in your life in union with Christ Jesus, I have become your father by bringing the Good News to you." Paul uses the father-initiator style in this case.[7]
comment	The father-initiator style is closely related to the obligation-persuasion style in that obligation (debt owed due to founding the work) is used as a power base. However, it differs from obligation-persuasion in that more than persuasion is used. The decision to obey is not left to the follower. It is related to the apostolic style in that it is apostolic in its force of persuasion.

---

[7]Note in this example the force of the two powerful figures: the absolute for the relative in verse 14 and the hyperbole in verse 15. See my **Figures and Idioms** available from Barnabas Publishers for help in identifying and decoding figures and idioms.

10 PAULINE LEADERSHIP STYLES continued

2 DIRECTIVE STYLES

introduction	There are two directive Pauline styles. They show concern for the follower yet bring strong influence pressure to bear upon the follower.

4. Obligation-Persuasion

definition	An <u>obligation-persuasion</u> leadership style refers to an appeal to followers to obey some recommended directives which • persuades, not commands followers to heed some advice, • leaves the decision to do so in the hands of the followers, but • forces the followers to recognize their obligation to the leader due to past service by the leader to the follower and • strongly implies that the follower owes the leader some debt and should follow the recommended advice as part of paying back the obligation and finally • reflects the leader's strong expectation that the follower will conform to the persuasive advice.
example	See the book of Philemon where Paul uses this style with Philemon on Onesimus' behalf.
example	Paul uses obligation-persuasion in combination with other styles in 1 and 2 Corinthians.
comment	One method of influencing followers over which there is no direct organizational control involves persuasion. The leader persuades but leaves the final decision to the follower. This is a particularly powerful influence technique because it uses normal appeal techniques coupled with a sense of obligation on the part of the follower due to past relationship/ experience with the leader.
comment	This is a directive style. The expectation is high though the actual decision to do so passes to the follower.

--------- x ---------

10 PAULINE LEADERSHIP STYLES

2 DIRECTIVE STYLES continued

5. Father-Guardian

definition
: The <u>father-guardian style</u> is a style which is similar to a parent-child relationship and has as its major concern protection and encouragement for followers.

example
: 1 Thessalonians 2:10,11 reflects this style. "You are our witnesses, and so is God, that our conduct toward you who believe was pure, right, and without fault. You know that we treated each one of you just as a father treats his own children. We encouraged you, we comforted you, and we kept urging you to live the kind of life that pleases God, who calls you to share in his own Kingdom and glory."

comment
: Usually this style is seen when a very mature Christian relates to very immature followers. This style is usually directive but because of the caring relationship between leader and follower and the follower maturity level (low maturity, that is, immaturity) it does not seem directive since influence behavior always seems to have the follower's best interest at heart.

10 PAULINE LEADERSHIP STYLES continued

2 NON-DIRECTIVE STYLES

introduction Two non-directive styles involve influence which leaves the final follow-through more in the hands of the followers. If they are mature they will most likely follow the influence. If not, they may or may not.

6. Maturity Appeal

definition A <u>maturity appeal leadership style</u> is a form of leadership influence which counts upon

- Godly experience, usually gained over a long period of time,
- an empathetic identification based on a common sharing of experience, and a recognition of the force of imitation modeling in influencing people

in order to convince people toward a favorable acceptance of the leader's ideas.

example Peter in 1 Peter 5:1-4 uses this style. John does so especially in 2, 3 John. Paul uses it in 2 Corinthians (see especially 2 Corinthians 11:16-33 and 12:1-10).

comment The book of Proverbs indicates that all of life is an experience that can be used by God to give wisdom. And those who have learned wisdom should be listened to by those needing yet to learn. Maturity in the Christian life comes through time and experience and through God-given lessons (as well as giftedness--see word of wisdom gift). Leaders often influence and persuade followers by citing their *track record* (learned wisdom) with God.

comment This style borderlines between directive and non-directive but is usually non-directive.

---------- x ----------

10 PAULINE LEADERSHIP STYLES

2 NON-DIRECTIVE STYLES continued

7. Nurse Style

definition	The nurse leadership style is a behavior style characterized by gentleness and sacrificial service and loving care which indicates that a leader has given up rights in order not to impede the nurture of those following him/her.
example	The primary example is 1 Thessalonians 2:7, "But we were gentle among you, even as a nurse cherisheth her children."
comment	Paul uses the figure of a nurse to describe this gentle caring sacrificial style. This is the only use of this particular word in the New Testament though related cognates do occur. The essential idea of the figure is the gentle cherishing attitude of Paul toward the new Christians in Thessalonica with a particular emphasis on Paul's focus on serving in order to help them grow.
comment	This is a non-directive style.
comment	It is interesting to note that in the very latter stages of his ministry, Paul exhorts Timothy to use this gentle leadership style in confronting people in the Ephesian church. See 2 Timothy 2:24,25. "And the servant of the Lord must not strive, but be gentle unto all men, apt to teach, patient, in meekness, instructing those that oppose him, if God, perhaps will give them repentance to the acknowledging of the truth."

10 PAULINE LEADERSHIP STYLES continued

3 HIGHLY NON-DIRECTIVE STYLES

8. Imitator Style

definition	The <u>imitator style</u> refers to a conscious use of imitation modeling as a means for influencing followers. The user model's appropriate thinking or behavior with an expectant view that followers must, will, and should be encouraged to follow his/her example.
example	Philippians 4:9 captures this thrust. "Put into practice what you learned and received from me, both from words and from my actions. And the God who gives us peace will be with you."
example	Paul is conscious of the power of imitation modeling. See 2 Timothy 3:10,11.
comment	Paul seemed continually to sense that what he was and what he did served as a powerful model for those he influenced. He expected his followers to become like him in attitudes and actions. It is this personal model of being and doing as a way to influence followers that forms part of the foundational basis for Paul's spiritual authority.
comment	This style is highly non-directive.

--------- x ---------

9. Consensus Style

definition	<u>Consensus leadership style</u> refers to the approach to leadership influence which involves the group itself actively participating in decision making and coming to solutions acceptable to the whole group. The leader must be skilled in bringing diverse thoughts together in such a way as to meet the whole groups needs.
example	Acts 13 involving Paul and Barnabas and the launching of the deliberate missionary movement.
example	Acts 6 and Acts 15 illustrate this highly non-directive style.

10 PAULINE LEADERSHIP STYLES

3 HIGHLY NON-DIRECTIVE STYLES continued

10. Indirect Conflict

definition	The <u>indirect conflict leadership style</u> is an approach to problem solving which requires discernment of spiritual motivation factors behind the problem, usually results in spiritual warfare without direct confrontation with the parties of the problem.
example	See 1 Corinthians 5:3-5.
comment	See the context of Matthew 16:21-23, especially verse 23. This is an example of indirect conflict leadership style.
comment	Mark 3:20-30 gives the underlying idea behind this style. See especially verse 27. "No one can break into a strong man's house and take away his belongings unless he first ties up the strong man; then he can plunder his hose."
comment	See also Ephesians 6:10-20 in which Paul points out the need for this style. "For we are not fighting against human beings but against the wicked spiritual forces in the heavenly world, the rulers, authorities, and cosmic powers of this dark age."

ADAPTED TREE DIAGRAM FOR INFLUENCE, POWER, AUTHORIT

introduction   Influence, power, and authority are important terms that are sometimes used interchangeable in leadership literature. I follow Dennis Wrong's basic schema for relating these concepts though I have adapted it to fit my understanding of spiritual authority. Influence is the most embracing of the concepts. Power is intended use of influence. And authority is one kind of power usually associated with tight organizations.

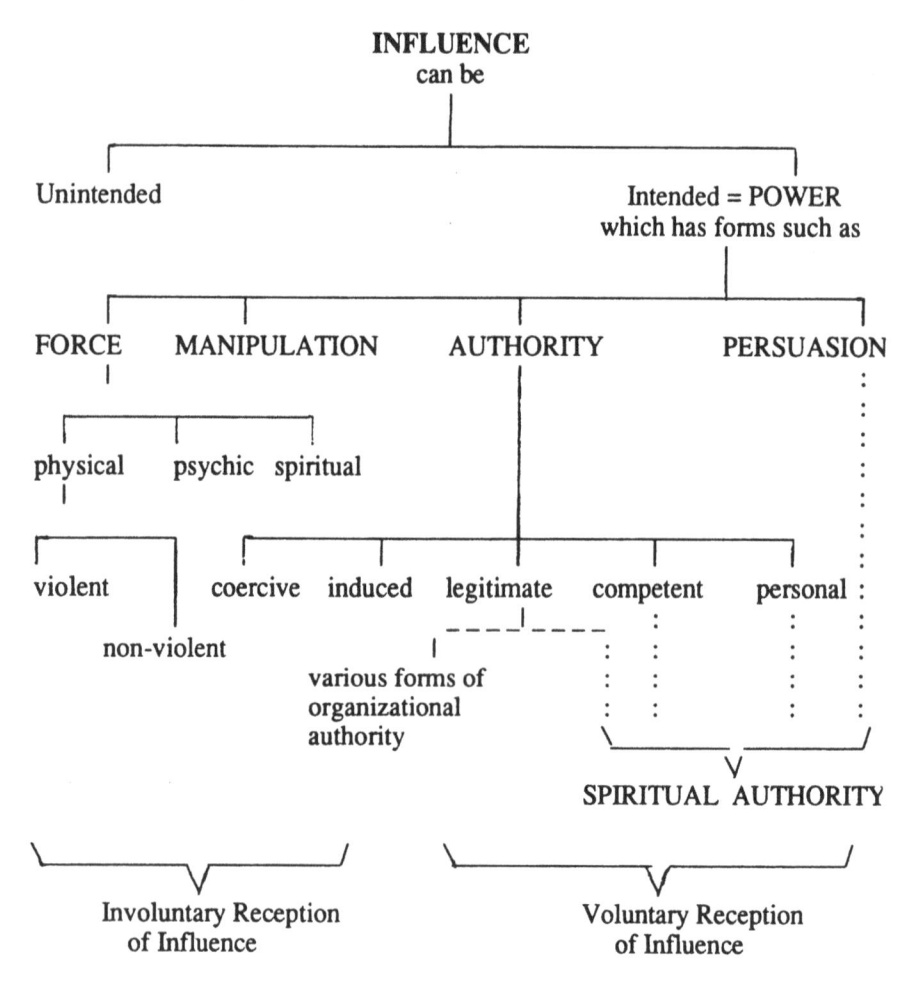

```
                           INFLUENCE
                            can be
                               |
        ┌──────────────────────┴──────────────────────┐
   Unintended                                    Intended = POWER
                                              which has forms such as
                                                     |
                       ┌──────────────┬──────────────┼──────────────┐
                     FORCE      MANIPULATION     AUTHORITY       PERSUASION
                       |              |              |
                ┌──────┼──────┐       |              |
             physical psychic spiritual             |
                |                                    |
          ┌─────┴─────┐      ┌────────┬──────────────┼──────────┬──────────┐
       violent   non-violent coercive induced    legitimate  competent  personal
                                                     |
                                              various forms of
                                              organizational
                                                 authority

            _____/          _____/
                       V                                    V
           Involuntary Reception                 Voluntary Reception
              of Influence                          of Influence

                                   SPIRITUAL AUTHORITY
```

(Tree diagram: INFLUENCE can be Unintended, or Intended = POWER which has forms such as FORCE (physical: violent, non-violent; psychic; spiritual), MANIPULATION, AUTHORITY (coercive, induced, legitimate — various forms of organizational authority, competent, personal), PERSUASION. Legitimate, competent, personal, and persuasion together = SPIRITUAL AUTHORITY (Voluntary Reception of Influence); the others = Involuntary Reception of Influence.)

POWER DEFINITIONS: POWER BASE AND AUTHORITY

introduction	Leaders have a right to influence. The ability to influence comes through the control of power bases.
definition	<u>Power base</u> refers to the source of credibility, power differential, or resources which enables a leader (*power holder*) to have authority to exercise influence on followers (*power subjects*).
definition	<u>Authority</u> refers to the right to exercise leadership influence by a leader over followers with respect to some field of influence.
examples	Power is manifested in power forms which bring about compliance. The four major power forms in our tree diagram include FORCE, MANIPULATION, AUTHORITY, AND PERSUASION. Authority is further sub-divided into coercive, induced, legitimate, competent, and personal. Spiritual authority is a combination of persuasion and legitimate, competent, and personal authority.
examples	Power forms depend upon power bases. Bases come from power resources--those individual and collective assets such as organization, money, reputation, personal appeal, manipulative skills, interpersonal skills, kinds of knowledge, information, indwelling Holy Spirit, giftedness.
central concept	The central concept of authority is the right to exercise influence. That right is recognized both concept by leader and follower. It is based upon common assumptions about the *field of influence*. For a spiritual leader the *field of influence* has to do with God's purposes and His directions for accomplishing specific aims that He reveals. Morality, corporate guidance, and clarification of truth, are three aspects within the *field of influence* which define the leader's range of use of authority.

POWER FORMS synonym: influence means, power instruments

introduction	The following definitions are prerequisite for understanding the range of power used by a leader.
definition	Power forms refer to four general terms of influence means: force, manipulation, authority, and persuasion.
definition	A force power form refers to the use of physical and psychic influence means to gain compliance.
definition	A manipulative power form refers to any influence means whereby a leader gains compliance of a follower where the follower does not have awareness of the leader's intents and therefore does not necessarily have freedom to exert moral responsibility in the situation.[8]
definition	A persuasive power form refers to any influence means such as arguments, appeals or exhortations whereby the leader gains compliance of the follower yet protects the freedom of the follower to exercise moral responsibility.
definition	An authority power form refers to influence means such as: coercive authority, induced authority, legitimate authority, competent authority, personal authority and spiritual authority.
definition	Coercive authority is the form of power in which a leader obtains compliance by using influence means such as threat of force or of punishment.
definition	Induced authority is the form of power in which a leader obtains compliance by using influence means of promise of reward or some gain for the follower.
definition	Legitimate authority is the form of power in which a leader obtains compliance by using influence pressure consonant with common expectations of the role or positions held by the follower and leader.

---

[8] Manipulation in general usually has only negative connotations in Western societies since it usually implies influencing against some one's wishes. While it is true that manipulation is usually bad it does not have to be so. The definition above is neutral. It is the motivation behind and the ultimate purpose of the influence that is the key.

POWER FORMS continued

definition	<u>Competent authority</u> is the form of power in which a leader obtains or can expect (but not demand) compliance by virtue of acknowledged expertise in some field of endeavor. The authority is limited to that field of endeavor.
definition	<u>Personal authority</u> is the form of power in which a leader obtains or expects compliance (but can not demand it) by virtue of the follower's recognition of the leader's personal characteristics.
comments	Machaivelli posited two real ultimate motivations: fear and love. For him, fear was the stronger of the two and hence a vital part of effective leadership. Jesus advocated love as the stronger. On the power continuum, those forms to the left of inducement all utilize the motivation of fear. Those from induced authority to the right all have in essence love as the primary motivation.
comments	Hersey and Blanchard give terms which help us understand further the *competent* sub-form. They use the term *expert* to indicate a person who has expertise, skill and knowledge about something so as to command respect from followers. In addition, they define *information* to indicate the leader's possession of information that is valuable to followers. Competent power includes this as well.
comments	Two terms from Hersey and Blanchard help us understand further the *personal* power sub-form. *Referent* power is a type of power based on the leader's personal traits. Such a leader is usually liked and admired by others because of personality, sincerity, or the like. *Connection* power refers to a type of power that arises because a leader has connections to influential or powerful people.
comment	Leaders will need the entire range of power forms and authority sub-forms in order to lead followers. It is helpful to know this as well as the negative and positive aspects of these forms.[9]

---

[9]See Dennis Wrong, **Power--Its Forms, Bases, and Uses**. New York: Harper and Row, 1980. He gives an excellent treatment of definitions as well as the dynamics of the forms. When certain forms are overused they tend to change to other types of forms.

SPIRITUAL AUTHORITY

introduction   One of the major trans-Biblical lessons is stated as one of the seven major leadership lessons. **EFFECTIVE LEADERS VALUE SPIRITUAL AUTHORITY AS A PRIMARY POWER BASE.** While it will take a whole range of power forms to accomplish God's purposes to take immature followers to maturity it should be the goal of spiritual leaders to move people toward the right on the power continuum so that they voluntarily accept leadership and follow for mature reasons. So, leaders who are concerned with developing followers should be continually moving to use spiritual authority when ever possible.

definition   <u>Spiritual authority</u> is the right to influence conferred upon a leader by followers because of their perception of spirituality in that leader.

comment   Spiritual authority is that characteristic of a God-anointed leader, which is developed upon an experiential power base that enables him/her to influence followers through: 1. Persuasion, 2. Force of modeling, and 3. Moral expertise.

comment   Spiritual authority comes to a leader in three major ways. As leaders go through deep experiences with God they experience the sufficiency of God to meet them in those situations. They come to know God. This *experiential knowledge of God and the deep experiences with God* are part of the experiential acquisition of spiritual authority. A second way that spiritual authority comes is through a life which *models godliness*. When the Spirit of God is transforming a life into the image of Christ those characteristics of love, joy, peace, long suffering, gentleness, goodness, faith, meekness, temperance carry great weight in giving credibility that the leader is consistent inward and outward. A third way that spiritual authority comes is through *gifted power*. When a leader can demonstrate in ministry gifted power--that is, a clear testimony to divine intervention in the ministry--there will be spiritual authority. Now while all three of these ways of getting spiritual authority should be a part of a leader, it is frequently the case that one or more of the elements dominates.

10 COMMANDMENTS OF SPIRITUAL AUTHORITY

introduction From a study of spiritual authority in general and observations on different leaders who have manifested it in particular the following observations about it have been derived.

1. **ESSENTIAL SOURCE.**
   One who learns spiritual authority as the power base for ministry must recognize the essential source of all authority--God.
2. **DELEGATED AUTHORITY.**
   God's delegated authority is His authority and does not belong to the person exercising it. That person is just a channel.
3. **RESPONSIBILITY.**
   The person through whom that delegated authority is channeled is responsible to God for how that authority is exercised.
4. **RECOGNITION.**
   A leader is one who recognizes God's authority manifested in real-life situations.
5. **SUBMISSION.**
   Subjection to authority means that a person is subject to God Himself and not to the channel through which the authority comes.
6. **REBELLION.**
   Rebellion to authority means that a person is not subjecting himself to God, though it may appear that the person is rejecting some impure manifestation of God's authority through a human channel.
7. **SENSITIVITY.**
   People who are under God's authority look for and recognize spiritual authority and willingly place themselves under it.
8. **ULTIMATE PURPOSE.**
   Spiritual authority is never exercised for one's own benefit, but for those under it.
9. **POWER BASE.**
   A person in spiritual authority does not have to insist on obedience or manipulate or coerce. Followers are responsible to recognize and follow God's spiritual authority in leaders.
10. **DEFENSE.**
    God is responsible to defend spiritual authority.

6 CHARACTERISTICS AND LIMITS OF SPIRITUAL AUTHORITY

1. Ultimate Source
Spiritual authority has its ultimate source in Christ. It is representative religious authority. It is His authority and presence in us which legitimates our authority. Accountability to this final authority is essential.

2. Power Base
Spiritual authority rests upon an experiential power base. A leader's personal experiences with God and the accumulated wisdom and development that comes through them lie at the heart of the reason why followers allow influence in their lives. It is a resource which is at once on-going and yet related to the past. Its genuineness as to the reality of experience with God is confirmed in the believer by the presence and ministry of the Holy Spirit who authenticates that experiential power base.

3. Power Forms
Spiritual authority influences by virtue of persuasion. Word gifts are dominant in this persuasion. Influence is by virtue of legitimate authority. Positional leadership (usually Type C, D, and E) carries with it recognition of qualities of leadership which are at least initially recognized by followers. Such authority must be buttressed by other authority forms such as competent authority, and personal authority.

4. Ultimate Good
The aim of influence using spiritual authority is the ultimate good of the followers. This follows the basic Pauline leadership principle seen in 2 Corinthians 10:8. Momentary judgment of leadership acts and influence means depends on this criterion.

5. Evaluation
Spiritual authority is best judged longitudinally over time in terms of development of maturity in believers. Use of coercive and manipulative forms of authority will usually reproduce like elements in followers. Spiritual authority will produce mature followers who will make responsible moral choices because they have learned to do so.

6. Non-Defensive
A leader using spiritual authority recognizes submission to God who is the ultimate authority. Authority is representative. God is therefore the responsible agent for defending spiritual authority. A person moving in spiritual authority does not have to insist on obedience. Obedience is the moral responsibility of the follower. Disobedience, that is, rebellion to spiritual authority, means that a follower is not subject to God Himself. He/she will answer to God for that. The leader can rest upon God's vindication if it is necessary.

FEEDBACK ON AUTHORITY/POWER DEFINITIONS

1. Consider again the definition of spiritual authority. <u>Spiritual authority</u> is the right to influence conferred upon a leader by followers because of their perception of spirituality in that leader. It is that characteristic of a God-anointed leader, which is developed upon an experiential power base that enables him/her to influence followers through: 1. Persuasion, 2. Force of modeling, and 3. Moral expertise.

   In your experience you most likely have observed leaders who in your opinion have utilized spiritual authority. Note the name of one such leader. What influence means stood out in this leader's life (persuasion, force of modeling, moral expertise)? Be prepared to share incidents which illustrate the influence means.

   name: Explanatory Comments:

2. For the leader noted in exercise 1 what aspects of his/her experiential power base are you aware of? Note any which you feel underlie his/her spiritual authority.

3. For the leader noted in exercise 1 and 2 check below power forms you have observed used by that leader to influence followers. Check any which apply.
   ___ a. force   ___ c. coercive authority   ___ e. legitimate authority
   ___ b. manipulation   ___ d. induced authority   ___ f. personal authority
                                                         ___ g. persuasion.

4. Power forms depend upon power bases. Bases come from power resources. What power resources have you observed in the leader described above? Check any which fit and be prepared to explain.
   ___ a. organization   ___ d. personal appeal   ___ g. special knowledge
   ___ b. money   ___ e. manipulative skills   ___ h. information
   ___ c. reputation   ___ f. interpersonal skills   ___ i. Holy Spirit presence
                                                        ___ j. giftedness

5. Suppose a leader was considering inviting you to be a part of his/her ministry and asked you the following question. What clear evidence do you have that you have spiritual authority? What would you say?

ANSWERS----------

I am not going to answer these due to the personal nature of the answers but will give them in my classes when we do these exercises.

LEADERSHIP VALUE

introduction	The motivational reasons underlying a leader's thought processes and behavioral activity are important to a Christian leader. Sometimes these reasons are clearly known and can be expressed. Sometimes the reasons are not clearly identified. Sometimes the reasons lie at deep level and are not even known to be a value. It behooves a Christian leader to explore and to seek to make explicit the individual reasons and patterning of these reasons into a systematic framework. Values are special principles of truth which control a leader's thought processes and behavioral activity as a leader.
definition	A <u>leadership</u> <u>value</u> is an underlying assumption which affects how a leader behaves in or perceives leadership situations.
example	Specific Pauline value--Paul felt that openness and careful procedures must accompany handling of church finances and gifts. Normative--a matter of conscience (see the Value Certainty Continuum which follows).
example	Abstract Pauline value--Leadership must be trained in life-contexts. Preferred personal style of operation (see the Specificity Continuum which follow).
example	Ministry must be personal.
example	Ministry flows out of being hence the development of the interiority spirituality component must be a priority.
example	Spiritual authority must dominate a leader's power bases.
example	Small group structures are necessary for believer's to learn about their spiritual gifts.
example	One-on-one face-to-face ministry for mentoring purposes should characterize a ministry.
example	Checks should be countersigned by more than just the senior leader in a church.

SPECIFICITY CONTINUUM

introduction　　Two continuums describe the range or specificity of values. The first, the specificity continuum indicates just how specific a value is. Values can be highly abstract and embrace a number of sub-values or they can be quite specific and apply only in some unique situation.

SPECIFICITY CONTINUUM

|--|
Very Specific　　　　　　　　　　　　　　　　　　　Very Abstract
4　　　　3　　　2　　　　　　　　　　　1

focus　　The specificity continuum describes the level of ideation of the value. Very specific describes values which are highly application oriented and use specific situational language. Very abstract refers to general language which gives an umbrella like statement under which several application statement might fit. The more specific the value the easier to understand it but the less likeliness of transfer to other diverse situations. The more abstract the easier it is transfer but the harder it is to understand it in a real application.

example　　1. Spiritual authority must dominate a leader's power bases.

example　　2. Small group structures are necessary for believer's to learn about their spiritual gifts.

example　　3. One-on-one face-to-face ministry for mentoring purposes should characterize a ministry.

example　　4. Checks should be countersigned by more than just the senior leader in a church.

comment　　The above 4 examples might be placed along the continuum as noted above.

VALUE CERTAINTY CONTINUUM

introduction — Two continuums describe the range or specificity of values. The second describes how the leader actually feels about the value. It can be something preferred and helpful but not worth fighting a major battle over with someone else who does not prefer it. Or it can be something that is normative for the leader whether or not someone else agrees. If a leader feels it to be normative he/she must keep it or violate his/her conscience. A value could be normative for a leader, but that leader could give freedom for others to not view it as normative.

VALUE CERTAINTY CONTINUUM

|--|

Preferential   Normative
            3   2   4   1   5

focus — The obligatory/depth continuum describes the intensity or importance of the value to the leader. Normative indicates that the value must be observed; it is a matter of conscience and integrity. Preferential means that the value is good and is wanted. But if it is not carried out there is no conscience problem. It is a goal to shoot for but failure to reach it is not as serious as would be the case with a normative value.

example — 1. Leaders ought to be sure that God has appointed them to ministry situations.

example — 2. Leaders must be concerned about leadership selection and development.

example — 3. Leaders should view personal relationships as an important part of ministry.

example — 4. Leaders ought to see God's hand in their circumstances as part of his plan for developing them as leaders.

example — 5. Leaders should not be deceptive in their dealings with followers but should instead be open, honest, forthright, and frank with them.

comment — The above 5 examples might be placed along the continuum as noted above.

COMMENTARY ON LEADERSHIP VALUES

values
and
formations

Over a lifetime God forms a leader in three areas: spiritual formation, ministerial formation, and strategic formation. In each of these areas critical incidents in life will impress upon the leader lessons of life. These lessons will become underlying values--the social principles, goals, or standards held or accepted by an individual leader which regulate conduct and thinking about leadership.

range of
values

Broadly speaking, leadership values relate to personal ethical conduct, or to personal feelings desired about situations or to ideas of what brings success or failure in ministry (standards for judging).

causal

A value can be rooted in personality shaping, in formative processing in the leadership emergence history, in heritage or environmental shaping.

EXAMPLES: PAULINE LEADERSHIP VALUES ABSTRACTED

introduction   Below are given Pauline leadership values identified in 2 Corinthians first in specific wording that fit Paul. These were then abstracted to a higher level to see if they might apply to leaders in general. These will help you see the ideas of values and how important they are in shaping a ministry philosophy.

Value 1. DIVINE APPOINTMENT
Leaders ought to be sure that God has appointed them to ministry situations.

Value 2. TRAINING METHODOLOGY
Leaders must be concerned about leadership selection and development.

Value 3. PERSONAL MINISTRY
Leaders should view personal relationships as an important part of ministry.

Value 4. SOVEREIGN MINDSET
Leaders ought to see God's hand in their circumstances as part of his plan for developing them as leaders.

Value 5. INTEGRITY AND OPENNESS
Leaders should not be deceptive in their dealings with followers but should instead be open, honest, forthright, and frank with them.

Value 6. ULTIMATE ACCOUNTABILITY
Leaders actions must be restrained by the fact that they will ultimately give an account to God for their leadership actions.

Value 7. SPIRITUAL AUTHORITY--ITS ENDS
Spiritual authority ought to be used to mature followers.

Value 8. LOYALTY TESTING
Leaders must know the level of followership loyalty in order to wisely exercise leadership influence.

Value 9. TRUE CREDENTIALS (COMPETENCY AND RESULTS)
A leader should be able to point to results from ministry as a recommendation of God's authority in him/her.

EXAMPLES: PAULINE LEADERSHIP VALUES continued

Value 10. TRUE COMPETENCE (ITS ULTIMATE SOURCE)
A leader's ultimate confidence for ministry must not rest in his/her competence but in God the author of that competence.

Value 11. TRANSFORMING MINISTRY
Followers who are increasingly being set free by the Holy Spirit and who are increasingly being transformed into Christ's image ought to be the hope and expectation of a Christian leader.

Value 12. PROMINENCE OF CHRIST IN MINISTRY
A leader must not seek to bring attention to himself/herself through ministry but must seek to exalt Christ as Lord.

Value 13. SERVANT LEADERSHIP
A leader ought to see leadership as focused on serving followers in Jesus' behalf.

Value 14. DEATH/LIFE PARADOX
The first fruits of Jesus' resurrection life ought to be experienced in the death producing circumstances of life and ought to serve as a Hallmark of spiritual life for followers.

Value 15 MOTIVATIONAL FORCE
Leaders should use obligation to Christ (in light of his death for believers) to motivate believers to service for Christ.

Value 16 TRUE JUDGMENT CRITERION
Leaders should value people in terms of their relationship to God in Christ and not according to their outward success in the world (even in the religious world).

Value 17 UNEQUALLY YOKED
Christian leadership must not be dominated by relationships with unbelievers so that non-Christian values hold sway.

Value 18 FINANCIAL EQUALITY PRINCIPLE
Christian leadership must teach that Christian giving is a reciprocal balancing between needs and surplus.

Value 19 FINANCIAL INTEGRITY
A Christian leader must handle finances with absolute integrity.

FOR FURTHER STUDY

The Way To Look At Leadership (1989), by Dr. J. Robert Clinton, gives an overview of the tree diagram of leadership with its three fundamental concepts of leadership basal elements, leadership influence means and leadership value bases. This is a short six page paper which gives a brief overview of what Chapter 1 of this Handbook is all about. This is available through Barnabas Publishers, the publishers of this Handbook.

A Short History of Leadership Theory (1986), by Dr. J. Robert Clinton, is a study of the five major leadership eras from 1841 to the present. This study features the five eras, leading theorists and works of each era, the basic leadership paradigms used to shape leadership during the phases, and leadership lessons seen in this historical survey. This is a 73 page technical treatment of the history of leadership theory in the United States from a paradigmatic perspective. This is the research that elicited the tree diagram of leadership basal elements, leadership influence means, and leadership value bases as an overarching leadership framework. This is available through Barnabas Publishers, the publishers of this Handbook.

Coming To Conclusions on Leadership Styles (1986), by Dr. J. Robert Clinton, examines the leadership style theories of the contingency and complexity eras of leadership history. It presents the major theorists (Blake and Mouton, Fiedler, Hersey and Blanchard) their views, and then synthesizes the basic notions into a set of concepts which can inform a Christian leader today. Included are insights from the Scriptures regarding Pauline leadership styles. This is a 65 page technical treatment of leadership style history. It gives application to Christian leaders. This is available through Barnabas Publishers, the publishers of this Handbook.

Reading In the Illusive Field of Leadership (1987), by Dr. J. Robert Clinton, defines some basic categories for organizing materials about leadership. Leadership is such a broad field that the question, "What one book should I read in leadership?" is not a valid question. What area of leadership are you interested? Having chosen one of several areas of leadership, you can see what basal book(s) may help you in that area. This is a 12 page paper.

See Marjorie Warkentin's 1982 book, **Ordination--A Biblical Historical View.** This helps in understanding the question of ordination for men or women. My focus on influence rather than position helps but does not totally bypass the ordination barrier and its implications for leaders--men or women.

CHAPTER 2. MODELS AND MISCELLANEOUS CONCEPTS

introduction In this chapter I give more perspectives to focus your leadership glasses. These are in the nature of models, smaller frameworks, and individual miscellaneous concepts. Some of these will be more helpful than others as we look in the Scriptures. All of them are used in one or more of the Handbooks for deriving some observation.

I first introduce 5 New Testament philosophical Models. These are laced with values that should under gird ministry.

I next offer a number of miscellaneous concepts which have already been discovered about leadership and which find frequent representation in the Scriptures. All of these are seen in the Scriptures when you look at various leaders or their leadership situations.

I then switch to a series of models applying to revelation in the Scriptures, ethnotheological[1] perspectives for viewing the Bible of which the *Starting-Point-Plus-Process* Model is one of the most important. I should say a further word about the ethnotheological models. These models have to do with assessing revelation. I include them her so that as you study through the Scriptures and watch God revealing Himself to and through these leaders you can see them in action. And then too they can be helpful to you as a leader today. The *starting-point-plus-process* model can help you assess how God eventually abrogates some things revealed in the Old Testament and yet remains consistent with Himself.

I also offer some models which deal with movement theory and cross-cultural transference of models and theories. Finally, I overview a social dynamic change model, Sower's, since it describes how change can happen in a situation. And the Bible has illustrations of just such a change process.

Glance again at the table of contents so you can get an overall picture of this hodgepodge of ideas--the types of models and miscellaneous concepts that you will meet in the chapter.

---

[1] This is a neologism coined by Dr. Charles Kraft in his book **Christianity in Culture**. It means the cross-cltural aspects of interpreting the Scriptures. We do not come to the Scriptures unbiased.

5 BIBLICAL LEADERSHIP MODELS

introduction   More New Testament philosophical models may exist, but the following five models are the most important ones noted in Christian literature. The framework below is built on a premise that foundational models apply widely while superstructural models apply less widely. The foundational models apply to all leaders. The superstructural models apply somewhat to all leaders but more specifically to certain gifted leaders.

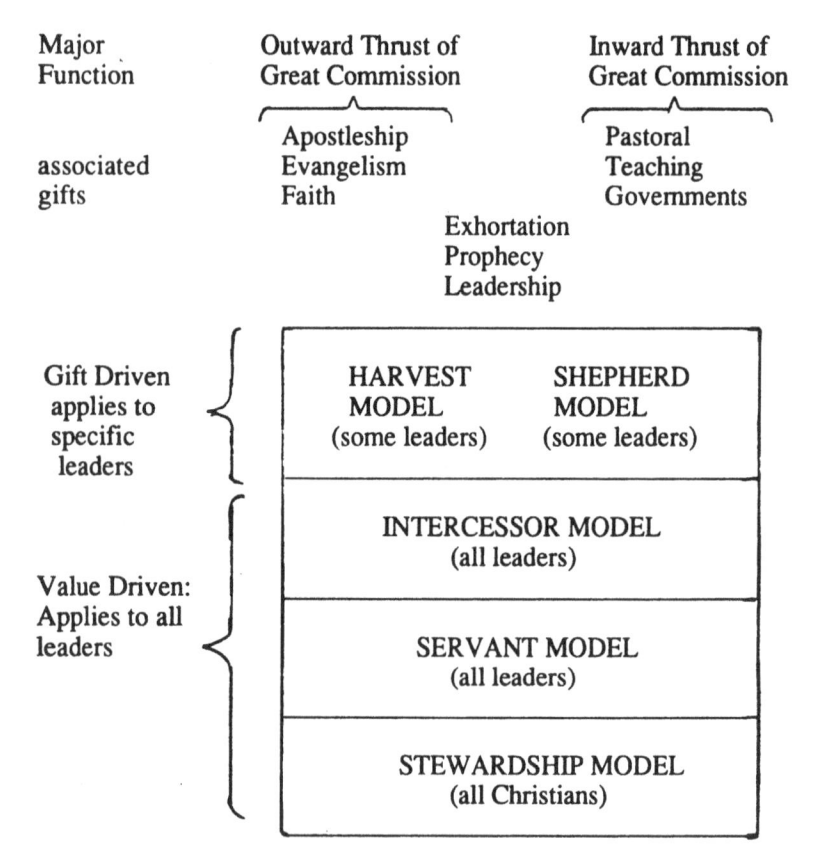

Major Function	Outward Thrust of Great Commission	Inward Thrust of Great Commission
associated gifts	Apostleship Evangelism Faith	Pastoral Teaching Governments
	Exhortation Prophecy Leadership	

Gift Driven applies to specific leaders:
- HARVEST MODEL (some leaders)
- SHEPHERD MODEL (some leaders)

Value Driven: Applies to all leaders:
- INTERCESSOR MODEL (all leaders)
- SERVANT MODEL (all leaders)
- STEWARDSHIP MODEL (all Christians)

comment   Value driven means the essence of the model is found in the values it promotes. It applies to all to whom the values are appropriate. Gift driven means that leaders with certain gifts will be drawn to the values of the models.

MINISTRY PHILOSOPHY MODEL--THE STEWARDSHIP MODEL

introduction	Ministry philosophy refers to a related set of values that underlies a leader's perception and behavior in his/her ministry. The values may be ideas, principles, guidelines or the like which are implicit (not actually recognized but part of perceptive set of the leader) or explicit (recognized, identified, articulated). For any given leader a ministry philosophy is unique. It is dynamic and related to three major elements: Biblical dynamics, giftedness, and situation. Though a ministry philosophy is dynamic there are core issues which are stable and apply to all leaders. The stewardship model is one such set of stable Biblical values.
definition	Ministry philosophy refers to ideas, values, and principles whether implicit or explicit which a leader uses as guidelines for decision making, for exercising influence, and for evaluating his/her ministry.
definition	The stewardship model is a philosophical model which is founded on the central thrust of several accountability passages, that is, that a leader must give account of his/her ministry to God.
passages	Accountability parables: Matthew 20 Laborers in the Vineyard, Matthew 24 The Waiting Servants, Matthew 25 The Ten Virgins, Matthew 25 The Ten Talents, Luke 16 The Worldly Wise Steward, Luke 19 The Pounds.
	General Judgment Passages: Romans 14:11,12, I Corinthians 3:5-9, 12-15, II Corinthians 5:10, Philippians 2:10,11, Hebrews 9:27.
	Special Leadership Responsibility: James 3:1, Daniel 12:1-3, Hebrews 13:17.
	Other Passages Indicating Accountability/ Rewards: I Corinthians 4:1-5, II Corinthians 4:1-6, Acts 20:17-38, I Peter 5:1-4.
	Cases: See Moses especially for severity of judgment due to leadership position and influence.

MINISTRY PHILOSOPHY--THE STEWARDSHIP MODEL continued

basic values
1. Ministry challenges, tasks, and assignments ultimately come from God.
2. God holds a leader accountable for leadership influence and for growth and conduct of followers.
3. There will be an ultimate accounting of a leader to God in eternity for one's performance in leadership.
4. Leaders will receive rewards for faithfulness to their ministry in terms of abilities, skills, gifts and opportunities.
5. Leaders are expected to build upon abilities, skills, and gifts so as to maximize potential and use them for God.
6. Leaders will be uniquely gifted both as to gifts and the degree to which the gift can be used effectively.
7. Leaders will receive rewards for their productivity in terms of zealously using abilities, skills, gifts, and opportunities fo God.
8. Leaders frequently must hold to higher standards than followers due to "the above reproach" and "modeling impact" they must have on followers.

implications
1. Leaders must be persons who maintain a learning posture all of their lives--growing, expanding, developing.
2. Leaders must make certain of ministry tasks, challenges, and assignments in terms of God's guidance (calling) for them.
3. Leaders must perform in ministry as unto the Lord in all aspects of ministry.

comment   The Stewardship Model is the most general of the New Testament Philosophical models in that it applies to followers as well as leaders. Servant leadership applies only to leaders as does the Shepherd and Harvest Models. Believers in a loving relationship do not see Stewardship Values as harsh and legalistic but lovingly serve their Lord knowing that service to Him will be the most fruitful and satisfying life they could have. They do not fear Him as a judge. He will judge fairly and with mercy for those who love Him and follow Him.

FEEDBACK ON STEWARDSHIP MODEL

1. Scan the list of values for the Stewardship Model. Assess your own personal preference for these values by placing an "x" in the appropriate column for each value. (MP = my personal ministry philosophy)

values	Column 1 Does not affect MP	Column 2 Loosely Held in MP	Column 3 Definitely affects MP	Column 4 Deliberately used and vital to MP
1.				
2.				
3.				
4.				
5.				
6.				
7.				
8.				

2. What other values has God taught you that are not listed but somewhat compatible with the central thrust of this philosophical model?

3. For any one of the values in exercise 1 for which you checked the right most column (deliberately used and vital to my personal ministry philosophy) suggest implications of this value for your ministry.

<u>Value Number</u>   <u>Implication for Me</u>:

4. Which value or implication is God now impressing upon you?

ANSWERS----------
   1. all of mine are column 4.   2. your choice.   3. Value 8. Implication: Particularly in disputed practices I must sometimes forego a Christian liberty for the benefit of others. That is, I must adhere to a more strict standard than I think is Biblical. This is necessary because my actions as a leader are constantly under scrutiny by followers and may be harmful to a *weaker brother*.   4. Values 1 and 7.

MINISTRY PHILOSOPHY MODEL--THE SERVANT LEADER

introduction Ministry philosophy refers to a related set of values that underlies a leader's perception and behavior in his/her ministry. The values may be ideas, principles, guidelines or the like. Each Christian leader will have a unique ministry philosophy that generally differs from others due to values God has taught experientially. But there will be some items in common with other leaders. The Servant Leader Model provides a set of values that should be common to the ministry philosophy of each Christian leader. Its central thrust says in essence that a leader's main focus is to use leadership to serve followers. A leader is great whose leadership capacities are used in service vertically to God and horizontally to followers.

definition The servant leader model is a philosophical model which is founded on the central thrust of Jesus' teaching on the major quality of great Kingdom leaders. That is, a leader uses leadership to serve followers. This is demonstrated in Jesus' own ministry.

primary passages Matthew 20:20-28, Mark 10:35-45.

secondary passages Parable of the Waiting Servant--Matthew 24:42-51, Luke 12:35-40, 41-48
Parable of the Unprofitable Servant--Luke 17:7-10.
Isaiah's suffering Servant--Isaiah 52:13-53:12.

basic values
1. Leadership is exercised primarily as service first of all to God and secondarily as service to God's people.
2. Service will require sacrifice on the leader's part.
3. Servant leadership is dominated by an imitation modeling leadership style. That is, the dominant form of influence is modeling for the followers and setting expectancies for them to do the same.
4. Abuse of authority, "Lording it" over followers in order to demonstrate one's importance, is incompatible with servant leadership.
5. A major motivational issue for leadership is anticipation of the Lord's return.
6. One ministers as a duty expected because of giftedness. Hence, there is no expectancy or demand or coercion for remuneration--no demanding one's due.

MINISTRY PHILOSOPHY MODEL--THE SERVANT LEADER

implications
1. A servant leader does not demand rights or expect others to see him/her as one with special privileges and status.
2. A servant leader can expect God to give ministry affirmation and does not demand it from followers.
3. A servant leader expects to sacrifice. Personal desires, personal time, and personal financial security will frequently be overridden by needs of service in ministry.
4. The dominant leadership style to be cultivated is imitation modeling. While there is a place for other more authoritarian styles this style will dominate.
5. Spiritual authority, with its earned credibility, will be the dominant element of one's power-mix.
6. Leadership functions are performed always with a watchful spirit anticipating the Lord's return.
7. Finances will not dominate decision making with regard to acceptance of ministry.

comment
"Servanthood is an attitude and a set of values, not a specific job description, or form of organization, or leadership style." (Bennett 1988:7)

comment
Balance is important, for the servant leader must lead and must serve. The servant leader must maintain a dynamic tension by recognizing Butt's (1975) assertion that a leader leads by serving and serves by leading.

comment
The servanthood Model is a general leadership model which applies to all leaders.

comment
Kirkpatrick (1988) identified eight common characteristics of Biblical leaders in the Old and New Testaments whom he considered servant leaders. While these commonalities do not give values that define what servant leadership is, they do identify broad areas of processing that can be expected and some character traits that will surface in servant leaders. These nine commonalities include: called by God, cleansed by God, commissioned by God, preserved by God, empowered by God, guided by God, humble in service, rejected by the world, triumphant in mission. The leaders he studied included: Isaiah, Jeremiah, Daniel, Ezekiel, Peter, John, Paul, Jesus.

FEEDBACK ON THE SERVANT LEADER

1. Scan the Servant Model values. Place an "x" in the appropriate column for each value. (MP = my personal ministry philosophy)

values	Column 1 Does not affect MP	Column 2 Loosely Held in MP	Column 3 Definitely affects MP	Column 4 Deliberately used and vital to MP
1.				
2.				
3.				
4.				
5.				
6.				
7.				
8.				

2. What other values has God taught you that are compatible with the central thrust of this philosophical model?

3. Choose <u>one</u> of the values in exercise 1 checked in the right most column suggest implications of this value for your ministry.

Value Implication for Me:

4. Which value or implication is God now impressing upon you?

ANSWERS----------

1. Column 1 = value 5. Column 2 = values 2, 6. Column 3 = value 1. Column 4 = values 3, 4.   2. Your choice.   3. Value 3--I must deliberately use what happens in my life (positive and negative lessons) as a means towards influencing my students.   4. In reviewing the values and implications for this model I have been convicted by how little the Servant Model has affected my leadership. I need to make the values and implications of this model real for me.

MINISTRY PHILOSOPHY MODEL--THE SHEPHERD LEADER

introduction — Each Christian leader will have a unique ministry philosophy that generally differs from others due to values God has taught experientially. Leaders whose giftedness and calling line up with the central function of the Shepherd Leader Model will find that its values are enmeshed in their own unique ministry philosophy. Leaders not so gifted may or may not have experienced processing leading to these particular ministry philosophy values. In any case the values are worth evaluation. Shepherd leaders tend to have a leadership style bent which is fundamentally relational in nature.

definition — The <u>shepherd leader model</u> is a philosophical model which is founded on the central thrust of Jesus' own teaching and modeling concerning the responsibilities of leadership in caring for followers as seen in the various Shepherd/ Sheep metaphors in scripture.

central thrust — Its central thrust is concern and care for the welfare of followers--that is, growth and development of the members in the Kingdom so that they know God's rule in their lives and can in turn productively impact on God's righteousness in society. This model is concerned primarily with the inward aspects of the Great Commission--teach them to obey all that I have commanded.

primary passages —
Matthew 28:19,20, Great Commission, Inward Aspect.
Matthew 9:36,37 Shepherd Aspect of the Analogy.
Matthew 18:12 Parable of Lost Sheep.
Luke 15:1-7 Parable of Lost Sheep.
John 10:1-18 The Good Shepherd.
John 21:15-17 Feed My Sheep.
I Peter 5:1-4 Peter's View, Shepherd Leadership.
Acts 20:17-38 Paul's View, Watching for the Flock.

archetypes — Peter and Barnabas are significant examples of the shepherd leaders in the New Testament.

values —
1. Shepherd leaders value personal kingdom growth in each follower. They want to see realization of kingdom truth in followers to increasingly experience the rule of God in their lives. (Matthew 28:20, John 21, Acts 20)

MINISTRY PHILOSOPHY--THE SHEPHERD LEADER continued

values
2. Shepherd leaders empathize with followers seeking to assess where they are and to help meet their needs and develop them toward their kingdom potential. (Matthew 9:36,37)
3. Shepherd leaders value each follower as important to the whole body and want to keep them incorporated in the body. (Acts 20:28 Luke 15:1-7, Matthew 18:12,13)
4. Shepherd leaders value personal relationships with followers. (John 10:3, 4, 14)
5. Shepherd leaders guide followers by setting examples-- particularly in the area of kingdom values. They value imitation modeling as an influence means. (John 10:4)
6. Shepherd leaders protect followers from deviant teaching by giving positive truth that will aid them in assessing counterfeit teaching. (John 10:5, 10, 12 Acts 20:28)
7. Shepherd leaders want followers to experience abundant life in Christ. (John 10:10)
8. Shepherd leaders willingly sacrifice their own personal desires, time, and financial security to meet needs in ministry. (John 10:11)
9. Shepherd leaders persevere through persecution or hard times in order to better the condition of followers. (John 10:11)
10. Shepherd leaders are open with followers exposing weaknesses and strengths and their heart with followers. (John 10:14)
11. Shepherd leaders value unity in body and wider body. (John 10:16)
12. Shepherd leaders willingly take responsibility for followers. (I Peter 5:2)
13. Financial gain is secondary to performing ministry in the values of a Shepherd leader. I Peter 5:2)

implications
see feedback exercise

comment
Gift-mixes of leaders which correlate strongly with the Shepherd Leader model include the various combinations of: the word gifts of pastor and teaching; the love gifts of mercy and helps and governments; the power gifts of healing and word of wisdom.

comment
The word gifts of prophecy and exhortation and leadership can operate with both Shepherd and Harvest leader models.

FEEDBACK ON SHEPHERD MODEL

1. Scan the Shepherd Model values. Place an "x" in the appropriate column for each value. (MP = my personal ministry philosophy)

values	Column 1 Does not affect MP	Column 2 Loosely Held in MP	Column 3 Definitely affects MP	Column 4 Deliberately used and vital to MP
1.				
2.				
3.				
4.				
5.				
6.				
7.				
8.				

2. Suggest one or two implications that in your opinion are necessitated if one is to hold these values with a high preference.

3. Is God impressing a need for you to learn more about or apply more definitely in your life one or more of the values or implications of this model? If so which?

ANSWERS----------

1. No Column 1 entries. Column 2 = values 3, 6, 9, 13. Column 3 = values 8, 11. Column 4 = values 1, 2, 4, 5, 7, 10, 12.
2. Implication of value 10: Leaders must share openly of God's processing in their lives. Implication of Value 4 (in my culture): Leaders must be on a first name basis with as many followers as practical.
3. Value 7 has been reaffirmed for me. Just this summer God gave a special word to me on this.

MINISTRY PHILOSOPHY MODEL--HARVEST

introduction | Ministry philosophy refers to a related set of values that underlies a leader's perception and behavior in his/her ministry. The values may be ideas, principles, guidelines or the like. Each Christian leader will have a unique ministry philosophy that generally differs from others due to values God has taught experientially. Leaders whose giftedness and calling line up with the central function of the Harvest Leader Model will find that its values are enmeshed in their own unique ministry philosophy. Leaders not so gifted may or may not have experienced processing leading to these particular ministry philosophy values. In any case the values are worth evaluation. Harvest leaders tend to have a leadership style bent which is fundamentally task oriented in nature.

definition | The harvest leader model is a philosophical model which is founded on the central thrust of Jesus' teaching which seeks to expand the Kingdom by winning new members into it as is demonstrated in the agricultural metaphors of growth in scripture.

central thrust | Its central concern is expansion of the Kingdom so as to bring to new members into the Kingdom as forcefully commanded in the outward aspect of the Great Commission--Go ye into all the world and make disciples of all people groups.

primary passages | Matthew 28:19,20: Great Commission--Outward Aspect. (See also Mark 16:15, Luke 24:46,47, John 20:21, Acts 1:8).

Kingdom Growth Parables:
    Matthew 13:24-30 Tares.
    Matthew 13:31,32 Mustard Seed.
    Mark 4:30-32 Mustard Seed.
    Matthew 13:33-35 Leaven.
    Luke 13:33-35 Leaven.
    Mark 4:26-29 Mysterious Growth of Seed.

Sending Passage:
    Luke 10:1-12 Sending of 70.

archetype | Paul is the archetype of a harvest leader in the New Testament.

values | 1. Harvest leaders have a strong concern for those outside the kingdom and want to give them a choice to hear and enter the kingdom. (Great Commission Passages)

MINISTRY PHILOSOPHY MODEL--HARVEST continued

2. Harvest leaders have a strong desire to motivate followers to take the kingdom message to others. (Luke 10:1-12)
3. Harvest leaders have a strong concern for power in ministry--they know the value of power to gain a hearing for the gospel of the kingdom. (Matthew 28:20, Mark 16:16,17, Luke 24:49, Acts 1:8)
4. Harvest leaders are more concerned with the ultimate destiny of those outside the kingdom than the present state of those in the kingdom. (Matthew 28:19 emphasis on outward not inward)
5. Harvest leaders recognize that Kingdom expansion means will not always sift out the real from the unreal but know that ultimately there will be resolution. (Matthew 13:24-30)
6. Harvest leaders by and large exercise faith. They believe God will accomplish His expansion work and hence are not afraid of small beginnings. (Matthew 13:31,32, Mark 4:30-32)
7. Harvest leaders recognize the evangelistic mandate as taking priority over the cultural mandate since the cultural mandate will require large numbers before impact on a non-kingdom society can be made. (Matthew 13:33-35, Luke 13:20-21)
8. Harvest leaders value receptivity testing in order to discover movements of God. (Mark 4:26-29)

implications   see feedback exercise

comment   Gift-mixes of leaders which correlate strongly with the Harvest Leader model include the various combinations of: the word gifts of apostle, faith, evangelist; the love gifts of mercy; the power gifts of healing, miracles, word of knowledge.

comment   The word gifts of prophecy and exhortation and leadership can operate with both Harvest and Shepherd leader models.

comment   See Wagner's **Leading Your Church To Growth** and **Church Growth and The Whole Gospel** which espouse Harvest leader values. See also Tippett's **Verdict Theology in Missionary Thought**.

FEEDBACK ON HARVEST MODEL

1. Scan the Harvest Model values. Place an "x" in the appropriate column for each value. (MP = my personal ministry philosophy)

values	Column 1 Does not affect MP	Column 2 Loosely Held in MP	Column 3 Definitely affects MP	Column 4 Deliberately used and vital to MP
1.				
2.				
3.				
4.				
5.				
6.				
7.				
8.				

2. What other values has God taught you that are not listed but somewhat compatible with the central thrust of this philosophical model?

3. Suggest one or two implications that in your opinion are necessitated if one is to hold these values with a high preference.

4. Which value or implication is God now impressing upon you?

ANSWERS----------

1. Column 1 = value 4. Column 2 = values 1, 2, 3, 6. Column 3 = value 7, 8. Column 4 = value 5 (Used in a negative way. I am vitally concerned with the sifting process. My strong bias to the Shepherd Leader Model makes me want to assess genuineness of those professing to be in the kingdom.)
2. Your choice. 3. If one held value 8 on receptivity high then that person would by necessity do studies in futurology--future trends, since receptivity is often correlated with various trends.
4. I don't feel like any of them are being impressed upon me at this time.

THE LEADER AS INTERCESSOR

introduction	One of the 39 macro-lessons identified in my first pass over the leadership eras is labeled, Intercession. Simply stated it says, Leaders called to a ministry are called to intercede for that ministry. It is seen in seed form in the Patriarchal Leadership Era in Abraham's intercession in Genesis 18. It is highlighted in Moses' Desert Leadership in the Pre-Kingdom Era. It is stated as a leadership value in Samuel's ministry, 1 Samuel 12, which is ushering in the Kingdom Leadership Era. It is relatively dormant in the Kingdom era except David's personal cries for help in leadership and for some praying by various prophets--especially Jeremiah. In the Post-Kingdom era it again is highlighted in Daniel's ministry. In the Pre-Church Era it is more exhaustively demonstrated in the life of Jesus. In the Church Era, Paul picks up the intercession torch and teaches it as well as does it. I was first introduced to it as a model by Dr. David Hubbard's leadership lectures on Hebrews given to the board of Fuller Theological Seminary.
definition	The <u>leader as intercessor model</u> is a philosophical/ spiritual model which is founded on the central prayer value: *If God has called you to a ministry, then He has called you to pray for that ministry.*
central thrust	Leader's called to ministry are responsible for and must find ways to adequately bathe their ministry in prayer. It is a responsibility solely between the leader and God.
Biblical statement	Samuel, the great intercessor in the transition from Pre-Kingdom to Kingdom leadership era states the principle clearly in his final public ministry as prophet-judge.
	As for me, far be it from me that I should *sin against the Lord* by failing to pray for you... 1 Samuel 12:23.
primary passages	There are many but these few are especially significant. 1. Genesis 18. Abraham's intercession for Sodom. 2. Exodus 32, 33. Moses' intercession for Israel. See also Numbers 11, 14, 27.

THE LEADER AS INTERCESSOR continued

3. Leviticus. Priestly intercessory role in each of the offerings.
4. 1 Samuel 12. Samuel's statement of the value and use of it in his own life.
5. 2 Chronicles 6. Solomon's intercession for Israel.
6. 2 Chronicles 14. Asa's prayer for Judah.
7. Isaiah 37. Isaiah's intercession for Hezekiah against Sennacherib's threatened invasion.
8. Isaiah 37. Hezekiah's own intercession for the problem.
9. Daniel' 9. Daniel's intercession to bring about the return.
10. Ezra 9. Ezra's intercession for his people concerning their neglect of God's word in their lives.
11. Nehemiah. Throughout the whole book Nehemiah frequently illustrates the model.
12. The Gospels. Jesus throughout the Gospels frequently demonstrates the central thrust of the model.
12. Paul throughout almost all his epistles demonstrates the reality of this model.
13. Hebrews. The book of Hebrews presents Jesus as the model leader/ intercessor. This is the key book and exhaustive treatment of leader as intercessor.

values

1. Leaders must sense a responsibility from God to pray for their ministries as part of their calling to that ministry.
2. Leaders must provide prayer covering for every aspect of their ministry.
3. Leaders must from time-to-time spend extended times alone with God to intercede for their ministry.
4. Leaders must use divine initiative praying to see God's leading and vision for their ministry.
5. Leader's should encourage their followers by specifically sharing their specific prayers for followers.
6. Leaders should pray for emerging leaders in their ministry.
7. Leaders should pray for blessing for their followers.
8. Leaders should use word of faith praying for their ministries.

gift-mix   All leaders are responsible for praying. Some will be more intense about this due to gifting (faith, word of knowledge, word or faith, discerning of spirits, miracles, healings, natural abilities of intuition, or introvertish personality, spiritual discipline skills). But all should insure that a prayer covering is over the ministry.

FEEDBACK ON THE LEADER AS INTERCESSOR

1. Scan the Leader As Intercessor Model values. Place an "x" in the appropriate column for each value. (MP = my personal ministry philosophy)

values	Column 1 Does not affect MP	Column 2 Loosely Held in MP	Column 3 Definitely affects MP	Column 4 Deliberately used and vital to MP
1.				
2.				
3.				
4.				
5.				
6.				
7.				
8.				

2. What other values of prayer has God taught you?

3. Take either one of the values from question 1 above or question 2 above and describe how the value works out in practice?

ANSWERS----------

1. Value 1 = Column 4; Value 2 = Column 2; Value 3 = Column 2; Value 4 = Column 3; Value 5 = Column 4; Value 6 = Column 3; Value 7 = Column 3; Value 8 = Column 2.
2. Everyday commonplace incidents, events, people should be valuable as prompts for spontaneous prayer. Application from 1 Thessalonians 5:17.
3. Sirens remind me to pray. Beautiful things do. I pray for a blessing for a church when I pass its building. I thank God for good water when I take a drink. I pray when I am going to answer the phone. And many others.

5 KINDS OF FINISHES

introduction	The Bible mentions a number of leaders. Some receive only scant notice.[2] Others receive prolonged treatment.[3] I did[4] research on 100 of the more prominent leaders.[5] These included major Old Testament types: patriarchal, military, civil, formal religious (priests), informal religious (prophets), charismatic. They also included major New Testament types: apostles, prophets, evangelists, teachers, pastors. Of the 100 listed only about half had enough information to tell how they finished.[6] When it was all said and done, how did they do? 5 Kinds of finishes were observed: 1. cut off early, 2. finish poorly, 3. finished *so-so*, *4. finished* well, 5. can't be sure. The one that is most important, *finished well*, deserved further treatment. Leaders who finished well were studied for characteristics of a good finish.
definition	<u>Cut off early</u> means they were taken out of leadership
examples	Abimelech, Samson, Absalom, Ahab, Josiah, James.
comment	Assassinations, killed in battle, prophetically denounced, or overthrown were common causes of being *cut off*.
comment	Some of these were traced directly to God's doing.
definition	<u>Finished poorly</u> means they were going down hill in the latter part of their ministry. This might mean in terms of their personal relationship with God or in terms of competency in their ministry or both.

---

[2] Such as the prophet Ahijah (I Kings 11), the unknown man of God (I Kings 13), Micaiah (I Kings 22), Nathan and Gad, two of David's personal prophets. These appear fleetingly on the Biblical stage, perform some leadership function or two and are heard of no more. Numerous Jewish local civil leaders in the Old Testament are listed in special lists, several in the Pentateuch and several in I Chronicles, with nothing more than a name mentioned. See also Nehemiah and Ezra for other such lists.

[3] Leaders like Moses, David, Paul, and Jesus have an overwhelming amount of material to analyze. Many have some data. Even those having data do not always give the data needed to ascertain how they finished.

[4] I listed Abraham, Isaac, Jacob, Job, Joseph, Moses, Miriam, Aaron, Eleazar, Joshua, Caleb, Othniel, Ehud, Deborah, Barak, Gideon, Abimelech, Tola, Jair, Jephthah, Iban, Elon, Abdon, Samson, Eli, Samuel, Saul, David, Absalom, Solomon, Jeroboam, Rehoboam, Abijah, Baasha, Asa, Omri, Ahab, Elijah, Micaiah, Jehosophat, Joram, Elisha, Obadiah, Jerhoram, Jehu, Joel, Ahaziah, Athaliah, Joash, Jehoahaz, Jehoash, Amaziah, Jeroboam II, Jonah, Amos, Uzziah, Zechariah, Shallum, Menaham, Jotham, Pekahiah, Pekah, Hosea, Micah, Isaiah, Hoshea, Ahaz, Hezekiah, Manasseh, Nahum, Amon, Josiah, Zephaniah, Habakkuk, Jeremiah, Jehoahaz, Daniel, Jehoakim, Jehoachin, Ezekiel, Esther, Mordecai, Zerubabel, Joshua, Zechariah, Haggai, Ezra, Nehemiah, Malachi, Jesus, Peter, James, John, Barnabas, Paul, Stephen, Phillip, Titus, Timothy.

[5] See my paper, *Listen Up Leaders! Forewarned is forearmed!* available from Barnabas Publishers, for an in-depth presentation of this research.

[6] I actually made judgments of this for 49.

5 KINDS OF FINISHES continued

examples	Some who in my opinion are typical examples of *finished poorly* include: Gideon, Samson, Eli, Saul, Solomon.
definition	Finished *so so* means they did not do what they potentially could have done or should have done. They did not complete what God had for them to do.
examples	Some who in my opinion are typical examples of finished *so so* include: David, Jehosophat, Hezekiah.
comment	This might mean that there were some negative ramifications from their ministry or reign which lingered on even though they were walking with God personally at the end of their lives.
comment	There are also many who seem to bridge more than one category (*cut-off* and finished *poorly*, *cut-off* and finished *so so*, finished *poorly* and *so so* or finished *so so* and *somewhat well*). The categories are not always mutually exclusive.
definition	Finished well means they were walking with God personally at the end of their lives and probably contributed to God's purposes at some high realized level of potential.
comment	Some who in my opinion are typical examples of *finished well* include: Abraham, Job, Joseph, Joshua, Caleb, Samuel, Elijah, Jeremiah, Daniel, Jesus, John, Paul, Peter.
definition	Not sure means we don't have enough data to know. Some leaders who receive scant treatment probably did finish well but data concerning their finish is not available in the Bible.
comment	Now the data isn't conclusive. And one might question what I mean by finish well. More on that later. But there is enough information to justify a first major observation from the Bible concerning leadership.

FEW LEADERS FINISH WELL!

comment	Of those on which information was available less than 30% finished well. Now that is a startling conclusion. It should frighten any present day leader who desires to count for God.

5 KINDS OF FINISHES continued

comment   Can we do anything about it? Yes, we can. One, we can study why these leaders failed to finish well. Two New Testament passages, I Corinthians 10:6 and Romans 15:4 point out to us that history in the Bible is meant to teach us today lessons for our own lives. Recognizing what it means to finish well is a major step forward. I'll identify 6 major characteristics of finishing well. Then I'll give 6 barriers hindering a good finish. I'll also give 5 things we can do to enhance a good finish. All of these can help us.

comment   But the most important thing we can do is take advantage of the warning that **few leaders finish well**, and believe that more can finish well if they are *determined under God to do so*. A natural challenge flows from this observation. **Set a lifetime goal to finish well.**

6 CHARACTERISTICS OF THOSE FINISHING WELL

introduction   Comparative study of leaders who have finishing well have identified 6 descriptors:

6 Characteristics

1. They maintain a <u>personal vibrant relationship</u> with God right up to the end.

2. They maintain a <u>learning posture</u> and can learn from various kinds of sources--life especially.

3. They evidence <u>Christ likeness in character</u> as evidenced by the fruit of the Spirit in their lives.

4. Truth is lived out in their lives so that <u>convictions</u> and promises of God are seen to be real.

5. They leave behind one or more <u>ultimate contributions</u> (saint, stylistic practitioners, mentors, public rhetoricians, pioneers, crusaders, artists, founder, stabilizers, researchers, writers, promoters).[7]

6. They walk with a growing awareness of a <u>sense of destiny</u> and see some or all of it fulfilled.

comment   The classic example in the Old Testament of a good finish is Daniel who manifests all six characteristics.

comment   The classic example in the New Testament other than Christ is Paul.

comment   There are gradations of finishing well. Some finish well but not quite having all six or lesser intensity on one or the other major characteristics.

---

[7] See position paper on *Ultimate Contribution* available from Barnabas Publishers for explanation of these types.

PIVOTAL POINTS

introduction	My preliminary study of some of these Bible leaders and in-depth study of others indicates that for many of them there were critical times in their lives in which decisions were made that affected all of the rest of their lives and ministries. I call these times pivotal points. A pivotal point in a leader's life is a critical time of God's dealing with that leader. The leader's response to God's processing will carry significant implications for the rest of the leadership. At the end of life one can trace back to that point in time and identify it as having done at least one of four things.
definition	A <u>pivotal point</u> is a critical time in a leader's life in which something happens, sometimes inadvertently, or a decision is made which can,

1. curtail further use of the leader by God or at least curtail expansion of the leader's potential.
2. limit the eventual use of the leader for ultimate purposes that otherwise could have been accomplished,
3. enhance or open up the leader for expansion or contribution to the ultimate purposes in God's kingdom or
4. serve as a guidance watershed which forever changes the direction of the life.

example	Saul typifies result one in two pivotal points which tested his integrity and obedience in I Samuel 13:7-14 and 15:10-35.
example	Moses exemplifies the second. His act in striking the Rock to provide water in Numbers 20:11,12 prevented God from allowing him to take the Israelites into the promised land-- which should have been the culminating ultimate contribution of his ministry.
example	Daniel's response to the integrity check in Daniel chapter 1 illustrates the third kind of pivotal point as was Joseph's response to temptation from Potiphar's wife in Genesis 39.
example	Moses' burning bush experience typifies the fourth kind.

3 CATEGORIES OF PIVOTAL POINTS

introduction A tentative categorization results in the following tree diagram for classifying pivotal points.

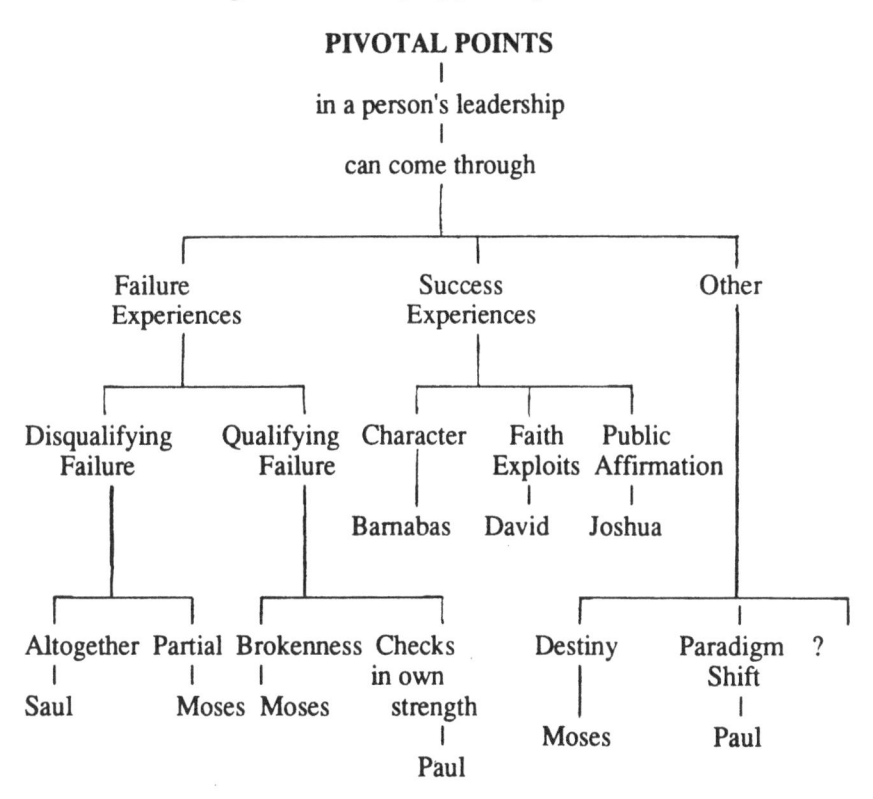

```
                        PIVOTAL POINTS
                              |
                     in a person's leadership
                              |
                        can come through
                              |
        ┌─────────────────────┼─────────────────────┐
      Failure              Success                Other
   Experiences           Experiences
        |                     |
    ┌───┴────┐         ┌──────┼──────┐
Disqualifying Qualifying  Character  Faith   Public
  Failure    Failure                Exploits Affirmation
    |          |            |         |        |
    |          |         Barnabas   David    Joshua
    |          |
┌───┴───┐  ┌───┴────┬─────────┐        ┌──────┼────────┐
Altogether Partial Brokenness Checks  Destiny   Paradigm   ?
   |        |       |         in own     |       Shift
  Saul    Moses   Moses      strength    |         |
                                |      Moses     Paul
                               Paul
```

6 OBSERVATIONS ON PIVOTAL POINTS

Some Observations About Pivotal Points

1. **RANGE.** Biblical leader's that I have meditated on so far seem to have a range of from 2 to 6 pivotal points. That is, there is frequently more than one pivotal point that serves as "conditional road map markers" in a life. Moses giving up of his rights to the throne, his slaying of the Egyptian, his sense of destiny experience at the burning bush, his mountain top experience testing and his striking of the rock are typical examples of pivotal points.

2. **INTENTIONAL SELECTIVITY.** Due to the highly intentional selection of Bible material, the New Testament commentary on an Old Testament leader probably will signal pivotal points.

3. **PERSPECTIVE.** Pivotal points probably can't finally be evaluated except with post-life retrospective reflection. However, even as we move through a major boundary we may well know that we have experienced a pivotal point.

4. **PURPOSE OF STUDY.** At this point studying and identifying pivotal points can furnish us with *warnings* for our own lives, can point out the ways that God frequently processes leaders at critical junctures of their lives which in turn may cause us to have a more sensitive awareness of the Spirit's daily processing in our lives. We may not be able to know at the moment if something happening to us is pivotal or not; hence we must exercise a Spirit-led caution as we respond to God. The more familiar we are with Biblical leaders and with the processes used by God in their emergence the more sensitive we will be to God's dealing with our own lives. That a single incident in my life may be strongly determinative for the rest of a person's leadership will certainly cause one to see the importance of a daily sensitive walk with God via the Holy Spirit. Forewarned is forearmed!

5. **BALANCE.** We must avoid two extremes. One is being afraid of running into a pivotal point every day and hence being so overcautious that we can not freely minister as we ought. The other is assuming that since for the most part we can't control when pivotal points come we just simply ignore the truth about them and go our merry way.

6. **BARRIERS.** The six barriers to finishing well usually are keyed by some negative experience and should serve to warn us. We can certainly avoid these negative pivotal points which may cause at worst disqualifying failure and at best qualifying failure.

6 BARRIERS TO FINISHING WELL

introduction — Several repeated kinds of pivotal points or critical processing has led to leaders not finishing well. While there are probably many others as well, at least these are major ones and should be known and avoided.

6 Barriers To Finishing Well

1. **FINANCES.** Leaders, particularly those who have power positions and make important decisions concerning finances, tend to use practices which may encourage incorrect handling of finances and eventually wrong use. A character trait of greed often is rooted deep and eventually will cause impropriety with regard to finances. Numerous leaders have fallen due to some issue related to money.
   Biblical Example: Gideon's golden ephod.

2. **POWER.** Leaders who are effective in ministry must use various power bases in order to accomplish their ministry. With power so available and being used almost daily, there is a tendency to abuse it. Leaders who rise to the top in a hierarchical system tend to assume privileges with their perceived status. Frequently, these privileges include abuse of power. And they usually have no counter balancing accountability.
   Biblical Example: Uzziah's usurping of priestly privilege.

3. **PRIDE.** Pride (inappropriate and self-centered) can lead to a downfall of a leader. As a leader there is a dynamic tension that must be maintained. We must have a healthy respect for our selves, and yet we must recognize that we have nothing that was not given us by God and He is the one who really enables ministry.
   Biblical Example: David's numbering.

4. **SEX.** Illicit sexual relationships have been a major downfall both in the Bible and in western cultures. Joseph's classic integrity check with respect to sexual sin is the ideal model that should be in leaders minds.
   Biblical Example: David's sin with Bathsheba was a pivotal point from which his leadership never fully recovered. It was all downhill from here on.

5. **FAMILY.** Problems between spouses or between parents and children or between siblings can destroy a leader's ministry. What is needed are Biblical values lived out with regard to husband-wife relationships, parent-children, and sibling relationships. Of growing importance in our day is the social base profiles for singles in ministry and for married couples.
   Biblical Example: David's family. Ammon and Tamar. Absalom's revenge.

6. **PLATEAUING.** Leaders who are competent tend to plateau. They can continue to minister at a level without there being a reality or Spirit empowered renewing effect. Most leaders will plateau several times in their life times of development. Some of the 5 things for enhancing a good finish will counteract this tendency. There again is a dynamic tension that must be maintained between leveling off for good reasons, (consolidating one's growth and/or reaching the level of potential for which God has made you) and plateauing because of sinfulness or loss of vision.
   Biblical Example: David in the latter part of his reign just before Absalom's revolt.

5 THINGS TO ENHANCE GOOD FINISHES

introduction　　There are also repeated items which help leaders continue well and to finish well in ministry.

1. **PERSPECTIVE.** We need to have a lifetime perspective on ministry. *Effective leaders view present ministry in terms of a lifetime perspective.* [8] We gain that perspective by studying lives of leaders as commanded in Hebrews 13:7,8.[9]

2. **RENEWAL.** Special moments of intimacy with God, challenges from God, new vision from God and affirmation from God both for personhood and ministry will occur repeatedly to a growing leader. These destiny experiences will be needed, appreciated. and will make the difference in persevering in a ministry. All leaders should expectantly look for these repeated times of renewal. Some can be initiated by the leader (usually extended times of spiritual disciples). But some come sovereignly from God. We can seek them, of course, and be ready for them.

3. **DISCIPLINES.** Leaders need discipline of all kinds. Especially is this true of spiritual disciplines. A strong surge toward spirituality now exists in Catholic and Protestant circles. This movement combined with an increasingly felt need due to the large number of failures is propelling leaders to hunger for intimacy. The spiritual disciplines are one mediating means for getting this intimacy.[10] Leaders without these leadership tools are prone to failure via sin as well as plateauing.

4. **LEARNING POSTURE.** The single most important antidote to plateauing is a well developed learning posture. Such a posture is also one of the major ways through which God gives vision. I will describe more about how to do this in the commentary which follows.

5. **MENTORING.** Leaders who are effective and finish well will have from 10 to 15 significant people who came alongside at one time or another to help them. Mentoring is also a growing movement in Christian circles as well as secular.[11]

---

[8] This is one of 7 major leadership lessons seen in effective leader's lives. More on this later.

[9] I have been doing intensive study of leader's lives over the past 13 years. Leadership emergence theory is the result of that research. Its many concepts can help us understand more fully just how God does shape a leader over a lifetime. My findings are available in two books, **The Making of A Leader,** published by Nav Press in 1988 and a lengthy detailed self-study manual , **Leadership Emergence Theory,** that I privately publish for use in classes and workshops. In addition, my latest research is available in position papers published by Barnabas Publishers. Chapter 3 of this Handbook gives a brief introduction to these findings.

[10] Such authors as Eugene Peterson, Dallas Willard, and Richard Foster are making headway with Protestants concerning spirituality. See also my section on spiritual guides and the appendix on the disciplines in **The Mentor Handbook,** available through Barnabas Publishers.

[11] See **Connecting--The Mentoring Relationships You Need To Succeed in Life.** See also **The Mentor Handbook** available from Barnabas Publishers.

COMMENTARY: ENHANCEMENTS

timing of renewal — Most leaders who have been effective over a lifetime have needed and welcomed renewal experiences from time to time in their lives. Some times are more crucial in terms of renewal than others. Apparently in western society the mid-thirty's and early forty's and mid-fifty's are crucial times in which renewal is frequently needed in a leader's life. Frequently during these critical periods discipline slacks, there is a tendency to plateau and rely on one's past experience and skills, and a sense of confusion concerning achievement and new direction prevail. Unusual renewal experiences with God can overcome these tendencies and redirect a leader. An openness for them, a willingness to take steps to receive them, and a knowledge of their importance for a whole life can be vital factors in heeding step two for finishing well. Sometimes these renewal experiences are divinely originated by God and we must be sensitive to his invitation. At other times we must initiate the renewal efforts.

discipline — We need to guard our inner life with God. The spiritual disciplines have proven helpful in this regard to many earlier generations of leaders. Spiritual disciplines can be generally defined to include activities of mind and body which are purposefully undertaken in order to bring personality and total being into effective cooperation with the Spirit of God so as to reflect Kingdom life. [12]

Pauline exhortations — I concur with Paul's admonitions to discipline as a means of insuring perseverance in the ministry. When Paul was around 50 years of age he wrote to the Corinthian church what appears to be both an exhortation to the Corinthians and an explanation of a major leadership value in his own

---

[12] Helpful categorizations for me which I derived from my study of Willard include the following: 1) Disciplines of abstinence such as solitude, silence, fasting, frugality, chastity, secrecy, sacrifice; 2) Disciplines of engagement such as study, worship, celebration, service, prayer, fellowship, confession, and submission; 3) Some other miscellaneous disciplines such as voluntary exile, keeping watch, sabbath keeping, practices among the poor, journalling, and listening. I have defined many of these disciplines and given some practical suggestions for them in my spiritual dynamics course I teach at Fuller Seminary. See Dallas Willard's **The Spirit of the Disciplines** and Richard Foster's **Celebration of Discipline**.

COMMENTARY: ENHANCEMENTS continued

life. We need to keep in mind that he had been in ministry for about 21 years. He was still advocating strong discipline. I paraphrase it in my own words.

> I am serious about finishing well in my Christian ministry. I discipline myself for fear that after challenging others into the Christian life I myself might become a casualty. 1 Corinthians 9:24-27

Lack of physical discipline is often an indicator of laxity in the spiritual life as well. Toward the end of his life, Paul is probably between 65 and 70, he is still advocating discipline. This time he writes to Timothy, who is probably between 30 and 35 years old.

> ...Take time and trouble to keep yourself spiritually fit. Bodily fitness has a limited value, but spiritual fitness is of unlimited value for it holds promise both for the present life and for the life to come. (II Timothy 4:7b,8 Phillips)

spirituality check-ups — Leaders should from time to time assess their state of discipline. I recommend in addition to standard word disciplines involving the devotional life and study of the Bible other disciplines such as solitude, silence, fasting, frugality, chastity, secrecy. My studies of Foster and Willard have helped me identify a number of disciplines which can habitually shape character and increase the probability of a good finish.

Learning posture — Another of the major leadership lessons is *Effective leaders maintain a learning posture all their lives*. It sounds simple enough but many leaders don't heed it. Two Biblical leaders who certainly were learners all their lives and exemplified this principle were Daniel and Paul. Note how Daniel observed this principle. In Daniel 9 when he is quite old we find that he was still studying his Bible and still learning new things from it. And he was alert to what God wanted to do through what he was learning. Consequently, Daniel was able to intercede for his people and become a recipient of one of the great

COMMENTARY: ENHANCEMENTS continued

messianic revelations. Paul's closing remarks to Timothy show he was still learning. "And when you come don't forget the books Timothy!" (II Timothy 4:13).

application — In western culture, maintaining a learning posture usually involves reading. Countless materials are available on leadership. You should acquire skills which will allow you to read broadly and selectively the many resources that are now being published. I have learned selective reading techniques[13] which have allowed me to learn what I need to know without reading every word of a book. This has helped me to increase the range and number of books I read.

buddy reading model — A helpful accountability model I have used is the buddy reading model.[14] I have a reading buddy. We covenant together to read a book, do certain exercises in conjunction with the book, and then meet to share our learning. We alternate choices of book. My buddy picks it for one month. I do so the next month.

Training events — There are many non-formal training events available such as workshops, seminars, and conferences covering a variety of learning skills. Take advantage of them. A good learning posture is insurance against plateauing and a helpful prod along the way to persevere in leadership. An inflexible spirit with regards to learning is almost a sure precursor to finishing *so so* or *poorly*.

mentors — Comparative study of many leaders lives indicates the frequency with which other people were significant in challenging them into leadership and in giving timely advice and help so as to keep them there.

---

[13] I have developed a reading continuum which identifies different techniques for approaching the reading of a book for information. The continuum moves from less intense and less in-depth reading to highly intense and in-depth reading. Methodologies along the continuum include scan, ransack, browse, pre-read, read and study levels. Each type of reading has different goals and employs different techniques for getting information leading to those goals. See my **Reading on the Run--A Continuum Approach to Reading** available through Barnabas Publisher.

[14] This model could be generalized to any kind of special learning activity like listening to tapes and experiential visits to ministry happenings or the like. The dynamics of the model include co-mentoring, accountability, committal to learning and some kind of learning experience.

COMMENTARY: ENHANCEMENTS continued

relational empowerment
The general notion of mentoring involves a relational process in which someone who knows something (the mentor) passes on something (wisdom, advice, information, emotional support, protection, linking to resources) to someone who needs it (the mentoree, protégé) at a sensitive time so that it impacts the person's development. The basic dynamics of mentoring include attraction, relationship, response, accountability and empowerment. My observations on mentoring suggest that most likely, any leader will need a mentor at all times over a lifetime of leadership. Mentoring is available if one looks for specific functions and people who can do them (rather than an ideal mentor who can do all). God will provide a mentor in a specific area of need for you if you trust Him for one and you are willing to submit and accept responsibility.

Simply stated a final suggestion for enabling a good finish is find a mentor who will hold you accountable in your spiritual life and ministry and who can warn and advise so as to enable you to avoid pitfalls and to grow throughout your lifetime of ministry.

FEEDBACK ON FINISHING WELL AND RELATED CONCEPTS

1. If you were to assess the 6 characteristics of finishing well at this present moment in your life, which one or two would do you feel needs the most attention?
   ___ a. maintain a <u>personal vibrant relationship</u> with God right up to the end.
   ___ b. maintain a <u>learning posture</u> and can learn from various kinds of sources--life especially.
   ___ c. give evidence <u>Christ likeness in character</u> as evidenced by the fruit of the Spirit in their lives.
   ___ d. truth is lived out in their lives so that <u>convictions</u> and promises of God are seen to be real.
   ___ e. leave behind one or more <u>ultimate contributions</u> (saint, stylistic practitioners, mentors, public rhetoricians, pioneers, crusaders, artists, founder, stabilizers, researchers, writers, promoters).
   ___ f. walk with a growing awareness of a sense of destiny and see some or all of it fulfilled.

2. For which of the barriers to finishing well are you the most vulnerable?
   ___ a. misuse of finances or tendency toward greed or materialism
   ___ b. abuse of power
   ___ c. pride
   ___ d. sexual
   ___ e. family
   ___ f. plateauing

3. Which of the 5 enhancements are you strongest on?
   ___ a. lifelong development perspective   ___ b. renewal
   ___ c. disciplines   ___ d. learning posture   ___ e. mentoring

4. Which of the 5 enhancesments do you need to work on the most?
   ___ a. lifelong development perspective   ___ b. renewal
   ___ c. disciplines   ___ d. learning posture   ___ e. mentoring

ANSWERS----------

1. Your choice. For me its d. 2. Your choice. For me its d. 3. Your choice. For me its a, d, e. 4. c. and d.

LEADERSHIP TRANSITION CONCEPTS

introduction   Transition times in movements, organizations and churches hard complex times. How leaders transition new leaders in is a special time of problems and opportunities. The process is best understood when viewed along a continuum.

definition   **Leadership transition** is the process whereby existing leaders prepare and release emerging leaders into the responsibility and practice of leadership positions, functions, roles, and tasks.

LEADERSHIP TRANSITION CONTINUUM

REPLACEMENT OF LEADER				REPLACEMENT OF LEADERSHIP	
the leader's role	major responsibility for functions	pick up some functions	role with many tasks	more or complicated task(s)	simple task

<-- Practicing Leader increasingly RELEASES
<-------------------------Emerging Leader increasingly accepts RESPONSIBILITY

Continuum Definitions

definition   A **task** is an observable assignment of usually short duration.

definition   A **role** is a recognizable position which does a major portion of the ministry. It probably has several on-going tasks associated with it.

definition   **Leadership functions** is a technical term which refers to the three major categories of formal leadership responsibility: task behavior (defining structure and goals), relationship behavior (providing the emotional support), and inspirational behavior (providing motivational effort).

comment   Each of these major leadership functions has several specific sub-functions.

definition   **Leadership release** is the process whereby an existing leader deliberately encourages and allows an emerging leader to accept responsibility for and control of leadership positions, functions, roles, and tasks.

LEADERSHIP TRANSITION CONCEPTS continued

definition	<u>Overlap</u> is that unique time in a leadership transition when the emerging leader and existing leader share responsibility and accountability for tasks, roles, and functions.
definition	<u>Tandem training</u> describes the training technique during overlap used by an existing leader with an emerging leader.
comment extremes	On the right of the continuum is the maximum limit of leadership transition, that is, the leader him/herself is replaced totally from the leadership situation. The emerging leader thus becomes the new leader and is totally responsible for the leadership situation. On the left is the minimum, the present leader turns over some small piece of leadership -- a simple task.
comment process	As one moves across the continuum faithful performance of simple tasks leads to increasing responsibility such as a role. Faithful or successful accomplishment of a role will lead to greater responsibility -- usually wider roles and responsibility for important functions of the ministry as a whole.
comment 2 tendencies	In between, various levels of transition are experienced. As you move from left to right on the continuum, the present leader is increasingly releasing more tasks, functions and finally major responsibility for the ministry. This is signified by the arrow moving toward the right. The function of release is a difficult one for most leaders. The tendency is to either over-control on the one hand (authoritarian defensive posture), or to give too much responsibility without adequate supervision or transitional training on the other (the quick release posture). The first tendency tends to suffocate emerging leaders and frustrate them. Such a posture usually drives them out to another ministry where they can be released. The second tendency overwhelms them and usually insures failure in their first attempt at leadership. This can be discouraging and cause some to decide not to move into leadership in ministry.

LEADERSHIP TRANSITION CONCEPTS continued

comment rate
The rate at which the release should occur ought to depend on the ability of the emerging leader to pick up responsibility for it and not an authoritarian posture or a quick release posture. The arrow moving to the right demonstrates that the emerging leader should be picking up responsibility for the tasks, roles, or functions. As this is done, the leader should be releasing.

comment
Overlap is the time in which both the leader and emerging leader are working together in an increasing way to release and accept responsibility. Overlap can occur anywhere along the continuum.

comment
Tandem training allows the younger leader to share the learning experiences of the older leader via modeling, mentoring, apprenticeship, or internships so as to leapfrog the younger leader's development.

LEADERSHIP TRANSITIONS IN THE BIBLE

introduction There are numerous instances in Scripture of leadership transitions. Most are not ideal as suggested by the transitional continuum. The Moses/Joshua transition which took place over an extended time does follow the description given above of the transitional continuum. It is one of the positive models of leadership transition in the Scriptures. Another positive model occurs in the New Testament -- that of Barnabas and Saul. Other leadership situations in Scripture are worthy of study, mostly for the negative lessons and identification of the items on the transitional continuum that are missing. Table 1 lists some of the instances of Scripture that provide data for observing the positive and negative effects of leadership transitions -- be they good or bad.

Examples of Leadership Transition

Joseph (sovereign transition)
Moses (sovereign transition)
Moses/Joshua (tandem transition)
Joshua/? (none)
Jephthah (other judges--negative)
Eli/sons (negative)
Samuel (sovereign transition)
Samuel/Saul (modified negative)
Saul/David (negative)

David/Absalom (aborted)
David/Solomon (negative)
Elijah/Elisha (minimum)
Daniel (sovereign)
Jesus/disciples
Apostles/deacons (Acts 6)
Barnabas/ Paul (leader switch)
Acts 20 Paul/Ephesian elders

Table 1. Some Instances in Scripture for Seeing Transition Insights

10 STEPS IN MOSES/JOSHUA TRANSITION

introduction   In the Moses/Joshua transition several steps, stages, or discernible events can be ordered. These give insights into why the transition was successful and led to a great leader being raised up to follow a great leader. The following are some observations which suggest why the transition was successful.

STEP	LABEL	DESCRIPTION
1.	Definite Leadership Selection	There was deliberate and definite leadership selection. Moses chose Joshua. Joshua came from a leading family with leadership heritage (note the march order in Exodus -- his grandfather prominent). Notice Moses Nepotism, see comment which follows these steps.
2.	Ministry Task	Moses gave him ministry task with significant responsibility: a. first, select recruits and lead battle among the Amalekites who were harassing the flanks of the exodus march. b. second, spy out the land (probably one of the younger ones to be chosen). Moses checked Joshua's (1) faith, (2) faithfulness, (3) giftedness (charismatic ability to lead) with these increasing responsibilities.
3.	Spirituality Tandem Training	Moses included Joshua in his own spiritual experiences with God. Joshua had firsthand access to Moses vital experiences with God. Moses took him into the holy of holies, frequently into the tabernacle into the presence of God, up on the mountain when he was in solitude alone with God. This was tandem training in spirituality using mentoring.
4.	Leadership Span	Moses recognized the complexity of the leadership situation toward the end of his life. He knew Joshua could not do it all. When transitioning him into leadership he saw that Joshua was a charismatic militaristic leader who needed a supportive spiritual leader. He set Eleazar as the spiritual leader. He publicly did this -- bolstered Eleazar in the eyes of the people, recognized Joshua's strengths and weaknesses. Moses knew that any leader coming into his position would have trouble -- most likely could not fill his shoes; he would need help. Actually Joshua developed real spiritual

10 STEPS IN MOSES/JOSHUA TRANSITION continued

STEP	LABEL	DESCRIPTION
		authority and became a spiritual leader in terms of inspiration.
5.	Public Recognition	Moses recognized the importance of followers knowing whom he had appointed to be the next leader. No ambiguity. No scramble of leaders for that position after Moses' death. He settled it ahead of time and gave a public ceremony stipulating his backing of Joshua.
6.	New Challenge	The new leader following an old leader must not look back and compare. One way of overcoming this tendency is to have a big challenge, a new task not done by the old leader. There was a big task to do. It would be his own contribution -- possess the land.
7.	Divine Affirmation	The new leader needed to know not only that Moses had appointed him as leader but that God had confirmed this appointment. Deut. 31:14-18 and Joshua 1 point out Joshua's experiences personally with God concerning the appointment.
8.	Public Ceremony	Not only must there be personal assurance that God has he appointment but there must be public recognition of this. God gives this in Joshua 3 (note Joshua 3:7, "What I do today will make all the people of Israel begin to honor you as a great man, and they will realize that I am with you as I was with Moses." See also Joshua 4:14, "What the Lord did that day made the people of Israel consider Joshua a great man"). They honored him all his life, just as they had honored Moses.
9.	Initial Success	A leader moving into full responsibility needs an initial success that can bolster spiritual authority and demonstrate that the leader can get vision from God in his/her own right. Joshua's experience with the Captain of the Lord's Army was a pivotal point that did this. It gave him vision -- tactical plan with strategic implications. Its success came early on and stimulated followers. With it there was assurance that brought closure to the whole transition experience.

10 STEPS IN MOSES/JOSHUA TRANSITION continued

STEP	LABEL	DESCRIPTION
10.	Initial Failure	A final thing that ensured a successful transition was the early failure -- Ai. Leaders must know they are not infallible. They must trust God in their leadership. An early failure after initial success was a major deterrent to pride, showed the moral implications of Godly leadership, and the notion that leaders must always move followers along toward God's purposes for them in God's way.

COMMENTARY ON MOSES/JOSHUA TRANSITION

transferable? Peculiar dynamics occur in this model. Its uniqueness may preclude its application in other situations. There was a long period of overlap due to the disciplining of the people in the wilderness. Joshua essentially led the next generation -- not his own. A mighty expectation existed for the new task that challenged. He a home grown leader, from leadership heritage who had proved himself in many ways. He was a charismatic/military leader with a good spiritual track record of sensing and obeying God. Certain of the underlying ideas of these observations will probably be applicable even if the overall dynamics are not identical.

comment Notice that Moses avoids the problem of nepotism.[15] Joshua was hand-picked early for leadership. Yet when final transition time arrived Moses did not just assume that Joshua was the Lord's choice but sought the Lord's confirmation. And when it came *he did all he could to give Joshua the best chance of success.* This leadership transition is the most successful in Scripture. Moses was well aware that if his ministry was to be established beyond his lifetime as he wished (Psalm 90:17) that providing leadership for it was necessary. He certainly exemplifies the *continuity* or *transition* macro-lesson.

Transition **Leaders must transition other leaders into their work in order to maintain continuity and effectiveness.**

implications
1. *Continuity.* No ministry can be expected to continue well without deliberate transition efforts.
2. *Nepotism.* Rarely can a leader replace his/her father/ mother with the same leadership effectiveness. The appropriate leader, gifted for the job, is the proper selection.
3. *Best Start.* Whenever leaving a ministry insure that the next leader has the best possible chance of success.
4. *Models.* Study negative and positive Biblical models for guidelines. The positive models include Moses/ Joshua, Elijah/ Elisha, Jesus/ Disciples, Barnabas/ Paul. A particularly negative one to see is Solomon/ Rehoboam.

---

[15]It is not clear but it appears from hints given that Moses really had family problems and probably was separated from his family for extended times during his desert leadership. His sons are never prominently mentioned anywhere. His wife and children visit him when Jethro comes. So perhaps he was never tempted to try to place them in leadership as many charismatic leaders do today.

REGIME TURNOVER

introduction   Frequently there are changes in upper leadership in organizations and churches which have ripple effects to all lower level leaders involved with that leadership. This can be seen when a new senior pastor comes into a church that has already existed. Or in governmental circles when a new political party comes into power. Or in a university or college situation when a new Dean of a School or a President of the whole college or university takes over. Many times the new leadership is not compatible with the lower levels of leaders carried over from the old regime. A form of leadership transition occurs in which the *new regime deals with the carry over leaders from the previous regime.* How that problem is dealt with tests Christian organizational ethics. Most Christian organizations do not handle *regime turnover* very well.

definition   <u>Regime turnover</u> refers to the process and practices involved in transitioning an old staff recruited under a former regime until it fits the new leadership's idea of what its people should be and do.

alternate form   When a new powerful player joins a leadership team and has the ear of the most powerful leader (i.e. referent power) then a pseudo-regime turnover will occur as that new powerful leader introduces his/her ideas into the situation.

<u>Principles Observed in Some Regime Turnovers</u>

1. **POWER DETERMINES THE RADICALNESS OF SOLUTIONS.**
The more power the new leader or regime has the more final (top down edicts) will be the solutions--layoff, firing, transferring, quickly getting rid of the old regime carryovers. The less power the new leader or regime has the more political solutions (compromise) or negotiations will dominate the situation.

2. **NEW LEADERSHIP MUST RECRUIT TO ITS VISION.**
A major dynamic is involved in this principle. New leadership will bring new vision. Old timers may not fit that vision. When that vision is unclear there is confusion as to who fits and who doesn't. Old regime people are sometimes caught in a bind not of their choosing and can not even know if they fit or could adapt to fit since standards are not clear.

REGIME TURNOVER continued

The new regime usually gets rid of the old based on how the old regime leaders were previously operating without giving a chance for them to adapt. That is, the new regime does not usually think of the old as a pool from which to recruit.

3. **CULTURAL DISSONANCE BETWEEN THE NEW ORGANIZATIONAL CULTURAL VALUES AND THE OLD REGIME'S (or individuals from it) IS THE MAJOR ISSUE THAT NEEDS TO BE RECOGNIZED.**
    The problems felt by old regime leaders is essentially at value level. These values may be implicit and not easily articulated. But the uneasiness and conflict that arises has root causes in values. Where the differences in values can be stated they can also be assessed and changes can be made toward those values or differences recognized.

4. **POLITICALLY ADROIT OLD TIMERS WILL FIND WAYS TO SURVIVE THE NEW REGIME.**
    They know that regimes and power in organizations come and go. Survival can allow changes in the future.

Some Solutions Observed

1. **Total Turnover of Leadership Right Off the Bat**
    All old regime leaders automatically resign when the new regime comes in. The new regime may choose to keep some but is free not to and to recruit to their new vision.

2. **Partial Turnover of Potentially Problematic Leadership**
    New leaders keep old regime maintenance people (minor administrative and dog work positions) but remove those in philosophical roles or who might provide opposition.

3. **Political Maneuvering--Complex Organization**
    There is organizational political warfare depending on vested interest, power and the complexity and age of the organization.

REGIME TURNOVER continued

4. **Developmental Solution**
   The new regime honors old contracts (implicit or explicit) and seeks a developmental solution for old regime leaders. This involves sequencing such as:
   a. The new regime first of all decides on values/ vision (core and periphery) and clarifies these to the organization.
   b. They evaluate performance of all (including old regime regulars) based on those standards
   c. They seek first to train and develop all old regime leaders who wish to be part of the new vision and values.
   d. They evaluate the results of this training.
   e. They assess fit after a reasonable time and these attempts to train.
   f. They reassign non-fit types into other parts of the organization if they can. That is, they seek to keep people within the organization somewhere where most compatible.
   g. As a last resort, transitions out of the organization are made. they help those moving on toward making a new start elsewhere and giving those exited leaders the best possible jump-start into the new situation.

comment   It is obvious that this last approach, the Developmental Solution, is the most desirable. While fairly radical, the first one, Total Turnover, is at least clean and clear to all.

comment   As a change agent when you are doing your linear history you want to be especially aware of any regime turnovers. Key informants can let you in on some of these situations. Many present problems in an organization are festering results from past regime turnovers.

FEEDBACK ON LEADERSHIP TRANSITION CONCEPTS

1. If you have gone through a major leadership transition in your situation, check the description which best fits it.
   ___ a. it was a time of turmoil, trauma, and problems
   ___ b. it was well planned
   ___ c. there was overlap between the major leaders concerned
   ___ d. there was tandem training between the major leaders concerned
   ___ e. it just happened
   ___ f. you describe it:

2. Did any of the Moses/Joshua steps occur in your change situation? If so, identify. If not could they have applied? Which ones?

3. If you have gone through a regime turnover which of the options best describe how the situation worked out.

   ___ a. Total Turnover of Leadership Right Off the Bat
   ___ b. Partial Turnover of Potentially Problematic Leadership
   ___ c. Political Maneurving--Complex Organization
   ___ d. Developmental Solution

Describe the situation.

ANSWERS----------

1. Ours was not well planned. There has been more trauma than we expected.
2. No. The situation as it stood did not allow for them.
3. c (somewhat)

7 MAJOR LEADERSHIP LESSONS

introduction Comparative studies of Biblical, historical, and contemporary leaders has led to the identification of 7 major lessons. The list is a composite synthesized across leaders. A given effective leader may have 4 or 5 of these operating in his/her ministry. Another leader may have 3 or 4 including some of the ones of the first but some different.

Lesson Label	Lesson Statement
1. Learning Posture	EFFECTIVE LEADERS MAINTAIN A LEARNING POSTURE THROUGHOUT LIFE.
2. Spiritual Authority	EFFECTIVE LEADERS VALUE SPIRITUAL AUTHORITY AS A PRIMARY POWER BASE.
3. Sense of Destiny	EFFECTIVE LEADERS DEMONSTRATE A GROWING AWARENESS OF THEIR SENSE OF DESTINY.
4. Leadership Selection	EFFECTIVE LEADERS RECOGNIZE LEADERSHIP SELECTION AND DEVELOPMENT AS A PRIORITY FUNCTION.
5. Lifetime Perspective	EFFECTIVE LEADERS INCREASINGLY PERCEIVE THEIR MINISTRY IN TERMS OF A LIFETIME PERSPECTIVE.
6. Empowerment	EFFECTIVE LEADERS PERCEIVE THE IMPORTANCE OF RELATIONAL EMPOWERMENT IN THEIR OWN AND IN THEIR FOLLOWER'S LIVES.
7. Ministry Philosophy	EFFECTIVE LEADERS WHO ARE PRODUCTIVE OVER A LIFETIME HAVE A DYNAMIC MINISTRY PHILOSOPHY.

examples Daniel is the classic Old Testament character demonstrating every one of these lessons. Paul is the New Testament church leader exemplifying all of them.

FEEDBACK ON LEADERSHIP LESSONS

1. Which of the leadership lessons are you strongest on?
   ___ a. Learning Posture
   ___ b. Spiritual Authority
   ___ c. Sense of Destiny
   ___ d. Leadership Selection
   ___ e. Lifetime Perspective
   ___ f. Empowerment
   ___ g. Ministry Philosophy

2. Which of the leadership lessons are you weakest on?
   ___ a. Learning Posture
   ___ b. Spiritual Authority
   ___ c. Sense of Destiny
   ___ d. Leadership Selection
   ___ e. Lifetime Perspective
   ___ f. Empowerment
   ___ g. Ministry Philosophy

3. Check any of the leadership lessons that you have observed in some leader you respect. Give his/her name if you can.
   ___ a. Learning Posture   Name:
   ___ b. Spiritual Authority   Name:
   ___ c. Sense of Destiny   Name:
   ___ d. Leadership Selection   Name:
   ___ e. Lifetime Perspective   Name:
   ___ f. Empowerment   Name:
   ___ g. Ministry Philosophy   Name:

ANSWERS----------

1. a   2. g
3.
   _x_ a. Learning Posture   Name: Paul Leavenworth
   _x_ b. Spiritual Authority   Name: Bob Munger
   _x_ c. Sense of Destiny   Name: Richard Clinton
   _x_ d. Leadership Selection   Name: Paul Stanley
   _x_ e. Lifetime Perspective   Name: Doug McConnell
   _x_ f. Empowerment   Name: Roger Bosch
   _x_ g. Ministry Philosophy   Name: Peter Wagner

BROKENNESS

introduction	Someone has said all real leaders of God *walk with a limp*. That, of course, is a reference to the Jacob all-night experience in which he wrestled with God. This all-night experience demonstrated Jacob's deep need for God in a crisis situation. Total dependence upon God was at the root of the need. Leaders almost always accomplish more lasting results for God when they have been deeply processed in terms of character and essential relationship to God. This kind of processing includes sometimes some very negative things such as conflict, crises--general and life threatening, leadership backlash, and isolation . It results in a leader who is stripped of the wrong kind of self-reliance and in its place knows utter dependence upon God. The experience of going through this high learning curve full of darkness is called brokenness. An understanding of brokenness allows for vicarious learning as well as responsiveness to God's purposes in it.
definition	<u>Brokenness</u> is a state of mind in which a person recognizes that he/she is helpless in a situation or life process unless God alone works.
comment	It is a state of mind in which a person acknowledges a deep dependence upon God and is open for God to break through in new ways, thoughts, directions, and revelation of Himself that was not the case before the brokenness experience.
example	Jacob in Genesis 32 faced a **life threatening situation** in which he was forced to desperately depend upon God.
example	Joseph in Genesis 37 was faced with **loss of life**. This was the first of numerous brokenness experiences that shaped Joseph for a great work for God.
example	Moses' attempt to save the Israelites in his own way was a shattering experience that broke him. See Exodus 2 for this **loss of vision.** Exodus 3, occurring many years later, is God's restoration of the vision. It is clear that dependence upon God was a major difference.

BROKENNESS continued

example	David's experience with sin unchecked in his life and his eventual confrontation by Nathan along with his **repentant response** to God illustrates brokenness. 2 Samuel 12; Psalm 51 (see especially verse 17).
example	Peter's 3 denial experiences shattered his **self-confidence**. Jesus' restoration completed the process. Luke 22:54-62; John 21.
example	Paul's experience on the road to Damascus was an awesome experience that broke through a mis-directed **perspective** of serving God. Acts 9.
example	Isaiah's **awesome experience** in seeing a holy God allowed him to see himself in a new light and as unworthy to serve.
example	Hagar's persecution and dismissal by Sarah broke her before God and caused her to despair of any hope at all. It was God who became her only hope. Genesis 21.
means used	God uses crises--general and life threatening, sickness, persecution, conflict, isolation, awesome revelations of Himself, conviction of sin, and the like to accomplish the brokenness. The happenings may be stretched out over an extended period of time or concentrated.
purposes	Brokenness can accomplish any or several of the following :

- **new perspective**--paradigm shifts allowing us to see dependence upon God and to see things we could not see before,
- a **release of the Spirit,**
- new awareness of the **inner life,**
- **maturity** in character,
- **spiritual authority** in our leadership,
- more **effective ministry.**
- a healthy respect for **sinfulness**

COMMENTARY ON BROKENNESS

comment	Classic studies in brokenness in the Old Testament include biographical analyses of Joseph, Daniel, Job and Jonah. In the New Testament analysis of leadership development of Peter and Paul give important insights.
comments	The following are encouraging words about brokenness adapted from Charles Stanley's teaching on the subject. (See Stanley tapes available from First Baptist Church of Atlanta.)

1. When God refines us it is because he loves us and is purifying the Gold. The Gold is never destroyed. Only the dross. Refinement is a sign of God's love for us.
2. God limits the refining process to only those things that will accomplish His purposes.
3. There is a goal in God's processing--brokenness and refinement is always to teach us something.
4. While it may seem to the contrary, God will never desert us in the process of refining us.
5. The ultimate end of brokenness/refinement will be victory if you will sense God's working in it and persevere with God in the process.
6. God is long suffering with us and will patiently refine us even if it takes a long period of time and many separate processes.
7. Brokenness will sometimes result in radical obedience which may frighten us. But remember, He is responsible for the consequences of obedience.

comment	John 12:24 is the picture of brokenness and release which Jesus uses to describe himself and the impending cross. But it is also the prototype of brokenness for all believers. It is this death/life process that is involved in the brokenness process.
comment	There is a difference between negative or hard times and brokenness experiences. Negative or hard times don't necessarily lead to brokenness. It is one's response to God in the refining process that determines whether the pruning brings brokenness along with its fruitful results.

THE ULTIMATE CONTRIBUTION

introduction   When it is all said and done a leader leaves behind the results of his/her ministry. Over a lifetime God will lead a Spirit-led leader to sensitively recognize and more narrowly focus in on those things that are more important and will have lasting impact. The concept of ultimate contribution deals with this kind of guidance.

definition   An <u>ultimate contribution</u> is a lasting legacy of a Christian worker for which he/she is remembered and which furthers the cause of Christianity by one or more of the following:

- setting standards for life and ministry,
- impacting lives by enfolding them in God's Kingdom or developing them once in the Kingdom,
- serving as a stimulus for change which betters the world,
- leaving behind an organization, institution, or movement that can serve as a channel for God to work through, or
- the discovery of ideas, communication of them, or promotion of them so that they further God's work.

example   a godly life: Samuel Brengle, Jim Elliot, Hudson Taylor

example   a significant ministry model: A. J. Gordon, E. Stanley Jones

example   relational empowerment of individuals: R. C. McQuilkin, Florence Allshorn, Rufus Anderson, Paul Devanandan, Dawson Trottman

example   public ministry which impacted many: D. L. Moody, C. H. Spurgeon, W. W. Harris, D. T. Niles

example   founded a new work: J. O. Fraser, Robert Jaffray, V. S. Azariah, D. Livingstone, F. C. Laubach

example   left behind important classical writings: K. S. Latourette, John Bunyan, Stephen Neill

12 PRIME TYPES OF ULTIMATE CONTRIBUTION

introduction   A comparative research study of some very effective missionary and pastor types to identify what kinds of legacies they left behind resulted in the categorization of 12 prime types of ultimate contribution. The study also identified patterns of discovery of one's ultimate contribution types as well as various categories of ultimate contributions as to nature and short or long term contributions. But it is the prime types are helpful in long term goal setting and decision making for personal ministry.

definition   A prime type is a classification label that helps one identify a stereotype identity and its ultimate contribution thrust.

definition   An ultimate contribution set is the collection of prime types that any given leader will actually accomplish over his/ her lifetime.

Prime Type	Explanation
1. Saint	Person lived an exemplary life. Thought of as a saint or model for others to emulate. The person is usually thought of as having a very intimate relationship with God. Frequently mystical experiences occur. He or she demonstrates the fruit of the spirit. There is a zealousness for God that is beyond the ordinary. The thrust of this accomplishment is vertical, upward, toward God. *The ultimate contribution is a model life that others are attracted to and want to emulate.* Examples: Samuel Brengle, Jim Elliot, Hudson Taylor
2. Stylistic Practitioner	Person exemplified an important or unique ministry model. *A ministry model considered worthy of emulation is the ultimate contribution.* Examples: Stanley Jones, A. J. Gordon
3. Mentor	This is a person who has impact on individuals. He or she relates ministry down to a personal level. They are thought of as mentors, disciplers, and people who have a network of close followers. They will spend

12 PRIME TYPES OF ULTIMATE CONTRIBUTION continued

Prime Type	Explanation
	time developing individuals. There is heavy intensive and comprehensive sphere of influence. *The people developed are the ultimate contribution.* Examples: Robert McQuilkin, A. G. Hogg, Florence Allshorn, Rufus Anderson, Paul Devanandan, Dawson Trottman
4. Public Rhetorician	This is a person who has public exposure and whose ministry is thought of as to the masses or large groups of people. They are usually mass communicators. They shine before large groups. They will motivate a large following. There is broad extensive sphere of influence though comprehensive and intensive influence may be nil. *The changed lives are the ultimate contribution..* Examples: W. W. Harris, D. L. Moody, C. H. Spurgeon, D. T. Niles
5. Pioneer	This is a person who creates something like a new religious structure, new religious institution, new church or denomination or organization, or works in a place where no one has gone or sees a special need and finds a way to meet it or breaks new ground by showing some new way to do something. *The thing created or done is left behind as the legacy.* Examples: Robert Jaffray, J. O. Fraser, V. S. Azariah, D. Livingstone, F. C. Laubach
6. Crusader	This is a person whose desire is to correct things. They see problems in society or the church or a Christian organization and set about to bring change. Some operate more from compassion for those in need than for motives to make things better. *The people ministered to or the changed situation left behind comprises the legacy.* Examples: Mother Theresa, Theresa of Avila, John Woolman, Ida S. Scudder, C. F. Andrews, Alexander Duff, William Paton

12 PRIME TYPES OF ULTIMATE CONTRIBUTION continued

Prime Type	Explanation
7. Artist	This is a person with creative talent who introduces new products of various kinds into Christianity. It may be art forms, new music, a new genre of writing or some other innovative creation. Frequently, people leaving this kind of contribution have a brilliant natural talent which is the base of their giftedness set. *The artistic product--hymn, new genre of writing, poetry, painting, drama, dance or whatever is the contribution.* Examples: Philip Bliss, Charles Wesley, Eliza Hewitt.
8. Founder	This is a person who begins a new organization in order to embody a movement into an on-going institution. This person may or may not be good at running an organization but very good at getting one going. *The contribution left behind is the organization.* Example: Samuel Mills, Cameron Townsend
9. Stabilizer	This is a person who builds an organization and brings stability to it so that it will survive and will be effective. *The stable organization or on-going institution is the contribution.* Example: Barbara Hendricks, Henry Venn, Rufus Anderson, Max Warren, A. J. Brown
10. Researcher	This is a person who sees a situation and seeks to understand it and comes up with a framework for understanding it. This framework is usually considered a break through which aids the Christian church as a whole. The research can focus on a contemporary issue and applies uniquely only to that time or it can deal with fundamental dynamics which are more timeless in their application. *The basic thrust of the contribution is conceptualization.* Example: Donald McGavran, William Carey, Roland Allen, Pierre Charles, H. Kraemer

12 PRIME TYPES OF ULTIMATE CONTRIBUTION continued

Prime Type	Explanation
11. **Writer**	This is a person who produces a body of literature that affects a significant portion of Christianity either in a time bound way or in a timeless way--it is continually read by later generations. Sometimes one single work--a book, a tract, a sermon, an article--is significant enough that it lives on as an ultimate contribution. *The basic thrust of the contribution is the written product.* Example: K. S. Latourette, John Bunyan, Stephen Neil, Wilhelm Schmidt
12. **Promoter**	This is a person who may or may not have originated some conceptualization but who is adept at marketing it across the Christian market. *The contribution then is the widespread acceptance and use of the ideation by Christians.* Example: John Mott, S. Zwemer, Robert Speer, A. J. Gordon

COMMENTARY ON ULTIMATE CONTRIBUTION

categories   Ultimate contributions essentially involve:

1. example lives that set standards for others,
2. ministry focusing on development of individuals, or word ministries to the masses,
3. ministries that identify needs and find a way to meet them,
4. ministries that focus on organizations and institutions,
5. ministries involved in finding, communicating, and using ideas.

identification   Some of these are more easily seen during the lifetime of the individual as they are before the public eye-- ministry lifestyles that serve as examples for other ministries, word ministries to the masses, some artistic endeavors involving music, some of the ideation sub-categories such as writing and publicizing of ideas. Some may not be known till after the person's life is finished--such as meeting of social needs, changing of society or institutions, or starting a pioneering work. Some may never be known unless others (sometimes disciples or other followers) deliberately identify and publicize them--a holy life style, personal ministry to individuals, a   founding work, an organizational stalwart, a researcher.

importance   One prime type is not necessarily more important than another; all have their place and are needed in the on-going drama of redemption. SAINTS and STYLISTIC PRACTITIONERS give us models that inspire us. MENTORS and PUBLIC RHETORICIANS show us the power of spiritually focused ministries. PIONEERS show us that God still challenges us to identify needs and create works of God to meet them. CRUSADERS carry on the prophetic function that interweaves across Old and New Testaments. They try to correct situations that are oppressive in a fallen world. ARTISTS break old patterns and show the importance of diversity and creativity to leadership. STABILIZERS give themselves to preserving and improving organizations, institutions, and movements

COMMENTARY ON ULTIMATE CONTRIBUTION

so that they can be channels for God's further working. In a time of vast numbers of changes, there is a need for demonstration of stability. Organizations do that. STABILIZERS seek to develop organizations so that they remain faithful and effective over their lifetimes. They seek to overcome the degenerative tendencies of organizations, institutions and movements. RESEARCHERS show us the importance of assessment of situations and development of ideas that help us understand them. Christian leaders need perspectives based on facts as well as feelings. WRITERS disseminate needed information. RESEARCHERS discover. Writers communicate those discoveries to others in ways that make them useful. PROMOTERS take the best of ideas that are being researched and communicated and recruit followings to these ideas. All prime types have their place. All are needed.

FEEDBACK ON ULTIMATE CONTRIBUTION

1. In your opinion what would be Daniel's ultimate contribution set? Check those which you think fits his ministry.
   - ___ a. Saint
   - ___ b. Stylistic Practitioner
   - ___ c. Mentor
   - ___ d. Public Rhetorician
   - ___ e. Pioneer
   - ___ f. Crusader
   - ___ g. Artist
   - ___ h. Founder
   - ___ i. Stabilizer
   - ___ j. Researcher
   - ___ k. Writer
   - ___ l. Promoter

2. At this point in your life, which of the ultimate contribution prime types seem most likely to fit you?

3. In what way should knowing your ultimate contribution set make any difference in your leadership?

ANSWERS----------

1. In my opinion Daniel was a Saint, Stylistic Practitioner, Stabilizer, Writer
2. Your choice. Mine is Saint, Stylistic Practitioner, Mentor, Researcher, Writer
3. You can proactively make choices in guidance decisions which move towards roles that will enhance ultimate contribution. You can do goal setting which will focus on your ultimate contribution set. Your set should help you write your personal mission statement.

PARADIGM SHIFTS

introduction	Paradigm shifts occur throughout the Bible. Some people can embrace new paradigms and others can't. Any information that can help a leader understand what paradigms are, how shifts happen, and how they can influence followers to go through paradigm shifts is welcome information. Much of influence deals with attempts at getting people to go through paradigm shifts. Paradigms are important to leaders for several reasons including stimulus to growth and a major means for getting new vision.
definition	A <u>paradigm</u> is a controlling perspective which allows one to perceive and understand REALITY.
	symbolically r --->R
definition	A <u>paradigm shift</u> is the change of a controlling perspective so that one perceives and understands REALITY in a different way.
	symbolically r ---> r' --->R
example	conversion to Christianity
example	a Lordship committal in which Christ becomes the one in charge of or directing a life
example	moving from a mono-cultural perspective to a cross-cultural perspective
example	moving from not accepting women in leadership due to Biblical convictions to accepting women in leadership because of new Biblical convictions.
example	going through a brokenness experience

COMMENTARY ON PARADIGM SHIFTS

why needed — Many pastors, parachurch workers and especially missionaries find themselves in a paradoxical position. They need to be strong willed people with strong convictions in order to carry out their leadership with power. People who do this and do it well also find themselves frequently people who are inflexible. Such strong leaders frequently have major tendencies toward inflexibility in their leadership. Unfortunately inflexible leaders have a downside. They

- have a tendency to plateau,
- tend not to be life long learners
- tend to be naive realists,[16]
- do not perceive paradigm shifts very easily, and
- tend not to finish well.

importance — Now how can we help these inflexible leaders to both enjoy the strength that generally comes with inflexibility and yet make them more amenable to change. I believe we can do so by helping them understand what paradigms are, the nature of paradigm shifts, how they happen and most importantly how God uses them to develop leadership character, leadership skills, and leadership values. Paradigm shifts are God's way of breaking through inflexibility and expanding a leader. They are an antidote to the negative or down side of inflexibility.

---

[16]See the position paper on *Paradigm Shifts* available from Barnabas Publishers which explains several of these epistemological positions. Epistemology refers to the way we know things.

BIBLICAL EXAMPLES OF PARADIGM SHIFTS

PARADIGM SHIFTS

Who	Where In Bible	Paradigm Before	Paradigm After
1. Job	book of Job	Suffering is the result of sin and is deserved. Righteous people should not suffer.	A righteous person can suffer as a part of God's plan for him/her.
2. Jonah	Jonah 1-4	God exclusively deals only with Israel in order to bless. God is basically against non-Israelites.	God is not exclusively for Israel. He has concerns for all nations--to show His mercy and grace to all who repent.
3. Hab.	Habakkuk 1-3	God is unjust and unfaithful in His dealing with groups of people in history. He does not keep His promises.	God is just. He is complex in His dealings with nations. Ultimately His purposes and justice will be seen by all.
4. Elisha's	2 Kings 6:8-23	See only natural situation. Fear of the physical warfare to come.	Sees supernatural, the unseen Angelic Band protecting. Now believes in unseen world.
5. Nicodemus	John 3	Kingdom of God is external and has expected political ramifications.	Must have an inner transformation by the Spirit in order to perceive God's rule.

BIBLICAL EXAMPLES OF PARADIGM SHIFTS continued

PARADIGM SHIFTS

Who	Where In Bible	Paradigm Before	Paradigm After
6. Apostles	Acts 2	No church. No one is sure of what will happen next.	Coming of Holy Spirit Church is born. Message is for others; salvation.
7. Whole Church	Acts 5	Moral issues are relative; can follow cultural ethics.	Dishonesty is against God whether inward or outwardly known; integrity is a thing of the heart. God wants whole hearted obedience.
8. Saul	Acts 9	Persecuted Christians; saw Christ as a leader of a cult opposing Judaism.	Saw Christ as the resurrected Lord; loved Christians; propagated Christianity.
9. Peter	Acts 10	Gentiles not acceptable to God; Jews should not fellowship with them.	Gentiles accepted by God. All Christians are one.
10. Woman At the Well	John 4	Believed Smaritans had religious views comparable with Jews. Lived an unsatisfied life. Religion not satisfying.	Saw Jesus as one sent from God who had access to supernatural revelation. Christ's religious views brought hope.

3 CATEGORIES OF PARADIGM SHIFTS

introduction A knowledge of kinds of paradigm shifts can help leaders understand better how to work to accomplish them.

Kind	Explanation
1. Cognitive Shifts	New Ideas (information, categories, etc.) on Seeing things. The heart of the shift has to do with a new idea for seeing things, a possibility not considered before. The cognition may also be accompanied by a volitional to use it but the heart of it is the discovery of the validity of the idea. Examples: • a mono-cultural to cross-cultural perspective, • getting church growth eyes • getting leadership style insights
2. Volitional Shifts	A committal by an act of a will to use some idea even though it may not be fully understood or experienced. The heart of the shift is a recognition of the importance of letting go and following the new perspective whether or not it is understood. Usually there is a surrender of the will involved and an acknowledgment to God of this. Examples: • radical adult conversion • leadership committal • call to ministry
3. Experiential Power Shifts	These have to do with experiencing the effects of something. After the experience there may be a growing awareness of its meaning. Usually these have to do with life power or gifted power or personal experiences with the supernatural--that is, unusual experience with the Holy Spirit and supernatural power break throughs. Examples: • infilling of Holy Spirit--Luke's description • a major healing experience, • experiences with prophetic,

COMMENTARY ON KINDS OF PARADIGM SHIFTS

explanation	Further explanation is probably needed on experiential power shifts. Life Power is the appropriation of God's power via the Holy Spirit to live a victorious Christian life and to experience holiness. Examples include: entire sanctification--Brengle's experience, baptism of Holy Spirit--Torrey's experience, deeper life experience, McQuilkin's experience, Union life shift--Taylor's experience of the exchanged life, infilling of Holy Spirit--Luke's description of several in Acts. Gifted Power is the appropriation of God's power via the Holy Spirit to use giftedness with effective power in ministry. Examples: a major healing experience, experiences with prophetic, confirmed experiences with word of knowledge or word of wisdom or discernings of spirits, miracles, tongues or interpretation of tongues verified, anointing of Holy Spirit for a ministry, experience of unusual effectiveness with giving, helps, mercy, teaching, evangelism, apostleship, pastoral, or any of the normally considered non-supernatural gifts. Other power experiences can vary all over the place but usually have to do with spiritual warfare and its manifestations. Examples include power encounters--Elijah's, Nee's experience, spiritual warfare--Paul on Cypress, spiritual authority, cosmic level issues, prayer power, unusual intercessory experiences involving divine initiative praying.

FEEDBACK ON PARADIGM SHIFTS

1. As you have been studying chapters 1 and 2 of this Handbook, are you aware of God's impressing you with some special information that will stretch your present paradigms? If so, what are they.

2. What paradigm shift, if it could be accomplished in your leadership situation, would revolutionize your leadership? That is, what seems impossible to do now but if it could be done would radically change your ministry.

3. Corporate groups as well as individuals go through paradigm shifts. What are the most recent one or two paradigm shifts that your group has gone through?

ANSWERS----------

1. Your choice. I am working on experiencing how to operate in the future perfect paradigm.
2. A radical view toward delivery systems and a view toward training for ministry not for academic education.
3. An experiential believe in the supernatural.

FUTURE PERFECT TIME PARADIGM

introduction — Christian leaders are those who influence specific groups of God's people toward God's purposes for them. Getting external direction from God, that is, vision for the future for the group, involves an act of faith. Leaders with vision are able then to interpret present happenings of today in terms of this future state which they envision as already having taken place. They can live in the tension of the *what shall be as if it were* with the *anomalies of the present.* Such a time paradigm is very helpful to a leader.

definition — The <u>future perfect paradigm</u> refers to a way of viewing a future reality as if it were already present which in turn,
- inspires one's leadership,
- challenges followers to the vision,
- affects decision making, and
- causes one to persevere in faith,

and results in the future reality coming into being.

FUTURE PERFECT TIME PERSPECTIVE

|--|
PAST PERFECT   FUTURE PERFECT

*- - - - - - - - -> AFTERMATH   BEFOREMATH <- - - - - - - *

definition — <u>Aftermath</u> refers to the after effects and ramifications of some past act or event which has continuing influence of the present.

definition — <u>Beforemath</u> refers to the effects and implications of some future event or state which has influence reaching back into the present, at least to the eye of the leader holding the future perfect vision by faith.

comment — Characteristics of those working from a future perfect paradigm include:
a. Working on the Beforemath
b. Recognizing the paradox, yet maintaining hope in the future reality.
c. Decision making in light of the future/ not past.
d. Affirmation of the future--always seeing progress.
e. Recognizing renewal--ministry and divine affirmation experiences--as stimulating the future perfect vision.

examples — Hebrews 11 illustrates this kind of thinking.

5 STAGES LEADING TO THE FUTURE PERFECT PARADIGM

introduction   It is helpful to recognize that arriving at a future paradigm viewpoint does not happen all at once for all people. For some this will happen. For others there is a process that brings about the paradigm shift.

5 Stages Leading to the Future Perfect Paradigm

1. Dream/ Vision

2. Destiny--Consciousness of God in it

3. The Inner Paradigm Shift
   a. Working on the Beforemath
   b. Recognizing the paradox, yet maintaining hope in the future reality.
      (1) Decision making in light of the future/ not past.
      (2) Affirmation of the future--always seeing progress.
      (3) renewal--ministry and divine affirmation experiences.

4. Living in the Paradox, present but not yet present

5. Realization--the Reality Present

example   World class athletes frequently envision the final act of their events in their minds before it actually happens. They actually go through the event twice, once in their mind--a future perfect way of thinking, and then when it actually happens. And they make decisions in the present based on that envisioned reality. Discipline in the present is in light of the future perfect reality they have seen.

examples   The Bible speaks of speaking a word of faith and bringing something into existence.

examples   Hebrews 11 details this kind of thinking as it highlights Old Testament saints who lived by faith. They moved toward something, a vision, which they kept always before them. Some did not reach these visions but they walked in light of them and toward them and with hope in them.

FEEDBACK ON FUTURE PERFECT TIME PARADIGM

1. What Biblical examples readily come to your mind of people who lived out of a future perfect paradigm model?

2. Examine the stages of entering into a future perfect paradigm. If you are in process on some future perfect paradigm, then check where you are. Identify the Future Perfect Paradigm by some descriptive label, then check the stage you are in.

   Future Perfect Paradigm:

   ___ a. Dream/ Vision
   ___ b. Destiny--Consciousness of God in it
   ___ c. The Inner Paradigm Shift
       ___ (a) Working on the Beforemath
       ___ (b) Recognizing the paradox, yet maintaining hope in the future reality.
       ___ (c) Decision making in light of the future/ not past.
       ___ (d) Affirmation of the future--always seeing progress.
       ___ (e) renewal--ministry and divine affirmation experiences.
   ___ d. Living in the Paradox, present but not yet present
   ___ e. Realization--the Reality Present

3. In your opinion, what is the most important or challenging thing about the future perfect paradigm?

ANSWERS---------

1. Moses, especially in the latter days. Ezekiel. Nehemiah.
2. I applied the paradigm to one of my weaker courses. I am simultaneously in Stage C and D.
3. It stresses vision and faith, two important Biblical concepts for leaders.

5 ETHNOTHEOLOGICAL MODELS

introduction   The following 5 models come from the field of ethnotheology[17] and aid us in understanding the on-going progress of revelation in the Scriptures and even today. The story of leadership in the Bible is tied to an on-going revelation of what God was doing and saying. These models help us appreciate the problems and opportunities that leaders had in embracing an on-going revelation from God.

Model	Name	Basic Thrust
1	The Bible-As-Yardstick	The Bible is the standard for judging on-going revelation.
2	Bible Allowing A Range of Variation	God allows less than perfect understandings of Himself and his ideals in terms of a range of categories: ideal, sub-ideal, outside.
3	Bible-As-Tether	The Bible provides the set radius within which contemporary revelational encounters may occur.
4	Bible-As-Inspired Casebook	The Bible provides inspired case studies which give not only content but processes.
5	Starting-Point-Plus Process	God works within the limitations of cultures to reveal Himself and His ideals to them.

---

[17] My Doctor of Missiology was done in ethnotheology under Dr. Charles Kraft who is the leading expert in this field. See **Christianity in Culture**. These models are my interpretations drawn from his seminal work.

MODEL 1. THE BIBLE-AS-YARDSTICK

introduction	The Bible serves an important yardstick-like function in measuring God's contemporary revelations of Himself. This same model can be extrapolated backwards to see God using this same basic process to reveal Himself to leaders in both the Old and New Testaments. The Biblical repository of previous revelation adequately screens so that contemporary messages from God will not fall outside the range there allowed.
descriptive analogy	Model 1, The Bible-As-Yardstick, provides a standard for judging contemporary revelation by its adequate repository of previous revelational examples just as a yardstick provides a linear standard of measurement.
MAJOR ASSERTION	THE BIBLE PROVIDES NUMEROUS EXAMPLES WHEREBY CONTEMPORARY REVELATION CAN BE JUDGED.
premises	1. This model is essentially the same as that currently used by evangelicals to test *application* of Scriptural truth. 2. This model labels and measures a contemporary application as divine revelation, not as something that is qualitatively different from God's past revelatory work. 3. This model emphasizes a difference between what the Bible is and how it is used.
example	George McBane (*Does God Allow For Belief In Other Gods*), uses the Bible-as-a-yard-stick to measure general revelational concepts of gods among the Meghwar people in Pakistan.
comment	The *Bible-As-Yardstick*, *Bible As Allowing A Range* and the *Bible-As-Tether* combine to give us a range within which God works and the borders at either extreme of that range. God often presents ideal understandings (e.g. Matthew 5:28 on adultery and 5:21,22 on murder), exhibiting one extreme of the range. But He also shows where He is willing to start at the other end of that range. The Biblical range, then provides the tether within which contemporary interaction with God can move and the yardstick by means of which it is possible to evaluate whether or not contemporary practices are Biblical.
bottom line of analogy	The Bible record of revelational activity provides the standard whereby we judge contemporary revelation.

MODEL 2. BIBLE ALLOWING RANGE OF VARIATION

introduction   The Bible clearly shows that God is content to accept human behavior, including understandings of Himself and His truth, that fall within a range of acceptable variation (See also Model 5 Starting Point Plus Process). Owing to the limitations of culture, individual experience, and sin, human beings seldom if ever live or understand at the ideal level. Even through inspired Scripture, it is highly unlikely that any, much less all, people will perceive exactly the same meanings from any given portion. It is here postulated that certain meanings are within a range of allowable variation as measured by the Bible-As-Yardstick, that is, reasonably equivalent to the original intent but not corresponding exactly.

description   <u>Model 2, Bible Allowing Range of Variation,</u> contains a major assertion, 2 important concepts (range, range variants), and 5 premises all relating to the idea that God allows for slippage in His communication across the Gap.

major assertion   THE BIBLE REVEALS THE PROCESS WHEREBY GOD ALLOWS LESS THAN PERFECT UNDERSTANDINGS OF HIMSELF, HIS TRUTH, AND HIS WILL FOR CULTURE-BOUND PEOPLE IN TERMS OF A RANGE (IDEAL, SUB-IDEAL, OUTSIDE).

premises
1. In revelation, slippage occurs between the communicator and the receptor in any communication.
2. Slippage also occurs due to limitations of encoding the divine intent in inadequate human language.
3. Understandings fall within the acceptable range as sub-ideal or ideal or outside the acceptable range.
4. Range is best illustrated at the culture-specific level where much cultural variation is seen in perception of the Gospel and its implications.

examples   Kraft mentions marriage customs, concepts of God, views of the Ten Commandments, concepts of leadership as examples seen in the Scriptures where range of variation occurs.

example   Kraft also discusses the New Testament use of quotes from the Old Testament as a possible example of God's honoring range of variation among the New Testament writers.

RANGE	synonym: range of variation
introduction	God does not expect perfection in our understanding and response to His revelation. God knows the limitations of communicating from His supracultural position to our limited cultural position. The Bible shows that He allows for and is content to accept human behavior and understandings of Himself and His truth that fall within a range of acceptable variation. Owing to the limitations of such factors as culture, individual experience, and sin, human beings seldom if ever live or understand at the ideal level. Certain meanings within a range of allowable variation as measured by the Bible-As-Yardstick Model, are posited as acceptable, i.e. reasonably equivalent to the original intent but not corresponding exactly.
definition	<u>Range</u> or <u>variation of range</u> refers to the area of belief and behavior and limits to them, which are imposed by the Bible-As-Yardstick Model within which contemporary revelation (both as to information and stimulus/ response) is judged to be acceptable and hence termed dynamically equivalent revelation.

CONTEMPORARY REVELATION
|
as manifested by
|
- belief--its informational base component
- behavior--its stimulus/ response component

can fall

within an Acceptable Range and hence be termed Dynamically Equivalent Revelation	fall in an Unacceptable Range and hence be evaluated as Not Dynamically Equivalent Revelation
if its items of belief and behavior as interpreted in its cultural context	if its items of believe and behavior as interpreted in its cultural context are
Functionally Equivalent In Meaning to what the Bible shows to have been acceptable (even though sub-ideal) in behavior and belief in its cultural context	Functionally Equivalent In Meaning to what the Bible shows to have been unacceptable in behavior and belief in its cultural context

RANGE VARIANTS

introduction The Bible indicates that God will at first judge as acceptable behavior and beliefs which He later judges as unacceptable. He will continually lead and reveal Himself and His truth so as to expose these sub-ideal areas concerning knowledge and behavior so as to move His people toward His ideals. Of course the Bible also shows that some beliefs and behavior are rejected outright by God in His revelation of Himself to a people. It is helpful to recognize these distinctions.

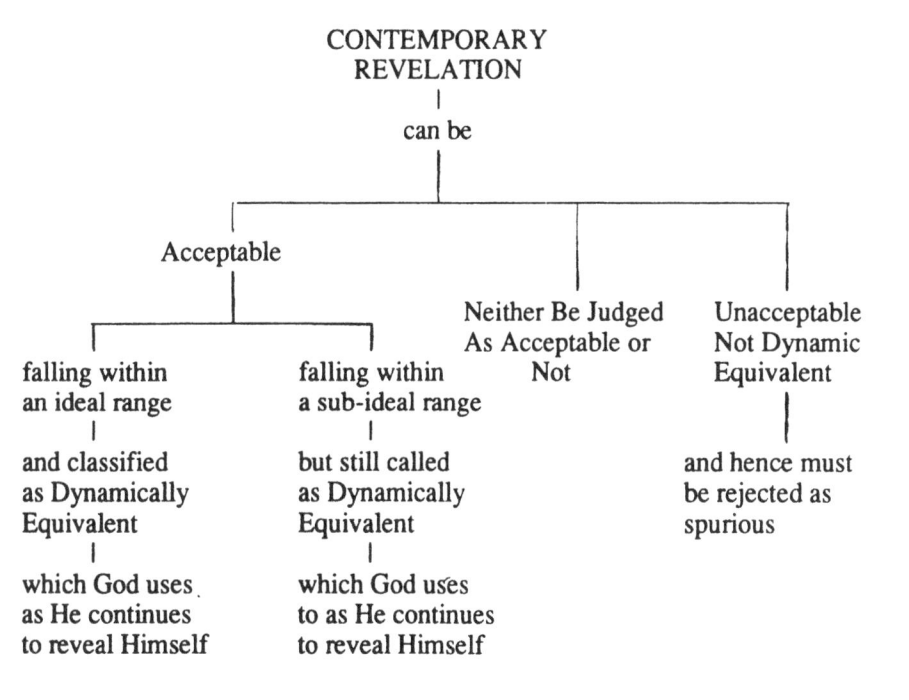

```
                    CONTEMPORARY
                     REVELATION
                          |
                        can be
                          |
        ┌─────────────────┼──────────────────┐
   Acceptable                                 
        |                   Neither Be Judged    Unaccceptable
   ┌────┴────┐              As Acceptable or     Not Dynamic
falling within  falling within       Not         Equivalent
an ideal range  a sub-ideal range                    |
     |                |                          and hence must
and classified  but still called                 be rejected as
as Dynamically  as Dynamically                   spurious
Equivalent      Equivalent
     |                |
which God uses  which God uses
as He continues to as He continues
to reveal Himself to reveal Himself
```

MODEL 3. THE BIBLE-AS-TETHER MODEL

introduction	As the confirmed inspired record of the way God works, the Bible provides the set radius within which contemporary revelational encounters may occur. Events that occur outside that range are by definition <u>not</u> revelational. Within this tether the contemporary repersonalization of the Scriptures is also to occur.
descriptive analogy	Model 3. The Bible-As-Tether Model, is analogous to a tether which is a means such as a rope or chain *by which an animal is fastened so that it can range only within a set radius.* a tether, then, provides both a circle within which one moves and a point at the center of that circle to which one is tied. The Bible is the *in-culture* point of reference that provides the *set radius* within which contemporary revelational encounters may occur and in terms of which all claims of divine revelation are evaluated.
assertion	THE BIBLE PROVIDES THE SET RADIUS WITHIN WHICH CONTEMPORARY REVELATIONAL ENCOUNTERS MAY OCCUR.
comment	The Bible-As-Tether Model is combined with the Bible-As-Yardstick and the concept of range of acceptable variation to conceptualize the fact that the Scriptures show us both the range within which God works and the borders at either extreme of that range. We recognize that God often presents ideal understandings (e.g. Matthew 5:28 on adultery and 5:21,22 on murder), exhibiting one extreme of the range. But He also shows where He is willing to start at the other end of that range. The Biblical range, then provides the tether within which contemporary interaction with God can move and the yardstick by means of which it is possible to evaluate whether or not contemporary practices can be considered Biblical.
bottom line of the analogy	The Bible shows the limits from ideal to non-acceptable. God will permit interaction anywhere within these limits.

MODEL 4. THE BIBLE-AS-INSPIRED-CASEBOOK

introduction	Model 4 likens the Bible to a casebook, a collection of descriptions of illustrative real-life exemplifications of principles to be taught. Case studies teach by analogy, assuming not only a closeness between the experience in the case and that of the learner but also that the learner has the ability to identify through the analogy that which is being recommended for personal application.
description	<u>Model 4. The Bible-As-Inspired-Classic-Casebook</u>, likens the Bible by analogy to a casebook--a modern methodology for teaching.
definition	The Bible is an inspired classic casebook in that: • the illustrative real-life exemplications were selected and canonized in a Spirit-guided process, • it contains time-tested and value-proven case studies which have wide applicability to human cultures, • it is a collection of divine-human interactions over a long period of time in which God's revelation of Himself fits each of the specific situational needs and yet has unifying relevance to God's overall plan for human beings.
major assertion	The Bible, God's inspired classic casebook, contains a collection of descriptions of illustrative real-life exemplication of principles He wishes to communicate to others.

premises

1. God utilizes the principle of analogizing from the specific to the general.
2. God follows the basic principle: Interpersonal communication is by analogy.
3. In using the case study approach the Bible assumes that in spite of significant differences in culture, there are impressive basic human similarities between peoples so that the Bible cases become appropriate analogies.
4. The Bible cases are classic, i.e. they are selective in that they exemplify widely applicable principles and <u>not</u> just specific analogous situations.
5. That the Bible is multicultural, along with classic cases dealing with universal human problems, insures with certainty that anyone of any culture can identify with at least certain major portions of the material recorded.
6. The Bible as classic casebook remains personal. It describes and invites the reader by indirection to identify with the participants and become involved in discovery which produces the most effective impact-learning.

MODEL 5. STARTING POINT PLUS PROCESS

introduction — Model 5 builds upon Model 1 Bible-As-Yardstick, Model 2 Bible Allows Range of Variation and Model 3 Bible-As-Tether to detail how God works within the limitations of culture to apply these models. Model 4 The Bible As Inspired Classic Casebook is used to demonstrate the processes in God's past interactions with humans in culture.

description — <u>Model 5, Starting Point Plus Process</u>, outlines 4 major assertions suggesting how God outworks Models 1, 2, and 3 in cultures. The basic motif is that God begins where people are and progressively reveals Himself and applicable truth to move them toward supracultural ideals.

4 major assertions

1. Assuming a valid faith-allegiance response, God allows for a range of understanding of Himself for He starts where people are rather than demanding that they immediately conform to His ideals.
2. This range of understanding of God can assume a variety of potential starting points anywhere from sub-ideal toward ideal perception of God.
3. God then initiates a process which involves a revelational progression from a sub-ideal starting point toward the ideal.
4. This process of beginning with a range of sub-ideal starting points of perception and behavior and moving by revelational progression from the sub-ideal toward the ideal can be applied to any doctrine of Scripture and any Scriptural treatment of behavioral patterns.

example

Unacceptable Starting Points Concerning <u>Marriage Behavior</u>	Sub-ideal but acceptable starting points concerning <u>Marriage Behavior Patterns</u>	Toward Ideal Concerning <u>Marriage Patterns</u>
adulterous non-permanent unions	polygamous marriages common-law marriages monogamous serial marriages monogamous permanent unions	monogamous unions not only permanent but reflecting the ideals of Christ-church relationship

MOVEMENT

introduction	Christianity at its start was a movement as has been Islam, communism, the Protestant Reformation, the Industrial Revolution, the evangelical awakening, black power, women's liberation, Pentecostalism, and countless other developments. The Gospels and Acts portray movement theory. It is helpful to know the theoretical notions about a movement when reading these portions of Scripture and even some of the Old Testament history. The definition basically comes from Gerlach and Hine (1970:xvi).
definition	A movement is a group of people, • who are organized for, ideologically motivated by, and committed to a purpose which implements some form of personal or social change, • Who are actively engaged in the recruitment of others; • and whose influence is spreading in opposition to the established order within which it originated.
example	Numerous movements occur in the kingdom era of leaderships as factions tried to assert themselves or overthrow the leader in power. See Jereboam or Absalom or the faction led by Adonijah, Haggith, and Joab that attempted to take over in David's last days.
example	See especially the revival in Josiah's time.
commitments	Gerlach and Hine suggest that there are 5 commitments needed to participate in a movement: 1. Commitment to personal involvement. 2. Commitment to persuade others to join. 3. Commitment to the beliefs and ideals of the movement. 4. Commitment to participate in a flexible, non-bureaucratic cell-group organization. 5. Commitment to endure opposition and misunderstanding.
results	Movements can serve to, • heighten the consciousness of many outside the movement, • identify aspects of the cultural system that need change, and • experiment with possible new structures.

FEEDBACK ON MOVEMENT

1. Refer to the expansion of the Christian movement after the day of Pentecost up to the persecution of Acts 8 from the viewpoint of those waiting in the upper room in Acts 2. Analyze their level of commitment (your opinion of course) by checking the appropriate column.

Commitment to:	1 not committed	2 somewhat committed	3 very committed	4 not sure
a. personal involvement				
b. persuade other to join				
c. the beliefs and ideals of the movement				
d. participate in flexible, non-bureaucratic cell-group organization				
e. endure opposition and misunderstanding				

2. How would you evaluate the results of this movement?

Result	1 no progress	2 some progress	3 much progress	4 not sure
a. heighten the consciousness of many outside the movement				
b. identify aspects of the cultural system needing change				
c. experiment with new structures				

ANSWERS----------

1. I would put all in column 3. 2. a. 3,   b. 2,   c. 3

5 FACTORS FOR A SUCCESSFUL MOVEMENT

introduction   A movement is characterized by at least five key factors. The presence and interaction of these set the stage for a successful movement.

No.	FOCUS	STATEMENT OF FACTOR
1	STRUCTURE	A social organizational structure in the movement made up of many cell groups each with its own leader yet interrelated to each other by a network of personal, structural, and ideological ties.
2	RECRUITMENT	Personal face-to-face recruitment of new members by committed individuals in the movement who use their own pre-existing significant social relationships.
3	COMMITMENT	A personal commitment by each individual generated by an act or experience which, <ul><li>separates a convert in some significant way from the established order (or his previous place in it),</li><li>identifies him with a new set of values, and</li><li>commits him to changed patterns of behavior.</li></ul>
4	IDEOLOGY	An ideology which, <ul><li>codifies values and goals,</li><li>provides a conceptual framework by which all experiences or events relative to these goals may be interpreted,</li><li>motivates and provides rationale for envisioned changes,</li><li>defines the opposition, and</li><li>forms the basis for conceptual unification of a segmented network of groups.</li></ul>
5	OPPOSITION	Real or perceived opposition from the society at large or from that segment of the established order within which the movement has risen.

FEEDBACK ON 5 FACTORS FOR A SUCCESSFUL MOVEMENT

1. Refer to the state of the Christian movement by the end of Acts 8. Which of the five factors for a movement were present?

Commitment to:	1 not present	2 somewhat present	3 very present	4 not sure
a. Structure				
b. Recruitment				
c. Commitment				
d. Ideology				
e. Opposition				

2. How would your answer change if you evaluated it after Acts 19?

3. How would your answer change if you evaluated it at the time 2 Peter was written?

4. Suppose you were evaluating Christianity at its earliest stages, say looking at it in the Gospel of Mark. Which of the factors are stronger? Which are weaker? Which are missing?

ANSWERS----------

1. a. 2,   b. 3,   c. 3,   d. 2,   e. 3
2. the structure was much more in place, a. 2 would become a. 3
3. all would be in column 3. The opposition is even more in view.
4. The structure is not yet in place. The development of the church as the structure which will institutionalize the movement happens after Jesus' death. The last 4 factors are there, though the ideology will yet develop as the New Testament canon is worked out.

SOWER'S 5 STAGE BRIDGING MODEL

introduction   Sower was a social scientist who studied change processes in urban renewal, inner city projects and the like. He saw major problems stimulating certain radical people to consider bringing about change. These few spread the dissatisfaction and recruited others to the team to bring about change. As more people join the effort the potential solution is broadened in order to gain their support. It is essentially a momentum model

description   Sower's[18] model involves 5 stages:

Stage	Name	Essence of Stage
1	Convergence of Interest	There is discontent within the present situation. A problem is identified. This discontent can be amplified so that others see it and want to become part of changing the situation.
2	Establish an Initiating Set	The problem is defined more carefully. An initial strategy for changing the situation is formulated by a group of people--called the initiating set.
3	Develop A Support Group	The initiating set must be enlarged if it is to have enough clout to bring about change in the social situation. In addition, the actual quality of the change solution is strengthened with the inclusion of more people and their ideas. The enlarged group is organized and contains people of various expertise.
4	Establish An Execution Set	This is a critical stage marking the boundary between advocating change and implementing it. Resources must be mobilized which will actually bring about the change.
5	Freeze The Change	The changes must become institutionalized, that is, part of the on-going system.

comment   This model is seen in almost classic form in Absalom's attempted take over from David.

---

[18] Schaller describes Sower's model in a running narrative format in his book **The Change Agent**, pages 89-11? See also the original discussion by Sower et al (1958), pages 306-314 in Community Involvement. See also my manual, **Bridging Strategies--Leadership Perspectives for Introducing Change,** which introduces 2 other bridging models and gives numerous concepts about introducing change into a Christian situation.

FEEDBACK ON SOWER'S MODEL

1. Read 2 Samuel 12-19:8 which tells the story of Absalom's movement to dethrone David. What element of Sower's model is missing?

2. What reason does the Bible give to explain why that element is missing?

3. Why is an understanding of Sower's model important to a Christian leader?

ANSWERS----------
1. The last stage, freezing the change, was missing. And it was the critical stage.
2. See 2 Samuel 15:31 and 17:14. Absalom should have followed Ahithophel's advice and in a Patton-like exploitation wipe him out before he could regroup. Or he could have simply consolidated his hold on the country and forced David to come back and attack. In either case, he did not freeze the change.
3. These dynamics of change are true today for local churches and parachurches. Wise change leader's recognize the need for ownership of change. The Sower model builds ownership as it goes.

FOR FURTHER STUDY

See Charles H. Kraft's **Christianity in Culture** for follow-up to the ethnotheology models.

See Wagner's **Leading Your Church To Growth** and **Church Gorwth and The Whole Gospel** for teaching based on the Harvest Model.

Study the paper, *Listen Up Leaders!*, available from Barnabas Publishers, for follow up on how leaders finish.

Study the manual, **The Mentor Handbook**, by J. Robert Clinton and Richard Clinton, in order to identify the mentoring you need and the mentoring you can give in order to take advantage of the Mentoring Enhancement for finishing well.

Study the *Ultimate Contribution* position paper available from Barnabas Publishers which gives a full treatment only partly alluded to here.

See Davis' basal article *Transforming Organizations: The Key to Strategy Is Context in* **Organizational Dynamics**, Winter 1982. This article lays out the basic idea of Future Perfect thinking as an underlying approach to strategic thinking. It is radically different from any other approach based on extrapolation or interpretation.

See also Davis' **Future Perfect: A Startling View of the Future We Should Be Managing Now**. Addison-Wesley. It looks as if this time paradigm will be a major view if not the major view underlying strategic planning in the future.

(This page is deliberately left blank)

Chapter 3. Life Long Development

introduction
Chapter 3, will give us some perspectives for viewing the individual development of a leader by God. We see the value of looking at the whole life through a time-line, of identifying processes in the life, and of generalizing patterns from this total display. Whereas chapters 1 and 2 help us, in general, in approaching any kind of leadership source material, this chapter especially helps us as we approach the biographical source of leadership information.

The chapter introduces you to 3 major umbrella concepts useful in describing how God develops a leader over his/her lifetime: the time-line, processing, and patterns of response.

I first describe in a narrate article how the three major concepts fit together to describe the shaping of a leader. In this article, I give a table with 12 of the process items listed, the name for specific instances of God's processing in a life, along with the major idea of the item. I also discuss the notion of response patterns, the tracing of a leader's development over the time-line.

God shapes a leader in terms of three kinds of formation: spiritual formation (character), ministerial formation (leadership skills), and strategic formation (philosophy and purpose). I next define these three formations. Finally I give actual definitions for the 5 most important process items and 4 most important patterns. These will serve as references as you study characters in the Bible.

what to do
You will not be expected to remember all of the concepts introduced in this chapter. I suggest that you get a feel for the overall. The article should do that. Then glance through the other information remembering where it is. Then simply use it as reference information. Later in this manual when you run across the process terms you will be able to refer back to the table or the definitions given here.

theory
Leadership Emergence Theory is the technical name for the theoretical model which describes life long development.[1]

---

[1] My PhD Dissertation was done on the study of the development of leaders over their lifetimes. Leadership Emergence Theory developed out of about 7 years of research. The research has continued. The manual

LIFE LONG DEVELOPMENT OF A LEADER--AN OVERVIEW

> Remember your former leaders. Imitate those qualities and
> achievements that were God-Honoring, for their source of
> leadership still lives -- Jesus! He, too, can inspire and enable
> your own leadership today. Hebrews 13:7,8 (Clinton paraphrase)

Many of us who are Christian leaders know full well how our lives have been significantly impacted by stirring examples of past missionaries or pastors or other Christian leaders. Early in my own development I was deeply challenged by reading about Hudson Taylor--particularly his many faith-challenging exploits. I learned that I could trust God in my ministry to supply funds and to open doors. I learned that I needed to listen to what God wanted to do through me and then to trust Him to do it. It is true! Jesus is the same. He is the source of leadership. What He did for past leaders He can do for today's leaders--and tomorrow's.

I like to interpret the command in this leadership mandate this way. *Think back on how they have lived and died and learn vicariously for your own lives.* At the School of World Mission[2] we have taken this leadership mandate very seriously. Studies in leadership at the School of World Mission now date back 12 years. Numerous lives of Christian leaders-- Biblical leaders, historical leaders and contemporary leaders--have been examined. And we have learned lessons which have been transferable.

We have comparatively examined more than 700 cases histories of leaders. Biblical cases include such characters as Joseph, Moses, Joshua, Jephthah, Samuel, David, Daniel, Jeremiah, Nehemiah, Barnabas, Paul, Peter and many others. Many historical leaders have been studied including such giants as Hudson Taylor, Andrew Murray, A. B. Simpson, Phineas Bresee, Henrietta Mears, Mary Slessor, Maria Atkinson, J. O. Fraser, and many others. By far the majority of case studies have been of contemporary leaders--current missionaries and national leaders from around the world.

What have we learned? Several important items. One, our definition of a Christian leader is becoming clearer. A Christian leader is a person with God-given capacity and God-given responsibility who is influencing a specific group of God's people toward God's purposes. Two, life long

---

Leadership Emergence Theory, available from Barnabas Publishers, contains most of the findings of this research. The book, **The Making of A Leader**, published by NavPress, gives a popularized version of the theory.

2The School of World Mission is one of three schools under the umbrella of Fuller Theological Seminary, Pasadena, Ca. It trains mid-career missionary leaders and national leaders as well as trains young missionary candidates.

LIFE LONG DEVELOPMENT OF A LEADER continued

development (leadership emergence) is a lifetime process in which God intervenes throughout in crucial ways to shape that leader towards his purpose for the leader. In fact, it is a life long developmental process. Three, when viewed from a whole life perspective it can be seen that God's intervention or shaping is intentional. His processing shapes character.[3] His processing develops the leader's capacity. It moves the leader to operate at realized potential in terms of giftedness--natural abilities, acquired skills and spiritual gifts.[4] His shaping includes guidance into a focused ministry.[5] The shaping processes allows for the leader's response to it. Life long development can be thwarted. Four, we are beginning to get an overall picture of how a leader develops or fails to do so.

A theoretical framework for organizing, interpreting, and perhaps even predicting a leader's development is emerging. This framework looks promising as an aid to personal growth and the selection and development of Christian leaders.

Overview of Life Long Development
The Leadership Emergence Framework

God works in a leader's life. The explanation of that working, that is, the development of the leader, can be explained to a large extent by the use of and relationship between three important umbrella-like concepts: processing, time analysis and patterns of response.

Processing

Processing describes the intervention incidents which God uses to shape leaders. Though each individual's processing is unique and situationally specific, there are common items shared with other leaders. We call those common items process items--items in the course of daily life which God uses in a special way to *process* a leader toward development. To date, we have identified and labeled about 50 of these process items. Their descriptive labels suggest their intent or use by God in the shaping process.

---

[3] We call this shaping process spiritual formation. It builds convictions in the inner-life, the heart of which is integrity.

[4] This shaping process is called ministerial formation. This shaping helps the leader learn how to influence others. Development of giftedness is a major part of this.

[5] The accumulation of values from various shaping activities along with guidance and destiny processing leads to a ministry philosophy and focused ministry. This totality of shaping is called strategic formation.

LIFE LONG DEVELOPMENT OF A LEADER continued

Character is crucial in a leader. God uses many process items to work on the development of a leader's character. *Integrity checks* contribute to early character shaping. God often uses a life incident to test or check a leader's character regarding consistency with inner convictions. Sensitivity to this processing and a successful response usually leads to God's expansion of the leader's capabilities and responsibilities. Lack of sensitivity or an unwillingess to respond usually leads to remedial processing on the same issue.

A second example involves guidance processing. Leaders must learn to get guidance from God if they are to learn to influence God's people toward God's purposes. There are a number of guidance process items. *Double confirmation* is an unusual guidance process item for crucial decision-making moments in a leader's life. It is not a frequent process but a very important one as the whole direction of a career may hinge upon it. God directs a leader toward some specific direction in a spectacular way. he first gives the leader indications of the intended direction. This direction may be given in a variety of ways including personal use of the written Word, the use of the Word by some one else, inward conviction, circumstances or various combinations of these. God next gives someone else confirmation of this same guidance totally apart from the original person and situation. God then brings the two together so that the second person can *externally* confirm the direction given to the leader. This double confirmation (internally to the leader, externally confirmed by another) gives a firm basis for a life-changing decision. God double confirms his direction for Moses through Aaron (Exodus 3 and 4) and for Paul through Ananias (Acts 9).

Barnabas, Paul's mentor, recognized early on the first missionary journey to Cyprus, that Paul needed to be released in order to develop his God-given potential. The *leadership switch* from *Barnabas and Paul* on Cyprus to *Paul and his companions* at Perga is one of the great illustrations of a *relationship insight*. This relationship insight concerns leadership transition. Few leaders seem to catch this important lesson of releasing a talented and perhaps threatening emerging leader. It is only one of many kinds of relationship insights that leaders must learn if they are to be effective. The majority of early ministry problems concern the leader's attempts to influence followers many of which have to do with relationships.

Relationship insights refer to life incidents in which a leader learns a valuable lesson concerning working with people--either followers or other

LIFE LONG DEVELOPMENT OF A LEADER continued

leaders. This lesson can be learned through either a negative or positive situation. The end result of a relationship insight is a tool, or attitude, or guideline which becomes part of a leader's arsenal and value system for future leadership. Barnabas' selfless mentoring attitude was at least partially responsible for Paul's ongoing development as a leader. The three process items just introduced--the integrity check, double confirmation, and relationship insights are typical of many that have been identified and described.[6] Having labels to describe one's experience is in itself a step forward in development and often gives reassurance and affirmation to a developing leader. Further, knowledge of the wide variety of process items and how they have been used in the past carries an exhortive punch for the present. This knowledge often sensitizes leaders in both their personal lives and in their leading others to grow.

Process items can be analyzed individually. Then, these special God-interventions can be correlated to the development of each of the concepts of a Biblical leader. Some process items focus on identifying and developing God-given capacity. Some relate more directly to the instilling of God-given responsibility to lead. Others relate to expansion of influence means. Still others can be seen to direct toward the specific groups of followers. And some refer to guidance that reveals God's purposes.

Process items should also be viewed cumulatively, that is, the effect of all of the process items taken together over a lifetime. This type of overall analysis of processing yields a three-fold result. Overall analysis suggests that processing moves toward three major leadership development goals: spiritual formation, ministerial formation and strategic formation. Spiritual formation essentially refers to the development of leadership character. Ministerial formation has as its essence the development of influence and ministry skills. Strategic formation focuses on development of leadership values which culminate in a ministry philosophy. That leadership philosophy, developed over a lifetime, compels the leader to an ultimate contribution in accordance with the purposes of God.

Time Analysis--The Ministry Time-Line

Time analysis, the second of the umbrella-like concepts that helps explain the development of a leader, refers to chronological analysis of the processing of a leader. Time analysis does three things. It forces the

---

[6] Appendix A provides a glossary of all of the process items we have labeled to date.

LIFE LONG DEVELOPMENT OF A LEADER continued

emerging leader to se present processing in terms of a larger picture. It also allows a means for integrating the processing experienced to date into some sort of coherent overall picture. Finally, it sets expectations. A coherent picture of a leader can be compared to a common time analysis synthesized from comparative study of many unique time-lines.

Every leader may analyze his/her development over time. This results in a unique time-line, that is, an analysis of development which recognizes natural time increments of development called development phases. Identification of one's time-line allows a means of integrating the processing experienced to date. Process items can be located as to when they happened on the time-line. An orderly presentation of processing along a time-line is the prelude to obtaining a more comprehensive view of the leader's development. Patterns begin to emerge. Overall lessons can be seen.

Comparison of a leader's unique time-line with a generalized *ministry time-line* helps orient and evaluate a leader's development. Further it sets future expectations. Figure 1 gives a simplified version of a generalized ministry time-line which represents a typical full time Christian worker.

Phase I	**Phase II**	**Phase III**	**Phase IV**
Ministry Foundations	General Ministry	Focused Ministry	Convergent Ministry

|_____|_____|_____|_____|

A_1 B_1 A_2 B_2 C_2 A_3 B_3 A_4 B_4

A_1 Sovereign Foundations (13-20 years)
B_1 Leadership Transition (3-6 years)

A_2 Provisional Ministry (2-6 years)
B_2 Growth Ministry (6-8 years)
C_2 Competent Ministry (2-6 years)

A_3 Role Transition
B_3 Unique Ministry (total $A_3 + B_3$ is 3-12 years)

A_4 Special Guidance (?)
B_4 Convergence (?)

Figure 1. THE MINISTRY TIME-LINE

LIFE LONG DEVELOPMENT OF A LEADER continued

All the processing that precedes entry into full-time Christian ministry is located and described in Phase I, the Ministry Foundations Phase. This phase can last from 16 to 26 years or sometimes longer.

The second phase, the General Ministry Phase, describes the time of development in which the leader is now in full time ministry. During the first two sub-phases (Provisional and Growth) the primary thrust of the ministry is for growth of the leader not on ministry accomplishments, though many great things may in fact be accomplished. God primarily teaches the leader about leadership--leadership character, leadership skills, and leadership values. During the first sub-phase the leader is learning about giftedness and looking for a niche that fits early development. During the third sub-phase, Competence, the leader knows who he or she is and what capabilities are present and begins to operate with competence.

The third phase, Focused Ministry, describes a time of very effective productivity by the leader. Prior to moving into this phase, usually the leader will have gone through some difficult character processing which shows the need for a deepened relationship with God. This deepened relationship adds to the leader's spiritual authority. The leader moves from a competency base to a character base as the foundation for this effective ministry. The leader has matured in leadership character as well as leadership skills but ministers dominantly out of a *being base* rather than a *doing base*. This shift, along with a much more narrowed ministry thrust which fits the leader's unique giftedness, characterizes the phase. Experiences gained both in the Ministry Foundation Phase and the General Ministry Phase fit into place. Leaders usually do not enter into the Focused Ministry Phase until between 40 and 55 years of age after 15-25 years of growth ministry.

Response Patterns

Comparative study of processing integrated along many unique time lines has also resulted in the identification of patterns describing various aspects of a leader's development. These *response patterns* make up the third of the three umbrella-like concepts which help explain how a leader

LIFE LONG DEVELOPMENT OF A LEADER continued

develops. More than twenty patterns have been clearly identified.[7] Another 10 or so have been suggested but need further confirming data.

Four foundational patterns describe the backgrounds out of which leaders emerge. Three transitional training patterns correlate to these foundational patterns. These foundational and transitional training patterns give a framework from which one can assess current emerging leaders. These patterns describe generally the flow of early emergence. Each of these early foundational patterns and transitional training patterns has advantages and disadvantages. Knowledge of these advantages and disadvantages is helpful to mature leaders for assessing and counseling young potential leaders.

Two early testing patterns focus on character. Two early patterns indicate giftedness. Specific ministry situations require various kinds of entry patterns. A giftedness development pattern which spans the entire General Ministry Phase describes how a leader discovers and uses spiritual gifts from the first use of one spiritual gift to the identification of a gift-mix and finally the development of the gift-mix into a gift-cluster.

A faithfulness pattern occurs throughout the General Ministry Phase. Faithfulness in ministry tasks and ministry assignments along with positive response to the testing element of many of the ministry process items leads to expanded ministry and re-testing of faithfulness at that new ministry level. This pattern along with overall comparisons of many entire life analyses has led to a hypothesis.

RESPONSE PREMISE
The time of development of a leader depends upon response to processing. Rapid recognition and positive response to God's processing speeds up development. Slower recognition or negative response delays development.

This hypothesis, if it can be shown to be true, gives added impetus to the leadership mandate of Hebrews 13:7,8.

Several later patterns describe various stages of character maturity and convergence toward effective ministry. A destiny pattern spans an entire

---

[7] I have deliberately left information concerning these patterns vague. To discuss these patterns even in an introductory manner would lengthen this article beyond its original intent. In the paragraph which follows I have simply indicated that there are different kinds of patterns and that each can be useful in understanding a leader's emergence.

LIFE LONG DEVELOPMENT OF A LEADER continued

lifetime and increasingly ties in God's plans and purposes for a leader beginning with the time of destiny preparation until the time of destiny revelation and finally culminating in destiny fulfillment.

The identification of all of these patterns has given power to the whole explanatory framework of leadership emergence. Current leaders can see where they are in their life long development by pinpointing their place on a number of these patterns. The patterns may also predict and help set expectations for leaders. When leaders can see their own development in terms of how God has developed previous leaders there is that compulsion to follow the leadership mandate and *imitate their faith*. Such a desire must rest on the fact that Jesus will respond to such obedience and supply the divine element that will bring fulfillment to one's leadership efforts.

Some Specific Findings That Can Be Applied

One can readily apply these concepts, especially some of the more common process items, the ministry time-line, and the early response patterns.

Some of the process items serve to explain and help leaders respond to God's present processing. Current data indicate that more than half of the fifty process items identified thus far will occur in more than seventy percent of leaders. Table 1 points out the 15 most common process items and the central thrust of their definitions or use.[8]

TABLE 1. SOME OF THE COMMON PROCESS ITEMS

Process Item	Central Thrust
Integrity Check	Early test of character
Obedience Check	Early test of volition and response to God
Word Check	Early test of sensitivity to God's speaking

---

[8] I realize that these process item terms are technical terms which are not defined in this article. However, the thrust of the definition shows the intent of the processing. The nature of this article is introductory. I recognize and hope that you will do some further study into these concepts. See **The Making of A Leader** or **Leadership Emergence Theory**. Later in this Handbook I do give detailed definitions for important process items.

LIFE LONG DEVELOPMENT OF A LEADER continued

TABLE 1. SOME OF THE COMMON PROCESS ITEMS continued

Process Item	Central Thrust
Giftedness Discovery	Finding out one's natural abilities, acquired skills, and spiritual gifts and how these relate to ministry.
Paradigm Shift	A breakthrough of a new perspective which radically changes how one perceives something
Ministry Insights	A discovery of lessons on how to effectively impact in one's ministry
Leadership Backlash	A recognition that followers may rebel against some intended action after its success even when they initially approved it
Double Confirmation	A sovereignly confirmed instance of guidance where the confirmation comes externally from an unexpected source
Isolation	A process of being set aside for deepening
Conflict	Negative processing that may affect character, skills or values
Crises	Severe threats concerning ministry or life
Destiny	Intimations of God's ultimate purposes for a leader which can be preparatory, clarifying, and leading to fulfillment

The ministry time-line can prove useful as a means for orienting one's counseling with an emerging leader. Most leaders go through a provisional time in which they struggle to learn early ministry lessons, find their giftedness profile, and find a role which suits them as to personality and giftedness. This awareness can pave the way for corrective advice and suggestions for the future.

Suggestive patterns which can be utilized right away include the *positive and negative testing patterns*, the *like-attracts-like gift pattern* and the *giftedness drift pattern*.

LIFE LONG DEVELOPMENT OF A LEADER continued

The *positive testing pattern* points out that God often tests a leader in order to build character. This is true early in a leader's development, particularly in the transition from non-leadership to leadership. There is the incident that tests, the recognition that the test is from God, and the positive response which deepens the character. Expanded leadership usually follows a positive test. The *negative testing pattern* is similar but ends with different results. There is the incident that tests, the refusal of the test, and the lack of character formation. The negative test almost always requires repeated remedial testing to correct the deficient character element.

Frequently, an emerging leader is attracted to the ministry of a more developed leader. Often those so attracted have one or more embryonic gifts corresponding to an important gift already developed in the mature leader. This pattern is called the *like-attracts-like* pattern.

The *giftedness drift pattern* refers to the tendency of an emerging leader, if not directed otherwise, to drift toward roles or functions or responsibilities which intuitively match embryonic gifts which will later emerge and be developed.

Using The Framework

I have only briefly introduced the notions underlying the framework for analyzing emergence or life long development of a leader. While one can use some of the concepts almost immediately as described in the previous section, extended study is needed if one wants to carefully mentor others. A detailed grasp of the theoretical framework allows one a personal orientation that can significantly affect a career track. Such an understanding gives a basis for counseling mid-career leaders. It is particularly useful in early selection and development of potential leaders.

Several courses and written materials including several manuals, a book, and several dissertations attest to the fact that in the School of World Mission the leadership mandate of Hebrews 13:7,8 has been taken seriously.

SPIRITUAL FORMATION

introduction — A leadership emergence study seeks to assess the emergence of leadership potential. It utilizes a life-history analysis of a leader which integrates internal, external, and divine influences upon the development of a leader. Spiritual formation refers to the inner development of character of a leader. Internal, external, and divine influences all affect that inner development.

definition — <u>Spiritual formation</u> refers to development of the inner-life of a person of God so that,
- the person experiences more of the life of Christ,
- reflects more Christ-like characteristics in personality and in everyday relationships, and
- increasingly knows the power and presence of Christ in ministry.

comment — Spiritual formation is one of four major components in Holland's Two-Track analogy (Clinton 1983b:41), a model for evaluating balance in training. There is input, experience, dynamic reflection, and spiritual formation. Holland stresses that spiritual formation is the end result of training and therefore must be designed into training programs and accounted for explicitly not implicitly. These same four components can be applied to life activities as well as formal and non-formal training.

comment — Spiritual formation is the application of the process of Romans 8:28,29 to a leader's life. It recognizes that God utilizes life processes to "conform a leader to the image of Christ." That conformation process is spiritual formation.

comment — Spiritual formation relates directly to a leader's power base for influencing. Power base refers to the source of credibility which enables a leader to have authority to influence followers. Spiritual authority is that source of credibility perceived as from God which permits leaders to influence followers. Spiritual authority characteristics presuppose spiritual formation. While there are other power bases which are legitimate for a Christian leader, spiritual authority is foundational and should be the central means of power for influencing followers.

MINISTERIAL FORMATION

introduction
Spiritual formation has to do with *being*. Ministry formation is concerned with *doing*. It focuses on the leader's ability to function as a leader. It seeks to identify and measure the skills, abilities, and knowledge needed to operate as a leader in ministry. These skills have to do with *innate* skills as well as *acquired skills*. They have to do with spiritual gifts. They have to do with sensitivity to God's purposes in a leadership situation. They have to do with the use of influence means in order to motivate followers toward ministry goals.

definition
Ministerial formation refers to development of ministry skills and knowledge, which are reflected by a leader's
- growth in experiential understanding of leadership concepts,
- growing sensitivity to God's purposes in terms of the leadership basal elements (leader, follower, and situation),
- identification and development of gifts and skills and their use with increasing effectiveness with followers,
- ability to motivate followers toward beneficial changes which will harmonize with God's purposes.

comment
Experiential understanding of leadership concepts means the ability to dynamically reflect on and use concepts dealing with leadership basal elements, leadership influence means, and leadership philosophy in local situations. This may be a studied thing or it may be intuitive.

comment
At every level of influence a leader must be able to sense the important elements of the leadership triangle--leader, follower, and situation. Crucial leadership decisions should reflect an awareness of important patterns of interplay between these elements.

comment
Deliberate development of natural abilities and acquisition of skills not only indicates maturity in ministerial formation but also a responsible attitude toward God-given capacities.

comment
By definition, the central ethic of a leader is the motivation of followers toward God's purposes. An increased ability to do this indicates development in ministerial formation.

STRATEGIC FORMATION

introduction — Strategic formation, the third formational thrust, refers to an overall ministry perspective.

definition — <u>Strategic Formation</u> is the shaping of an overall ministry perspective, a ministry philosophy, which interweaves lessons learned into an increasingly clear ministry framework that gives direction and focus and ultimate purpose to a leader's life.

comment — The heart, or idealized goal, of strategic formation is its end result--a well articulated lived-out ministry philosophy.

<u>Stage</u>	<u>General Description</u>	<u>Some Functions</u>
I. Osmosis	Leader learns implicit philosophy experientially.	(1) Operate with implicit philosophy of sponsoring group.
II. Baby Steps	Leader discovers explicit philosophy through experience.	(2) Personal lessons in ministry.
		(3) Questioning/ evaluation of implicit philosophy of ministry.
		(4) Evolving of a modified philosophy; some implicit some explicit.
III. Maturity	Leader formulates, uses and articulates his/her ministry philosophy. He/she passes on to others the key ideas and retrospective reflection of what ministry is about.	(5) Develops a growing sense of uniqueness and ultimate accountability. (6) Sees need for evaluation of ministry. (7) Recognition of need for focus and unique ministry. (8) Formulation of focused ministry philosophy. (9) Internalization of the philosophy. (10) Articulation of the philosophy. which has been worked out in paractice.

comment — Lessons learned from three clusters of process items--discernment. guidance, and destiny--are most significant in the shaping of strategic formation.

FEEDBACK ON THREE FORMATIONS

1. The root concept underlying all of the three formations is spirituality. Most leaders do not have an adequate understanding of their own view of spirituality. Nevertheless they are controlled by their uninformed implicit view of spirituality. Spiritual formation deals primarily with the vertical aspect of spirituality, as it applies to character. Ministerial formation deals with the horizontal aspect of spirituality as it applies to performance in ministry and relationship to others. Strategic formation deals with spirituality and ultimate contribution. A step forward for any leader is to identify an explicit *informed* theology of spirituality.

   a. define spirituality:

   b. How does spirituality relate to the Kingdom?

2. It is not unusual for a leader to be developed further in one formation than another. Comparatively evaluate your general overall development in terms of the three formations.
   a. Further along in development of:
   b. Next further along in development of:
   c. Least further along in development of:
   d. Other:

3. If failure in leadership can be attributed to lack of development in one of the formations more than the others, which one would it to be?

ANSWERS----------

   1. a. In my opinion spirituality is a measure of control by the spirit of my whole being and is a state of relationship with God in which God is manifested through me, a total being, to accomplish His purposes in me and to others so that Kingdom values are proliferated. b. The Kingdom is the realm of God's rule. Spirituality is a measure of that rule in an individual.

   2. In my opinion, comparatively, my development would rank the three formations in this order: spiritual formation, ministerial formation, and strategic formation. It is not unusual for strategic formation to lag behind. Most leaders when they first start out are ahead in spiritual formation. But in their growth ministry--provisional and competent ministry sub-phases ministry formation usually moves ahead (doing takes precedence over being). Strategic formation lags well behind. Toward the end of the competent sub-phase spiritual formation again usually overtakes ministerial formation with significant development having taken place in strategic formation. In the unique ministry phase the three usually come into balance.

   3. Spiritual formation is usually considered to be more foundational although all are necessary. People can have power in ministry and maintain an apparently outward success and yet fail fundamentally in character development. Sooner or later it will catch up.

THE MINISTRY TIME-LINE AND FORMATIONS

THE MINISTRY TIME-LINE

Phase I Ministry Foundations		Phase II General Ministry			Phase III Focused Ministry		Phase IV Convergent Ministry	
A. Sovereign Foundations (13-20 yrs)	B. Leadership Transition (3-6 yrs)	A. Provisional Ministry (2-6 yrs)	B. Growth Ministry (6-8 yrs)	C. Competent Ministry (2-6 yrs)	A. Role Transition <-- (3-12 yrs) -->	B. Unique Ministry	A. Special Guidance ?	B. Convergence ?
	S.F.	M.F.	M.F.	M.F.	S.F.	ST.F.		ST.F., S.F., M.F.
	M.F.	(S.F.)	S.F.	S.F.	ST.F.	S.F., M.F.		
	(ST. F.)	(ST.F.)	(ST.F.)	ST.F.	M.F.			

INTEGRITY CHECK PROCESS ITEM Symbol: P(IC)

introduction At the heart of any assessment of biblical qualifications for leadership lies the concept of integrity--that uncompromising adherence to a code of moral, artistic or other values which reveals itself in utter sincerity, honesty, and candor and avoids deception or artificiality (adapted from Webster).

definition An <u>integrity check</u> refers to the special kind of process test which God uses to evaluate heart-intent, consistency between inner convictions and outward actions, and which God uses as a foundation from which to expand the leader's capacity to influence.

example Daniel (Daniel 1,5); Joseph (Genesis 39), Paul (Acts 20:22,23)

kinds
- temptation (conviction test)
- restitution (honesty testing)
- value check (ultimate value clarification)
- loyalty (allegiance testing)
- guidance (alternative testing--better offer after Holy Spirit led commitment to some course of action)
- persecution (a steadfastness check; may come through prophecy or contextual situation)

uses
- to see follow-through on a promise or vow
- to insure burden for a ministry or vision
- to allow confirmation of inner-character strength
- to build faith
- to establish inner values very important to later leadership which will follow
- to teach submission
- to warn others of the seriousness of obeying God

timing Integrity checks usually occur early in the transition into leadership. Occasionally, later, there will be integrity checks at critical junctures of transition from one given ministry focus to another.

FEEDBACK ON INTEGRITY CHECK PROCESS ITEM

1. Check the kinds of integrity checks have you personally experienced.
   ___ a. temptation (conviction test)
   ___ b. restitution (honesty testing)
   ___ c. value check (ultimate value clarification)
   ___ d. loyalty (allegiance testing)
   ___ e. guidance (alternative testing--better offer after Holy Spirit led commitment to some course of action)
   ___ f. persecution (a steadfastness check)

2. Check any of the uses of integrity checks have you seen in your own life?
   ___ a. to see follow-through on a promise or vow
   ___ b. to insure burden for a ministry or vision
   ___ c. to allow confirmation of inner-character strength
   ___ d. to build faith
   ___ e. to establish inner values very important to later leadership
   ___ f. to teach submission
   ___ g. to warn others of the seriousness of obeying God

3. For any one item you marked in question 1, jot down the essentials.

The kind:
The background:

The challenge:

My response:

The result:

Effect on later leadership:

ANSWERS----------
1. Here are the ones for me: a., b., e. 2. Here are the ones for me: a., c., d.
3. Here is one I personally experienced: **The kind**: restitution **The background**: when I left the military I took some items of equipment (used) which were really not mine though they were assigned to me for my use. **The challenge**: God challenged me on honesty. **My response**: I did not know how to return the equipment. It was used material and would be thrown away. So I talked it over with a mentor with whom I was doing a personal bible study. I had assessed the value of it. He suggested I send the money to a servicemen's center in Texas who were ministering to those in the armed forces. I would at least be returning some value back to the military. **The result**: I did so. God blessed my efforts in my discipling ministry and continued to expand my sphere of influence.
Effect on later leadership: I saw first hand the value of restitution.

OBEDIENCE CHECK PROCESS ITEM Symbol: P(OC)

introduction	A leader must influence others toward obedience. A necessary first step is that the leader personally learns obedience including recognizing God's voice, understanding what God is saying, and obeying when obedience is called for. Usually the obedience process item is learned rather early in the development of the leader and then repeated throughout life. Often the first lessons come as checks, that is, the leader is tested as to obedience. A proper recognition and response leads to growth and further revelation.
definition	<u>Obedience checks</u> refer to that special category of process items in which God tests personal response to revealed truth in the life of a person.
examples	Ananias (Acts 9), Peter (Acts 10), Barnabas (Acts 4)
kinds	Some frequently seen obedience checks concern:

- learning about possessions/giving,
- learning about choice of mate and putting God first,
- willingness to be used by God in ministry
- willingness to trust a truth God has shown,
- willingness to forgive,
- willingness to confess something,
- willingness to right a continuing wrong,

order	Again the pattern is threefold. There is the demand for obedience by God in terms of an issue, there is the response by the leader, and there are the results. The demand for obedience may be in terms of the written Word or as the result of some spoken Word or in terms of application of what is already known. The response can be positive or negative. A positive response may be immediate obedience, or a desire to obey but with the need for further clarification. A negative response is a refusal to obey. The results for those who respond positively is usually enlightenment with more truth; negative responses most often result in some remedial action.
importance	To have credibility, leaders must continually model obedience if they expect others to recognize their spiritual authority and obey them.

FEEDBACK ON OBEDIENCE CHECK PROCESS ITEM

1. Can you identify an obedience check in your own experience? Check which category it fits in and then give a short explanation of how you see this obedience check being used to develop you as a leader.
   ___ a. learning about possessions and giving,
   ___ b. learning about choice of mate and putting God first,
   ___ c. willingness to be used by God in ministry,
   ___ d. willingness to trust a truth God has shown,
   ___ e. willingness to forgive,
   ___ f. willingness to confess something,
   ___ g. willingness to right a wrong,
   ___ h. some other kind, you name it:

How has this obedience check process item affected your leadership development?

ANSWERS----------

1. _x_ a. God tested me twice within my first week of Bible College concerning my sharing of finances with other students. God for the next three years met our financial needs. This perspective on God's ownership of all of *our things* and sharing and giving has influenced all of my ministry and those I have influenced.

WORD CHECK PROCESS ITEM Symbol: P(WC)

introduction	It is essential that leader is receive truth from God. This is a springboard to authoritative use of the word in ministry. It is also an integral part of a leader's methodology for getting guidance for the ministry. The process item used to describe this development is called the word process item. A special kind of word process item is a word check which launches a leader into other kinds of word processing.
definition	A <u>word</u> <u>check</u> is a process item which tests a leader's personal ability to understand or receive a word from God, to see it worked out in life, and to desire to know it.
example	Barnabas was sent to Antioch (Acts 11) to ascertain genuineness of the experience there. He had just been exposed to truth concerning God's acceptance of Cornelius. The test--Can he use this truth in a life situation?
example	Peter was told by the Holy Spirit (Acts 10) to go with the three gentiles to Cornelius' home. This happened concurrently with the thrice repeated vision concerning clean and unclean. He immediately perceived new truth. The Gentiles were not unclean. He was then ready for God's expansion of that truth in Cornelius' home. Peter was tested on two truths (Gentiles are clean and Jesus will baptize in the Holy Spirit).
development	A successful pass of a word check results in an increased ability to discern God's voice of truth, to clarify truth, and to apply it to life's situation. This will lead to more truth and authoritative use of truth.
other	The word check process item represents only one kind of word processing item. Over a lifetime a leader will see other kinds such as use of the word for guidance, for ministry, for formation of character and as a framework for interpreting life in line with the purposes of God. But God uses the word check usually in the early formative stages of an emerging leader, to test the leader's ability to understand the word, to use the word in one's own life and to transfer truth from it to life situations. By it, God cements in the young leader's life the authority of the Word and thus form life habits which will insure continued growth in acquiring truth.

FEEDBACK ON WORD CHECK PROCESS ITEM

1. Which of the following passages contains a Word Check Process Item?
   ___ a. Acts 11:27-30   ___ c. neither of the above
   ___ b. Acts 23:11 and 27:13ff   ___ d. both of the above

2. Identify a word check process item from your own experience. Describe it and show how it has been used to help develop you as a leader.

3. Interview a Christian leader concerning the word process item in general and word checks in particular. See if you can elicit a good example of a word check process item. Describe your findings.

ANSWERS----------
1. d. both of the above 2. In my early days of being discipled I was reading 5 Psalms and 1 chapter in Proverbs each day. I did this for about a year. God repeatedly brought attention to truth concerning my use of words. I have memorized many of the verses. God changed my use of my tongue through those many truths. I would find that it was often the case that I would be introduced to a truth in my quiet time and would be immediately confronted with its application at my job at Bell Telephone Labs. Usually the process would be: truth given, a failure at work involving that truth, recognition that God was testing, reaffirmation and progressive use of the truth. A leader must be careful concerning what he/she says. Because they influence others so much words take on added import. It is particularly true of one with an exhortation gift. I am continuing to learn to use words that not only encourage (an exhortive gift thrust) but also edify (a teaching gift thrust). 3. I interviewed Peter Kuzmic, a limited level 5 leader from Yugoslavia concerning the word process item. At one point in his life in which he was isolated from all other Christians in an isolated military post where the word of God was not permitted he memorized the Gospel of John. He had a small copy of the Gospel in his billfold. Other word process items were shared with me, enough to know that Peter is a man of the Word.

COMMENTARY: EARLY CHARACTER SHAPING PROCESS ITEMS

importance	As has been mentioned previously, failure in ministry dominantly is rooted in spiritual formation issues (spirituality) rather than ministerial formation and strategic formation issues. Most of these failures can ultimately be traced to basic failures of integrity checks early on in this transitional time.
order	There are three parts to an integrity check: the challenge to consistency with inner convictions, the response to the challenge, and the resulting expansion. Sometimes the expansion may be delayed or take place over a period of time but it can definitely be seen to stem from the integrity check. Delayed expansion is seen in Joseph's classic test with Potiphar's wife. Immediate expansion is seen in Daniel's wine test.
preparation for wider sphere of ministry	Integrity is the heart of character as can be seen by in-depth analysis of the biblical leadership trait lists in Timothy and Titus. God often prepares a leader for a wider sphere of influence by testing the leader's integrity. Intent of the heart and follow through on intent are checked in an integrity check. Usually a successful passing of an integrity check results in a stronger leader able to serve God in a wider sphere of influence.
ongoing integrity	Integrity checks occur as tests of entrance into leadership or entrance into particularly demanding ministries later in life. Normally, processing concerning integrity during ministry is usually not in the form of testing for leadership but in the form of continued molding of leadership character and occur in combination with processing concerning guidance and word or literary or other ordinary expansion items.
causal source property	Often the integrity check happens completely unknown to people around the emerging leader. That is because of its inward nature. The secondary causes may be events, people, etc. They may not even know that they are sources. The primary causal source is inward via the conscience. The Holy Spirit shapes the conscience.
obedience developmental	A leader must learn obedience in order to influence others in obedience. A will conditioned to obey God is a primary tool

COMMENTARY: CHARACTER SHAPING PROCESS ITEMS continued

focus — for all leaders. With it they have a fundamental basis for developing spiritual authority--experiencing the living God in their lives.

Abraham's classic obedience — God's request for Abraham to sacrifice Isaac in Genesis 22 illustrates several important characteristics of an obedience check.

1. Obedience checks may appear to contradict some earlier leading. This obedience check was especially difficult because of a series of destiny experiences and promises concerning Isaac. Abraham knew his future line depended on Isaac, but he was still willing (conative function) to obey God.
2. Obedience checks are not always logical. It is one thing to obey when it seems logical and necessary, but it is quite another when obedience calls for something that doesn't make sense. Obedience doesn't always hinge on understanding. Sometimes it is true we know in order to do but it is also sometimes true that we do in order to know.
3. God requires unconditional obedience. Obedience checks often test surrender of the will.
4. God is responsible for the results. They may or may not be anything we would expect from the obedience.
5. Larger purposes may be involved than is immediately seen in the outward act. Hebrews 11:17-19 shows that faith in the living God as the source of life, was being strengthened through this obedience check.

causal source — An obedience check tests obedience to God. The ultimate cause must be traced to the Lord no matter what the intermediate means. A leader must learn to know that it is the Lord's voice he/she is obeying.

John 7:17 — The Lord's statement in this passage is often tested in an obedience check. "If any man will do his will, he shall know of the doctrine, whether it be of God, or whether I speak of myself."

major lesson — Leaders will be responsible for influencing specific groups of people to obey God. They will not achieve this unless they themselves know how to obey the thrust of this early

COMMENTARY: CHARACTER SHAPING PROCESS ITEMS continued

major lesson: **OBEDIENCE IS FIRST LEARNED, THEN TAUGHT.**

word checks as bridges	Leaders usually have one or more word gifts (apostleship, evangelism, prophecy, teaching, pastoring, exhortation, faith, word of knowledge, word of wisdom) as part of their gift-mix (the set of primary spiritual gifts). The word check processing is usually a springboard leading to perception of one of these gifts and its use. Word checks usually lead to public sharing of a testimony concerning the check, a first step in experiencing use of a word gift.
timing	Word checks usually occur early in a leader's life in order to initiate habits of intake and appreciation for the written word.
love of word	Leaders greatly used of God have evidenced a love for truth. They study the written word to feed their own souls as well as to help those to whom they minister. They are quick to discern God's truth in everyday life. They learn to hear the voice of God through the ministry of other people. So then, one would expect God to develop a leader in his/her ability to appreciate truth, and to cultivate habits of intake.
trigger	Usually early word checks have a strong trigger incident which involves the written Word. Some verse, phrase or sentence seems to come alive and rivets one's attention until there is a recognition that it is the Lord speaking personally.
spiritual authority	Usually one aspect of perceived spiritual authority by followers is their respect for a leader's understanding and use of the word. When the word has made a powerful impact on a leader's life its spill over or by-product is spiritual authority.
balanced learning	Holland (1978) points out that balanced learning involves three goals: being, knowing, doing. The three process items, integrity check, word check, and obedience check, respectively, focus on these three learning goals for a young leader.
overlap	Sometimes it is not so easy to differentiate between integrity, obedience, and word checks. Often a test involves a combination of one or more of these three process items. Although it is good to identify a given process item it is much more important to see the testing's significance.

GIFTEDNESS DISCOVERY PROCESS ITEM Symbol: P(GD)

introduction — Apart from acquisition of general leadership skills, the most important development during the growth ministry sub-phase involves giftedness, especially the discovery of spiritual gifts and confident use of them. This process item focuses on the discovery of giftedness and its development.

definition — The giftedness set refers to the set of giftedness elements: natural abilities, acquired skills, and spiritual gifts.

definition — The giftedness discovery process item refers to any significant advancement along the giftedness development pattern and the event, person or reflection process that was instrumental in bringing about the discovery.

Example — Barnabas discovered his exhortation gift early in his ministry. A destiny experience affirmed this gift and set expectations for using it. (See Acts 4:32-37.) There were later significant discoveries in Acts 9 and Acts 11 which brought out manifestations of his apostleship gift. The Galatians 2:6-10 affirmation was another step forward in giftedness discovery.

general time-line — Giftedness development, the discovery process of identifying, adding to, and building upon one's natural abilities, acquired skills, and spiritual gifts, usually occurs somewhat in order--time-wise. Some stages may overlap; some may be skipped. But the general tendency flows from natural abilities to acquired skills to spiritual gifts to supplemental skills.

order
1. Natural Abilities
2. Basic Acquired Skills
3. Early Spiritual Gift Indications
4. Further Acquired Skills
5. Early Identification of Spiritual Gift(s)
6. Late Discovery of Latent Natural Ability (occasionally occurs)
7. Identification of Other Spiritual Gifts
8. Identification of Gift-Mix
9. Further Acquired Skills
10. Formation of Gift-Cluster
11. Discovery of Focal Element of Giftedness Set
12. Convergence of Giftedness

FEEDBACK ON GIFTEDNESS DISCOVERY PROCESS ITEM

1. It may prove helpful for you to indicate for which of the stages you have process incidents to show development.
   ___(1) Natural Abilities
   ___(2) Basic Acquired skills
   ___(3) Early Spiritual Gift indications
   ___(4) Further Acquired skills
   ___(5) Early Identification of Spiritual Gift
   ___(6) Occasionally late discovery of latent natural ability
   ___(7) Identification of Other Spiritual Gifts
   ___(8) Identification of Gift-Mix
   ___(9) Further Acquired Skills
   ___(10) Formation of Gift-Cluster
   ___(11) Discovery of Focal Element of Giftedness Set
   ___(12) Convergence of Giftedness

2. List your dominant natural abilities.

3. List the dominant acquired skills you are presently aware of.

4. List the spiritual gifts that you are presently repeatedly demonstrating in ministry. Identify the dominant one.

5. For any one stage you checked in exercise 1 above give the details of an incident(s) or analysis indicating giftedness discovery.

6. Which of the four New Testament philosophical models is most fundamental to the concept of the giftedness discovery process item?
   ___a. Stewardship ___b. Servant ___c. Shepherd ___d. Harvest

ANSWERS----------
1. I have incidents for the first 11. 2. Leadership and analytical sensitivity. 3. Ability to conceptualize through models. 4. exhortation, teaching, word of wisdom, leadership 5. I'll discuss stages 3, 5, 7, and 8 and 10. My first gift discovered was teaching in 1965. It came about through ministry tasks relating to

FEEDBACK: GIFTEDNESS DISCOVERY PROCESS ITEM continued

home Bible classes as assigned by Pastor Thompson. I increasingly accepted openings to teach. I have taught children classes, teen-age boy's classes, teen-age girl's classes, collegiate classes, couple's classes, single's classes, and old people's classes. I saw my effectiveness in teaching improve as I continued to have numerous opportunities to teach, as I gained a better understanding in regards to teaching methods, as I made efforts to develop my own teaching gift and as I experienced personal growth and maturity in my Christian development.

In 1968 I did a spiritual gifts paper for Dr. J. R. McQuilkin entitled, "My Spiritual Gift and How I Intend to Develop It." This outlined steps for development of my teaching gift which I have followed and added to. Books on practical communication as well as hermeneutics and writing skills have immensely aided me in improving effectiveness of the teaching gift.

In 1973,74 in conjunction with my study into spiritual gifts I recognized that I had the gift of exhortation (primarily admonition thrust). As I continued to utilize my teaching gift I began to see that my exhortation gift dominated all that I did in teaching. I found that I had already made significant efforts towards developing my exhortation gift since I had been so diligent in applying truth to my own life. I also recognized that the basic pattern which occurs with the exhortation gift was already happening within my ministry. I was increasingly shifting the admonition thrust to the encouraging thrust so that my exercise of that gift was more balanced. Today I have seen that God has also further balanced my exhortation gift into a comfort thrust.

In 1975,76 I began to increasingly notice, especially in small group settings, that I often would speak a word of wisdom for situations. I first noticed this gift in another member of the executive team of which I was a part. I then saw that the same occurrence was happening with me. My continued study of gifts identified this as the word of wisdom gift. In the past I have been very careful about this gift and would seek outside confirmation. Increasingly in recent times I have been more free to use it and even try to put myself in situations where I can, by faith, expect to use that gift. Since 1979 I have recognized a gift-mix of exhortation, teaching, and word of wisdom with exhortation being dominant.

The cluster has begun to take shape. The teaching gift provides the base from which exhortation takes off. Ideas arising in teaching stir people and open them for change. Exhortation strongly moves people toward use of ideas. Follow-up counseling after application leads to opportunity for word of wisdom.

A most recent discovery, due to my continued study of the Stewardship Model and its implications for my life, has been my realization of my leadership ability as a natural ability. This ability supplements and fits well with my spiritual gift-mix. Thus I am sensing a responsibility to use it.

6. a. The Stewardship Model is most fundamentally related to the giftedness discovery process item. Its strong central thrust on accountability is at the heart of discovering who we are and what we have been given by God to use for Him. Shepherd and Harvest models are very related in an applicational manner.

GIFTEDNESS TIME-LINE EXAMPLE

introduction "Post" discovery of giftedness development is stimulated by using a giftedness time-line. Below, a "generic time-line," followed by several examples of specific giftedness time-lines, is given.

General Giftedness Time-Line

Phase I	Phase II	Phase III	Phase IV
Ministry Foundations	General Ministry	Focused Ministry	Convergent Ministry

|_____|_____|_____|_____|

A_1 B_1 A_2 B_2 C_2 A_3 B_3 A_4 B_4

1. Natural Abilities
2. Basic Skills 3. Early Spiritual Gift Indicators
   4. Acquired Skills
   5. Spiritual Gifts
   6. Late Natural Abilities
   7. More Spiritual Gifts
   8. Gift-Mix
   9. Further Acquired Skills
   10. Gift-Cluster
   11. Focal Element
   12. Convergence

Example: Mo Whitworth (1989)

1959 1964 - 1977   1977-1981 1982   1983   1984   1985   1987-1989
| [K-12 grade] college   work   grad. ed.
||---

1)optimism   2)analyt-   2)resource   2)prayer 5)teach 5)giving   7)discern
1)perseverance   ical   linking   5)faith   ing/   5)word of ings of
1)high commitment thinking   3)govern-   5)proph- exhort- knowl-   spirits
1)compassionate   2)writing   ments   ecy   ation   ledge   8)gift-mi
1)diversity of   2)self-   3)faith   5)pastor 3)miracles identi-
  interests   disci-   ing   9) small   fied
2)organizational   pline   5)ruling business
  skills   1)see   skills
2)group dynamics   overall   9) event
  skills   picture   coordi-
    3)prophetic   nation
    impressions

COMMENTARY ON GIFTEDNESS DEVELOPMENT

discovery stimulus P(GD)
: Ministry achievement or other special ministry affirmation is frequently associated with the discovery of progress or advancement in giftedness.

forced discovery
: A ministry situation may demand gifts that the leader has not previously recognized. God will reveal in that leader the needed gift in response to a step of faith. The gift might have been there in embryonic form or might be entirely new.

early discovery
: Three patterns help one recognize early discovery of elements of the giftedness set. They are listed here in order to point out "discovery" stimuli for the giftedness discovery process item.

Pattern	Explanation
Like-Attracts-Like	Potential leaders are intuitively attracted to leaders who have like spiritual gifts.
Giftedness Drift	Potential leaders respond intuitively to ministry challenges and assignments that fit their spiritual gift even if not explicitly known.
Role/Gift Enablement	A role assigned to a person can be the stimulus for discovery of a latent gift or acquisition of new gift needed to function in the role.

further explanation
: For further information on spiritual gifts, especially definitions and developmental suggestions, see Clinton (1985). A **spiritual gift** is a God-given capacity to a leader for use in ministry. Leaders usually demonstrate several spiritual gifts over a life time. Some are more permanent and repeatedly used. Some occur for periods of time. Some only spontaneously appear. Those gifts which repeatedly appear make up the set of gifts called the **gift-mix**. The **gift-cluster** is a mature gift-mix in which a dominant gift is effectively supported by each other gift in the mix. The **focal element** of the giftedness set refers to the element--natural abilities, acquired skills, or spiritual gifts--which dominates the ministry behavior of a leader.

COMMENTARY ON GIFTEDNESS DEVELOPMENT continued

discovery
spiritual
gifts

Usually Type A and B leaders will discover spiritual gifts experientially by using them without knowing names for them, or even that they are spiritual gifts. They will eventually use effectively at least one gift. The gift may not be identified explicitly in terms of cognitive terms but usually implicitly in terms of intuitive drift toward ministry using the gift. Type C leaders will at least implicitly identify more than one gift and use at least one effectively. Type D and E leaders will explicitly identify at least gift-mix. Often they will identify a gift-cluster and will rearrange roles and priorities in terms of this gift-mix or gift-cluster, which is a major step toward convergence.

MINISTRY CONFLICT PROCESS ITEM Symbol: P(MCONF)

introduction — Conflict inevitably arises when people influence other people. Particularly this is true during the growth ministry period where many decisions are made by an immature emerging leader. The **conflict process item** is a general process item which describes any conflict that is used to process a leader in terms of spiritual or ministerial formation. The **ministry conflict process item** is the special process item which describes conflict which takes place in the growth ministry period and which has its primary focus on ministerial formation. Spiritual formation is also affected by such processing. Conflict is a mighty weapon in the hand of God and can be used to teach a leader lessons that could not be learned in any other way.

definition — The <u>ministry</u> <u>conflict</u> process item refers to those instances in a ministry situation, in which a leader learns lessons via the positive and negative aspects of conflict with regards to
1. the nature of conflict,
2. possible ways to resolve conflict,
3. possible ways to avoid conflict,
4. ways to creatively use conflict
5. perception of God's personal shaping via the conflict.

example — The Apostles in Acts 6 faced conflict from within the church between the Greek-speaking and Jewish-speaking converts.

example — Paul faced conflict from without in the Ephesian situation with the silversmith, Demetrius.

causal source — The conflict may come from without, that is, those who are not believers, or from within, those who are believers. Sometimes the conflict from within is the most difficult to face since a leader has higher expectations for believers.

focus — The ministry conflict process item, like the general conflict process item and the crises process items, generally tests maturity in the inner-life. Someone has said, "In a crisis we are what we really are." Therefore, conflict processing, in general, and ministry conflict processing, in particular are important not so much for lessons on problem solving but for their value in revealing one's character. For what we are in the conflict is probably much more vital than what we do.

FEEDBACK ON MINISTRY CONFLICT PROCESS ITEM

1. The following exercises will ask you to analyze several ministry conflict process items from your own personal experience. Jot down the last 5 or 6 conflict process items that have happened in your experience. Start with your most recent and work back. Perhaps previously you saw them only as problematic situations and didn't realize that God was in them and working for his purposes of developing you. This feedback will perhaps help you reflect on this conflict with new perspectives.

	When	Conflict Item	From Within	From Without
(1)				
(2)				
(3)				
(4)				
(5)				

2. <u>Ministry history</u> refers to the identification and cataloging of ministry tasks, ministry assignments, or other closure experiences sequentially so that certain aspects of leadership development can be analyzed. Notice those words *other closure experiences.* Ministry conflict processing is one kind of example of those *other closure experiences.* It is important enough that it should be traced and analyzed in a leader's life. A study of ministry history with a focus on just conflict processing can reveal important patterns. Often it is the case in conflict processing that *closure* is weak. Analyze your list of conflict items in terms of *closure.* Were they *successfully resolved, left unresolved, partially resolved,* or just *left?* For each item give your intuitive analysis of closure by putting a short word or phrase to capture how you feel about closure for the item.

(1)   (2)   (3)   (4)

3. Read again the definition of the ministry conflict process item. Note the five areas suggested for reflection. Closure in conflict processing involves two major aspects:
(1) closure with regard to the actual conflict
(2) closure with regard to learning leadership lessons from that conflict.

FEEDBACK ON CONFLICT PROCESSING continued

It is this second aspect that affects long term leadership development. One of the most important lessons to be learned in early growth ministry processing is awareness that God uses conflict for his purposes both for your ministry and for your personal life. It is bad enough just to go through conflict. It is worse to go through conflict and not profit from it. Take one of the items listed for exercise 1 and analyze it for closure 2.

a. List some positive or negative lessons learned:

b. What do you think was God's intent for leadership development for you in this conflict?

c. How do you think this processing will affect your future leadership?

ANSWERS----------
Because conflict is so personal and usually involves other persons I think it best if I don't put my ministry history in regard to five conflict items in print. However, I will share personally on this feedback when I use this manual for teaching. The important thing is that you regard conflict in terms of lessons for your leadership. And as you look at several taken together you may see some overall patterns that you did not previously see in the midst of an individual conflict item.

DESTINY PATTERN

introduction	Destiny experiences refer to those experiences which lead a person to sense and believe that God has intervened in a personal and special way toward some purpose of God during that leader's lifetime. A three stage pattern describes a leader's sense of destiny over a lifetime. The pattern begins in the ministry foundation phase of the ministry time-line, increases in intensity during the general ministry phase, and culminates either in the competent, focused, or convergence periods.
definition	<u>Sense of destiny</u> is an inner conviction arising from an experience or a series of experiences (in which there is a growing sense of awareness in retrospective analysis of those experiences) that God has His hand on a leader in a special way for special purposes.
description	The <u>destiny pattern</u> describes a spiritual leadership pattern in which there is a growing awareness of a sense of destiny, progress seen in that destiny, and finally, culmination as the destiny is fulfilled. These three stages take place over all three phases of the ministry time-line.

The Ministry Time-Line

Phase I	**Phase II**	**Phase III**	**Phase IV**
Ministry	General	Focused	Convergent
Foundations	Ministry	Ministry	Ministry
	_____	_____	_____	_____	

$A_1 \quad\quad B_1 \quad\quad\quad\quad A_2 \;\; B_2 \;\; C_2 \quad\quad A_3 \quad\quad B_3 \quad\quad A_4 \quad\quad B_4$

The Destiny Continuum

Destiny To Be Fulfilled   Destiny Fulfilled

time ------------->
emergence of leader unfolding ------------->

The Destiny Pattern

Stage 1	Stage 2	Stage 3
preparation --->	destiny revelation and confirmation --->	destiny realization--->

DESTINY PATTERN continued

explanation   Stage 1, involves God's preparatory work bringing a growing awareness of a sense of destiny. In Stage 2, the awareness moves to conviction as God gives revelation and confirmation of it. Stage 3, builds toward accomplishment of that destiny.

DESTINY PATTERN continued

Process items or incidents which correlate to the three stages include the following.

The Destiny Continuum

Destiny To Be Fulfilled   Destiny Fulfilled

time -------------->
emergence of leader unfolding -------------->

The Destiny Pattern

Stage 1	Stage 2	Stage 3
preparation --->	destiny revelation	destiny realization--->
P(DP)	P(DR)	P(DF)
• prophecy	• revelatory act	• promise realization
• name	• revelatory dream	• divine affirmation
• prayer	• revelatory prophecy	• obedience checks
• contract (oath)	• destiny insight	• word checks
• faith act	• word, obedience, integrity and faith checks	• faith acts
• contextual items	• divine affirmation,	
• mentor	• all forms of sovereign guidance: double confirmation, divine contacts, mentors	
• birth circumstances		
• preservation of life		
• heritage	• spiritual authority affirmation	
• parent's sense of destiny for child	• leadership backlash	
	• power items	
	• convergence	

NEGATIVE AND POSITIVE TESTING PATTERNS

introduction	God uses integrity, obedience, word, and faith checks along with ministry tasks to test and expand potential leaders. The pattern involves test, response, resultant action. Two sub-patterns occur. The success pattern involves test, positive response, and expansion. The failure pattern involves test, negative response, and remedial action.
definition	The <u>negative testing/remedial pattern</u> describes God's use of various process items to point out lack of character traits through a three step process which includes: 1. presentation of a test of character through a given incident in life experience, 2. a failure response in which the leader either does not perceive the incident as God's dealing and makes a poor choice or a failure response in which the leader deliberately chooses to go against inner convictions or that which pleases God's desires in the situation, 3. remedial action by God which re-tests the leader on the same or similar issue, restricts the leader's progress until the lesson is learned, or disciplines the leader.
definition	The <u>positive testing/expansion pattern</u> describes God's use of the testing cluster of items to form character in a leader via a three step process: 1. presentation of a test of character through a given incident in life experience, 2. response of the leader first to recognize the incident as God's special dealing with him/her and then the positive response of taking action which honors inner convictions and God's desires in the situation, 3. expansion in which God blesses the positive response by confirming the inner conviction as an important leadership value and by increasing the leader's capacity to influence or situation of influence.
negative example	King Saul's failure. See 1 Samuel 15. Disciplinary action involved eventual removal from office.
positive examples	Daniel 1 (wine issue), Daniel 3 (idolatry issue), and Daniel 6 (worship issue) contain positive examples of the testing pattern.

FEEDBACK ON TESTING PATTERNS

1. Demonstrate that you understand the testing-expansion pattern by analyzing it in conjunction with Daniel in chapter 1 of the book of Daniel. Note the three stages (test, response, expansion) of that pattern in your discussion.

2. Which testing patterns have you personally experienced?

　___a. T.1 Negative Testing. Circle the process items involved:
　　• integrity check　　• faith check
　　• obedience check　　• ministry task
　　• word check

　___b. T.1 Positive Testing. Circle the process items involved:
　　• integrity check　　• faith check
　　• obedience check　　• ministry task
　　• word check

ANSWERS----------

1. All three elements of the integrity check are clearly seen in the passage (Daniel 1:8-21). There is an inner conviction, a religious conviction about certain foods, and there is great pressure to violate this conviction. Daniel decided to stick to his convictions. An amazing thing is that this is a teen-ager away from home and parental influence who takes a stand on religious convictions learned early in life. God gave relationships that allowed him to work out a plan which did not compromise his convictions. God honored that firmness of character. Daniel and friends graduate with top honors. Notice the expansion of ministry. Daniel is given a top job offer. And God has strategically placed a leader who has character and will testify upon God's behalf in increasingly tough situations.
2. a. integrity check failed, b. obedience and faith check passed.

FOUNDATIONAL MINISTRY PATTERN

introduction	Jesus reveals an important principle in his remarks following the Unfaithful Steward Parable of Luke 16:1-13.

Luke 16:10 The Little-Big Principle
FAITHFULNESS IN A SMALL RESPONSIBILITY IS AN INDICATOR OF FAITHFULNESS IN A LARGER RESPONSIBILITY.

This basic principle seems to be foundational to all of ministry processing. From observations of repeated application of this principle comes the foundational ministry pattern.

description	The <u>Foundational Ministry</u> pattern describes the faithfulness expansion cycle that seemingly occurs throughout a life-time of ministry in which faithfulness in ministry tasks and ministry assignments along with positive response to the testing element of many of the ministry process items leads to expanded ministry and retesting of faithfulness at that new ministry level.
example	Lorne Sanny, Dawson Trottman's successor was cited by Trottman for this faithfulness quality. He became the architect for the second era of Navigator history.
Biblical theme	Paul's oft quoted leadership selection admonition to Timothy points out this important quality. "And the things that thou has heard of me among many witnesses, the same commit thou to faithful men, who shall be able to teach others also."
comment	A logical extension of implications of the two testing patterns, the foundational pattern, and the testing aspects of numerous process items is the response premise.

RESPONSE PREMISE
The time of development of a leader depends upon response to processing. Rapid recognition and positive response to God's processing speeds up development. Slower recognition or negative response delays development.

This premise needs verification testing but indications to date suggest strong plausibility.

FURTHER STUDY

Study **Leadership Emergence Theory** by Dr. J. Robert Clinton. Available through Barnabas Publishers. This is the in-depth treatment of life long development.

See also **The Making of A Leader** by Clinton, available from NavPress. This is a more popular treatment of life long development.

Chapter 4. The Bible And Leadership

Review
Chapters 1 and 2 provided leadership perspectives to use when coming to the Bible. Chapter 3, gives us many perspectives for viewing the individual development of a leader by God. We see the value of looking at the whole life through a time-line, of identifying processes in the life, and of generalizing patterns from this total display.

Chapter 4 now looks at the notion of Biblical leadership and provides an overall perspective for seeing the development of Bible leaders across 6 major leadership eras. It then takes a hard look at each of the 7 kinds of leadership source materials and tells what to look for and how to study it. The most important thing this chapter does is to define and give illustrations of the 7 kinds of leadership sources and show how to study them for leadership lessons.

The overview time-line of Biblical leadership eras is important for knowing the macro context for any given leadership source. When studying a given leadership source, the first thing one should do is to go to the leadership era and see what was going on. What kind of leadership was operating? What were its major challenges? Then you can begin to study the given source for its findings.

TIME-LINE OF BIBLICAL LEADERSHIP

I. PATRIARCHAL LEADERSHIP ROOTS	II. PRE-KINGDOM LEADERSHIP	III. KINGDOM LEADERSHIP	IV. POST-KINGDOM LEADERSHIP	V. N.T. PRE-CHURCH LEADERSHIP	VI. N.T. CHURCH LEADERSHIP
A. Abraham B. Isaac C. Jacob D. Joseph E. Job	A. Desert B. Conquering The Land C. Conquered By the Land	A. United B. Divided C. Single Kingdom	A. Exile B. Post Exilic C. Interim	A. Pre-Messianic B. Messianic	A. Jewish B. Gentile
FAMILY	REVELATORY TASK INSPIRATIONAL	POLITICAL CORRECTIVE	MODELING RENEWAL	CULTIC SPIRITUAL MOVEMENT	SPIRITUAL INSTITUTIONAL
BLESSING SHAPING TIMING DESTINY CHARACTER FAITH PURITY	TIMING PRESENCE INTIMACY BURDEN HOPE CHALLENGE SPIRITUAL AUTHORITY TRANSITION WEAKNESS CONTINUITY	UNITY STABILITY SPIRITUAL LEADERSHIP RECRUDESCENCE BY-PASS	HOPE PERSPECTIVE MODELING ULTIMATE PERSEVERANCE	TRAINING FOCUS SPIRITUALITY SERVANT STEWARD HARVEST SHEPHERD MOVEMENT	STRUCTURE UNIVERSAL GIFTEDNESS WORD CENTERED

These are key words that label the macro-lessons identified thus far. Those lessons that reoccur across Bible books. See Appendix C.

EXPANDED TIME-LINE OF BIBLICAL LEADERSHIP

	I. PATRIARCHAL LEADERSHIP ROOTS	II. PRE-KINGDOM LEADERSHIP	III. KINGDOM LEADERSHIP	IV. POST-KINGDOM LEADERSHIP	V. N.T. PRE-CHURCH LEADERSHIP	VI. N.T. CHURCH LEADERSHIP
	A. Abraham B. Isaac C. Jacob D. Joseph E. Job	A. Desert B. Challenge—The Land C. Decentralized By the Land	A. United B. Divided C. Single Kingdom	A. Exile B. Post Exilic C. Interim	A. Pre-Messianic B. Messianic	A. Jewish B. Gentile
Book	Gen, Job	Ex, Lev, Num, De Josh Judges	I, II Sam, I Chron Isa, Hos I, II Ki II Chron, Jer	Eze, Dan, Est Ezra, Neh, Hag Zech, Mal	extra biblical Matt Matt, Mk, Lk, Jn	Acts, 1,2 Peter Jas, Jn, 1,2,3 Jn Acts, Pauline
Cycle	decentralized	centralized centralized decentralized	centralized	decentralized	Quasi-centralized Centralized	centralized decentralized
Dominant Trait	heritage	spiritual authority military charismatic/ military	political pol/ proph pol/ proph	modeling renewal	religious spiritual movement	spiritual institutional
Nature	family	revelatory task crisis	unifying degenerate/ corrective	inspirational task	cultic movement Jewish Church	worldwide church
Kinds of Leaders	patriarchical tribal local priests local kings local military	spir/pol/mil clans judges prophets military	political formal relig informal relig prophets military various court	models prophets (priests) administrators military	Scribes, Lawyers Various Roman Rabbis, Priests Political Elders	Apostles Evangelists Prophets, Pastors Missionaries Elders, Overseers Deacons
examples	Abraham Judah Melchezedak Kedorlaomer	Moses, Miriam Joshua, Caleb Othniel Deborah	Saul, David Jereboam Hezekiah	Daniel Ezekiel Ezra Zerubbabel	Theudas Gamaliel Jesus	Peter, Paul, Barnabas Phillip Philemon Luke, Timothy

OVERVIEW--7 KINDS OF LEADERSHIP SOURCE MATERIALS

introduction   We can derive leadership finding from 7 kinds of sources.

1. **BIOGRAPHICAL:** which represents small narrative slices of life about a person. These narrative slices or vignettes gives information about the person which allows us to perceive processing, pivotal points, leadership acts or other such interpretations from this source material. The more slices there are the more we can build to a more complete biography.
    examples: Joseph, Moses, Joshua, Caleb, Jephthah, etc.

2. **HISTORICAL LEADERSHIP ACTS:** These represent one or more vignettes which go together to make up a slice of history in which a leader can be seen to influence followers toward some action. The data gives information that allows one to identify leader, leadership functions, leadership styles, and goals for the leadership influence.
    example: Samuel in 1Samuel 12, Paul's letter to Philemon.

3. **ACTUAL LEADERSHIP CONTEXTS:** These are usually small contexts in which the writer is describing actual leadership information or directing exhortations to leaders.
    example: 1 Peter 5:1-5

4. **PARABOLIC LEADERSHIP LITERATURE:** Parables or parabolic teaching, particularly in the synoptic Gospels provides teaching on character, behavior, Christian standards or values or information about God. This information applies to all Christians but even more so to leaders who must know and demonstrate these kind of things in their lives as well as propagate them also. Some parables are actually leadership parables. They are directed to the disciples in terms of future ministry.
    example: The Stewardship parables

5. **INDIRECT:** These are passages dealing with Christian character or behavior which also apply to Christian leadership as well.

6. **STUDY OF BIBLE BOOKS AS A WHOLE:** This refers to the use of whole books in the Bible as sources for large implications for leadership.

7. **STUDY ACROSS BOOKS OF BIBLE.** This uses all the books of the Bible in terms of comparative or contrastive or common themes and lessons on leadership.

BIOGRAPHICAL

introduction — Biographical data represents the single most important leadership source. There is much biographical information.

definition — <u>Biographical</u> data refers to that large amount of information in the Scriptures which is made up of small narrative slices of life about a person. These narrative slices or vignettes gives information about Bible characters which allows us to perceive processing, pivotal points, leadership acts or other such interpretations from this source material. The more slices there are the more we can build to a more complete biography

examples — Joseph, Moses, Joshua, Caleb, Jephthah, etc.

types — There are four major categories. There is some overlap in these at the borders between them.

1. **CRITICAL INCIDENT SOURCE.** A single incident or series of incidents taking place in a very short time. There may actually be a large amount of information but all focused on a short time-interval. The information can be interpreted for processing or for a leadership act or other such findings.
   example: Job, Habakkuk, Jonah

2. **MINI-SOURCES.** Multiple incidents over a period of time which allows the creation of an abbreviated time-line and the possibility to see some patterns over time.
   example: Asa, Jehoshaphat, Hezekiah

3. **MIDI-SOURCES.** Multiple incidents over the whole lifetime which allow not only the creation of an abbreviated time-line but some processing from the various time periods.
   example: Barnabas, Joseph, Daniel, Joshua, Peter, Jeremiah

4. **MAXI-SOURCES.** There is much information in the Scripture on the character.
   example: Moses, David, Jesus, Paul, Jeremiah

comment — Sometimes there is overlap between categories.

BIBLICAL LEADERS TO STUDY

introduction I list here those Biblical leaders who should be studied because they will give information essential or very helpful for leadership. Some of these lessons will be positive encouragement. Some will present warnings. There are three groupings that should be studied. I have not listed all that I could. You may want to add to these different lists.

I. ALL WHO FINISHED WELL (Mini, Midi, Maxi Types)

1. Abraham
2. Joseph
3. Moses
4. Joshua
5. Caleb
6. Samuel
7. Elijah
8. Elisha
9. Daniel
10. Jeremiah
11. (Jesus)
12. Paul
13. Peter
14. John
15. Jacob
16. Isaac

By finished well I mean that at the end of their lifetime they
1. were enjoying intimacy with God,
2. were still growing, had a learning posture,
3. left behind a legacy--achieved things for God that contributed to his on-going redemptive plan,
4. realized potential, achieved their destiny:
   a. fully   b. limited   c. somewhat
5. had Godly character
6. had lived out convictions about God's truth and promises and demonstrate them to be real.

II. SOME--NOT SURE ABOUT THEIR FINISH (Mini, Midi, Maxi Types)

1. Nehemiah
2. Jephthah

II. SOME WHO DID NOT FINISH WELL (Mini, Midi, Maxi Types)

1. Gideon
2. Saul
3. David
4. Solomon
5. Uzziah
6. Hezekiah
7. Asa
8. Jehoshaphat
9. Josiah
11. Samson
11. Others--you add them on:

III. CRITICAL INCIDENT TYPES

1. Job
2. Habakkuk
3. Jonah
4. Ezra
5. Esther
6. Abigail
7. Mordecai
8. Isaiah
9. Ezekiel
10. Hosea
11. Deborah
12. Barak
13. Timothy
14. Titus

12 STEPS FOR STUDYING BIBLE LEADERS

introduction   The following outline gives a basic approach to biographical study in the Bible. Not all 12 steps can be done with each leader but they provide the ideal framework that should be attempted. Do as much of the 12 as you can depending on the material available for a leader.

Step 1. IDENTIFY ALL THE PASSAGES THAT REFER TO THE LEADER.
    a. Use an exhaustive concordance to help you identify all such passages.
    b. There are two kinds of passages:
       (1) *Direct*, which refers to actual historical vignettes--a short literary sketch of a given slice of life, which gives raw data about the person and his/her actions. This is data that can be interpreted for leadership findings.
       (2) *Indirect*, not actual vignettes but references to the leader or accomplishments usually in retrospect such as summary passages, intentional selection which groups several important names, etc.
    c. For the *Direct*--actual historical vignettes--Number and label each vignette separately for reference.
    d. For the *Indirect*--note the commentary on the leader. What was said? Why important? Why remembered? Why selected? Ultimate contribution? Some trait or characteristic?
    e. Books written by the leader or prophecies made by the leader.

Step 2. SEEK TO ORDER THE VIGNETTES OR OTHER PASSAGES IN A TIME SEQUENCE.
    a. Bible dictionaries or encyclopedias usually have articles on most Bible characters. These articles usually help in establishing time of events in the life. Actual vignettes as given in the Bible may be out of chronological order.
    b. Remember the time period in the progress of redemption in which the leader is acting. Put the leadership in the broader time framework.
    c. Remember the leadership era in which the leader is acting. Remember what is expected of a leader in that era. Remember the kind of leader he or she is and the basic thrust of leadership for that kind of leader at that time.
    d. Note how the leader fits those stereotypes or doesn't.
    e. Notice if the leader is breaking new ground.

12 STEPS FOR STUDYING BIBLE LEADERS continued

Step 3. CONSTRUCT A TIME-LINE IF YOU CAN. AT LEAST TENTATIVELY IDENTIFY THE MAJOR DEVELOPMENT PHASES.
   a. Handbook II has examples of time-lines. See Joseph, Barnabas, and Joshua for examples.
   b. Sometimes not enough information is given to fill out the time-line completely. You can tentatively construct to fill in gaps as long as you know it is only suggestive.
   c. Be especially alert to how the leader finished.
   d. Check for the six major barriers to finishing well: sex, family, money, pride, power, plateauing and locate along the time-line.
   e. Check for any of the 5 major enhancements to finishing well: life time perspective, renewal experiences, guarding of the inner life with God-- spiritual disciplines, mentoring, learning posture. Locate along the time-line.
   f. See if the person's life illustrates or sheds light on any of the seven major leadership lessons: lifetime perspective, power base, ministry philosophy, learning posture, leadership emergence, relational empowerment, sense of destiny.

Step 4. LOOK FOR PROCESS ITEMS (CRITICAL EVENTS, PEOPLE, HAPPENINGS) IN THE LIFE.
   a. **The Making of A Leader** by Clinton or **Leadership Emergence Theory** defines process items in-depth. Chapter 3 of this Handbook gives an introduction to them. Appendix A has a glossary of process items. Usually a critical incident can be viewed through several process item grids.
   b. But even if you don't know the names of processes you can analyze what happened in some critical situation.

Step 5. IDENTIFY PIVOTAL POINTS FROM THE MAJOR PROCESS ITEMS.
   a. Seek to identify the kind of pivotal point it is.
   b. Seek to determine what might have happened or the after effects of the pivotal point. Various kinds of lessons can be learned from this analysis.
   c. How can knowing about this pivotal point be of aid to other leaders or emerging leaders?

12 STEPS FOR STUDYING BIBLE LEADERS continued

Step 6. SEEK TO DETERMINE ANY LESSONS YOU CAN FROM A STUDY OF THESE PROCESS ITEMS AND PIVOTAL POINTS. USE THE CERTAINTY CONTINUUM TO HELP YOU IDENTIFY THE LEVEL OF AUTHORITY FOR USING THE LESSONS YOU FIND.
   a. The case studies in Handbook II have examples of lessons. The Gideon Example in this chapter gives samples.
   b. Seek to identify specific lessons first (use wording of the specific situation ,time, place, and person concerned).
   c. Seek to abstract the specific lessons into wording that could apply more broadly.
   d. Assess the level of authority for application of the lesson.

Step 7. IDENTIFY ANY RESPONSE PATTERNS (OR UNIQUE PATTERNS).
   a. The **Leadership Emergence Theory** Manual identifies about 23 patterns. The Destiny Pattern is especially helpful. Use the patterns to help you see ideas and lessons in the leader's life. Chapter 3 of this Handbook gives an overview of patterns and lists 5 important ones. Appendix B gives a glossary of patterns.
   b. Look for unique patterns that only fit the leader's life.

Step 8. STUDY ANY INDIVIDUAL LEADERSHIP ACTS IN THE LIFE. USE THE APPROACH DEMONSTRATED IN THIS CHAPTER.
   a. Identify leadership style(s).
   b. Identify the situation--look for any dynamics, micro or macro that shed light on the situation.
   c. Study the folowership.

Step 9. USE THE OVERALL LEADERSHIP TREE DIAGRAM TO HELP SUGGEST LEADERSHIP ISSUES TO LOOK FOR.
   a. Use the basal elements to suggest things to look for.
   b. Use the influence means (individual) to help you suggest things to look for, i.e. look at the leader in terms of leadership style theory.
   c. Use the influence means (spiritual power) to help you suggest things to look for.
   d. Use the influence means (corporate) to analyze the power situations wrapped up in institutions, or tradition, or cultural family patterns.
   e. Use the value bases to help you identify values--philosophical or cultural or theological that are worth noting.

12 STEPS FOR STUDYING BIBLE LEADERS continued

Step 10. USE THE LIST OF MAJOR FUNCTIONS (TASK FUNCTIONS, RELATIONSHIP FUNCTIONS AND INSPIRATIONAL FUNCTIONS) TO HELP SUGGEST INSIGHTS. WHICH WERE DONE, WHICH NOT.
  a. Were there consideration functions in view?
  b. Were there initiation of structure functions in view?
  c. Were there inspirational functions in view? Usually you will always have something on this function.

Step 11. OBSERVE ANY NEW TESTAMENT PASSAGES OR COMMENTARY (indirect source--anywhere in Bible) ON THE LEADER. ESPECIALLY BE ON THE LOOKOUT FOR *BENT OF LIFE* EVALUATION.
  a. For example, Ezekiel refers to Daniel 3 times. This is actually a contemporary evaluation of Daniel. See Ezekiel 14:14,20; 28:3. Three names are listed in the first two: Noah, Daniel, and Job. These are intentionally selected--the focus is righteousness. The third commends Daniel's wisdom. This is bent of life testimony. This is what stands out as an important thing to be remembered about the character. These kinds of hints can then lead you back to the direct data for focused study. That is, now go back and study these three characters for ideas on righteousness. Study Daniel for ideas about wisdom in a leader.
  b. The New Testament references are usually bent of life types. See Romans 4:20,21 about Abraham and his faith. See Acts 7 for Stephen's comments. All of these indirect type of references give us focuses with which to go back and search the direct data.

Step 12. USE THE PRESENTATION FORMAT FOR ORGANIZING YOUR DISPLAY OF FINDINGS FOR STEPS 1-11.

  a. The presentation format is a technical layout for presenting the highlights of your data. The order of presentation is logically arranges.
  b. This standardized approach to presenting findings is used by me and by all that I teach in workshops, seminars, and classes. It makes for ease of referencing material.
  c. For popular consumption (articles, booklets, books, public preaching, etc.) you would not use this technical format but take out of it that which you want to use.

PRESENTATION FORMAT--FINDINGS ON BIBLE LEADERS

introduction   The following is a logical order of presenting data. It is standardized for reference purposes. When doing an actual study, the information available on the character and the nature of the findings will actually determine which of these categories are actually filled. Attempt to do them all.

1. *Biblical Name(s)*--Primary: Other:

2. *Biblical Data*:
Here list the direct contextual material on the leader studied, the indirect references to the leader, and note especially any summary passages on the leader (if an Old Testament leader look especially for New Testament references or assessment on that leadership).

3. *Abbreviated Time-Line*:
Construct a time-line with development phases--as much as possible from the data given. Recognize that the time-line is incomplete (if more data were given--more phases or sub-phases probably could be distinguished).

4. *Giftedness Indications*:
If Old Testament, then list areas of natural abilities, acquired skills or special anointings seen in the leader's life. If New Testament, attempt to identify gift-mix or gift-cluster.

5. *Sphere of Influence*:
Here give the followership being influenced. If possible note direct, indirect or organizational categories.

6. *Major Contributions*
Assess the leader's achievements in God's on-going redemptive program in the Bible.

7. *Biblical Context*
Here use the overview of Biblical Leadership Time-line, want to place this leader in terms of kind of leadership seen in the Bible for his/her time.

8. *Capsule*
Give a narrative overview of the leader's life in paragraph format based on a linear time organization of Bible vignettes or data. This narration should follow the time-line and give information that allows one to put the major findings in context.

PRESENTATION FORMAT--FINDINGS ON BIBLE LEADERS continued

9. *Major Lessons*
   A. Pivotal Points
   B. Major Processing
   C. Barriers to finishing Well
   D. Here include lessons learned from leadership acts--Give actual analysis in an Appendix attached to the presentation.
   E. General/ Other
   F. Major Lessons Stated

10. *Ultimate Contribution Set*
    Here use the categories from the ultimate contribution explanation to assess the long term achievement of this leader.

11. *Appendices*:
    Here you would include any leadership acts analyzed or any other pertinent information such as family tree diagrams, etc.

EXAMPLE: GIDEON

1. Biblical Name(s)--Primary: Gideon (5th judge)
   Other: Jerubbaal (6:31, 7:1, 8:29,35
   9:1,2,5,16,19,24,28,57)

2. Biblical Data: Direct: Judges 6:1-40   Indirect: Hebrews 11:32
   7:1-25
   8:1-35

See also Appendix A which identifies and lists the Scenarios contained in Judges 6-8

3. Abbreviated Time-Line:

```
I. Weak Foundations    II. Rise and Fall of A Leader
|_____|_____|
                   A. Power      B. Wartime    C. Compromised
                   Transition    Leadership    Leadership
                      P₁            P₂            P₃
```

Where the pivotal points are:

P_1 = is Gideon's encounter with the Angel of the Lord and the faith challenge which led to the power encounter with Baal and the change of name

P_2 = is the faith challenge and response concerning the use of only 300 warriors

P_3 = is the temptation to greed (collects gold earrings and makes golden ephod) which eventually leads to a compromised (divided loyalty to God and animistic gods)

4. Giftedness Indications: essentially none given; physical hardiness; anointed for power encounter and for recruiting the temporary army (6:34)

5. Sphere of Influence: own clan, the Abiezrites; Manasseh--particularly the western part; Asher; Zebulun; Naphtali; Ephramites.

6. Major Contributions:
   a. Modeled faith--see Hebrews 11:32
   b. Models God's patient dealing with a leader concerning guidance/ encouragement/ deliverance.

EXAMPLE: GIDEON continued

   c. Preserved portions of Israel during times of Judges.
   d. Models inspirational leadership.

7. Biblical Context

Gideon's leadership occurs in the third sub-phase of the pre-kingdom era. That sub-phase deals with the problems of decentralized leadership such as lack of unity, lack of communication, lack of overall challenge or purpose, loss of spiritual zeal, subtle enculturation by surrounding peoples, etc., enemies--raiding bands. There was a cycle seen throughout the sub-phase:

   (1) The Nation Serving God--at least to some degree, certainly not perfectly
   (2) The Nation Moves Away From Serving God--usually a drift toward other gods
   (3) The Nation Basically Forsakes God
   (4) God disciplines them through surrounding nations
   (5) They come under slavery or servitude to some conquering groups
   (6) The finally recognize their plight (some aspect of repentance and turning) and cry out to God for deliverance
   (7) God hears their cry and sends a deliver--a Judge
   (8) The people are delivered and there is peace for a time. Back to step one in the cycle.

The characteristics of ideal leadership for this sub-phase include:
a. courage/ as seen in mighty deeds of valor.
b. charismatic/ spiritual authority as the influence base for recruiting followers.
c. anointing from God.
d. military skills.
e. ability to organize regionally/ perhaps civil judging functions (e.g. Samuel).
f. highly directive leadership style/ use force and coercion as well as personal charisma as major power bases.
g. integrity is important--these leaders keep their word even in vengeance issues; if the make an oath they keep it.

8. Capsule

During the times of the Judges there is a basic cycle of God's people gradually turning away from Him, discipline by God, a turning back, deliverance through a Judge, and peace for a period of time. This cycle is

EXAMPLE: GIDEON continued

given 13 times in the Judges. Gideon is the 5th Judge to deliver. Only 4 of the 13 Judges have extended material (counting Barak and Deborah as one). Gideon is one.

During the beginning of Gideon's story the Israelites were under discipline from God via the Midianites. There had been seven years of oppression by the Midianites, Amalekites and other eastern peoples. This affected a limited number of the Israelite tribes including : Gideon's own clan, the Abiezrites; Manasseh--particularly the western part; Asher; Zebulun; Naphtali; Ephramites. The raiding bands came in when the crops were ready for harvest and took the crops and ravaged whatever else they wanted. Frequently, this also meant taking women to add to their households and others as slaves.

God raised up an unknown prophet to warn the people. Then He sends an Angel of the Lord (special heavenly messenger in human incarnate form--some theologians say this is Christ in a pre-incarnate form) to Gideon to recruit and empower him. The messenger challenges Gideon to deliver Israel from the oppression. In typical Eastern fashion Gideon bargains or negotiates with the messenger. He denies that he can do it. The messenger gives the all encompassing leadership ingredient--God says, "I will be with you." He gives authority to his message with a power display (food burned with heavenly fire). Gideon knows he has had a heavenly visitation.

God then gives a dream the very night of this first visitation. He challenges Gideon to get rid of worship symbols of Baal and Asherah. In effect, this is a challenge to a power encounter. Gideon takes the challenge and gets rid of the symbols. The people find out the next day and come to punish Gideon. His father makes the power encounter public by saying that the gods behind the symbols should do the punishing if they have any power. Gideon is renamed Jerub-babel (let Baal contend--meaning he won over Baal) from this incident. This name then signifies that God won a power encounter through Gideon and is with Gideon.

The Midianites, Amalekites and other eastern peoples then form a loose alliance, cross the Jordan, and mass their forces for a big attack. Gideon is anointed with power and recruits a delivering force from some of the tribes. Now it is time to act. This drives Gideon to some serious negotiation concerning guidance (the fleece incident) . God patiently deals with Gideon who is finally satisfied that God is really in the deliverance.

EXAMPLE: GIDEON continued

God pares down the army that Gideon has raised, from 32,000 to 300. This accentuates the faith challenge involved and shows that when deliverance comes it can only be God's work. Gideon gets a final confirmation via a night reconnaissance into the Midianite camp that he should attack at night and surprise the Midianites. He does this in one of the great military illustrations of a small force surprising and routing a larger force. The confusion in the night attack and lack of communication and the problems of a loose alliance all work to insure that the Midianites, Amalekites, and other eastern forces help eliminate themselves under the cover of darkness. They rout and flee the scene. Gideon follows to mop up and sends messages out to other Israelite tribes to help cut off the retreat paths. Gideon essentially wins the battle although he has some problems with Israelites in various local districts.

The end result of the battles is that Gideon is made a quasi-king, asks for booty (gold earrings) from the battle, makes a golden ephod (used to get supernatural directions from gods, other than God), and actually moves away from God in his judgeship. He has many children. The leadership transition is a disaster, one of his sons by a concubine--Abimelech, murders all the rest of the possible heirs to the leadership position and the cycle of the Judges continues again.

9. Major Lessons
    A. Pivotal Points
    There are three pivotal points in Gideon's life.

P_1 = is Gideon's encounter with the Angel of the Lord and the faith challenge which led to the power encounter with Baal and the change of name

P_2 = is the faith challenge and response concerning the use of only 300 warriors

P_3 = is the temptation to greed (collects gold earrings and makes golden ephod) which eventually leads to a compromised (divided loyalty to God and animistic gods)

The first pivotal point is the power encounter. Gideon follows God's commands and gets rid of the symbols at night in a surprise maneuver which foreshadows his major military triumph that is to come. It is a fait accompli. His father Joash makes it a spiritual matter by challenging openly the gods behind the symbols. This power encounter clearly won by God enhanced

EXAMPLE: GIDEON continued

Gideon's reputation and gave spiritual authority for his next exploit, the recruiting of the army. This was a stepping stone to a reputation he would need to recruit the army and deliver.

The second pivotal point, a major faith challenge, is accepted by Gideon, after the double confirmation guidance process item. (the external confirmation comes from the conversation in the Midianite camp.) This pivotal points actually allows for the major accomplishment in Gideon's destiny--the deliverance.

The third pivotal point, the aftermath of the victory temptation, curtails Gideon's future leadership. His desire for the gold and the ephod (usurping religious power) become his downfall in following hard after God. After this pivotal point we do not hear of anything spiritual in Gideon's life or ministry--just problems. The major lesson of this pivotal point is to expect temptation after a great victory. When you come down from a mountain top experience expect the smog in the valley. Forewarned is forearmed.

B. Major Processing

During Phase I, Weak Foundations, there was 7 years of *negative preparation*, oppression by the outside raiding parties, which readied Gideon and others for deliverance. There was the *destiny revelation*, prophetic utterance, given to the group as a whole of which Gideon was a part. The dream was both a *destiny revelation* (next step) and a *ministry task*. Gideon proved faithful. This is an example of the *positive testing pattern.* God expands his ministry anointing him with power so that he can recruit a following. Carrying out the ministry task led to a *power encounter*--God against spirit world forces (those spirit world beings represented by the symbols). The name change is a destiny revelation item--signifying that God was really with Gideon and contended with Baal. The anointing with power to recruit is an instance of *gifted power*. The fleece matter is an instance of certainty guidance, specifically an unusual form of *double confirmation*. The paring down of the army from 32,000 is both an *obedience item* and a *faith challenge*. Again we see the *positive testing pattern*. The command to go on the reconnaissance patrol into the Midianite camp is an obedience check. Responding positively to this Gideon gets confirmation from the enemy that the attack is strategic. It is clear that God is in this. The enemy gets the dream. Gideon was given a command to go there. There is the providential working out of timing and space to be at the right place at just the right instance to hear the interpretation of the dream.

EXAMPLE: GIDEON continued

The expansion phase of this positive testing pattern is two-fold: the information confirming the attack and the actual victory which comes with the surprise attack. The attack plan (we are not certain how he got this) is the functional equivalence of a *ministry insight*.. In the follow-up skirmishes after the battle there is the confrontation with Ephraim which becomes *authority insights* processing. Gideon handles this well. After the battle is totally done there is the issue of financial resources. Gideon wants a portion (relatively small) of the plunder, some of the golden earrings. I think this is actually an *integrity* test but it is difficult to pinpoint the processing. It certainly is a pivotal point which eventually turns Gideon away.

    C. Barriers to finishing Well
The financial barrier proved to be a snag for Gideon as did the family barrier. See the transition time for family issues.

    D. Leadership acts--there is no direct data which can be interpreted for a leadership act. We only have the final results of the leadership influence. We do not know how Gideon did these things or the reactions of the followers to his influence.

    E. General/ Other: We see in this incident the one of the essential lessons of this leadership sub-phase. God uses weak instruments as long as they are given over to him.

    F. Major Lessons Stated:

1. **SOURCE OF VICTORY.** God makes it clear for all time that leaders must depend upon Him for victory. No matter what a leader's giftedness or resources, ultimately victory is from the Lord.
2. **GUIDANCE.** God will patiently deal with a leader concerning guidance if the leader is sincere about the guidance and needs it to make major decisions.
3. **HOLINESS.** There must be spiritual preparedness before God will give His presence and power to a leader. Spiritual issues must be made right. Here, the major issue is spiritual. The prophet warns of the spiritual problem. God has Gideon destroy the symbols of the gods which the Israelites are worshipping. This is done first before the deliverance. See also Moses and the circumcision issue in Exodus 4:24-26. See also Joshua and the circumcision incident after the crossing of the Jordan (Joshua 5:2-12). This precedes the revelation of how to reach Jericho.

EXAMPLE: GIDEON continued

4. **HIGH/LOW PATTERN.** Leaders are often most susceptible to temptation after a great victory. After the highs comes the unexpected lows that can wipe a leader out. After a victory we should always be alert to special spiritual warfare or other subtle temptation.
5. **BARRIERS.** A leader can be thwarted from finishing well by greed or family situations.
6. **NO GUARANTEE.** A spectacular victory in which God is known in power and presence at one point in a ministry does not guarantee a successful leadership for the rest of one's days. To finish well a leader must continue to see God break into the life in renewal experiences as well as other ways.
7. **INSPIRATIONAL LEADERSHIP--AUTHORITY.** One of the most important motivating factors for a leader is to have spiritual authority that comes from some major experience with God. When followers perceive spiritual authority in a leader, they will tend to be motivated by that leader.
8. **INSPIRATIONAL LEADERSHIP--PRESENCE.** The most important motivational factor a leader can have is a conviction about the presence and power of the Lord in a vision that is to be carried out. That conviction is one of the most important influence means of a leader.

10. Ultimate Contribution Set. Direct ministry--large public/ deliverance of a portion of Israel during oppressive times.

11. Appendix A. Vignettes in the Gideon Story

Scenario	Reference	Title
1	Judges 6:1-10	Background/ Setting
2	Judges 6:11-24	Leadership Call/ Encounter with God
3	Judges 6:25-32	Power Encounter with Baal
4	Judges 6:33-40	Gideon-Certainty Guidance
5	Judges 7:1-8a	Test--Dependence upon God Alone
6	Judges 7:8b-15a	Double Confirmation--The Encouragement
7	Judges 7:15b-25	Victory--God Delivers
8	Judges 8:1-3	Opposition of Ephraim--Who gets the credit?
9	Judges 8:4-7	Elders of Succoth--Defiance
10	Judges 8:8,9	Elders of Peniel--Defiance
11	Judges 8:10-12	Final Defeat of Midianites
12	Judges 8:13-17	Elders of Succoth and Peniel Taught Lesson
13	Judges 8:18-21	Zebah and Zalmuna Executed
14	Judges 8:22-27	Gideon's Golden Ephod; financial barrier
15	Judges 8:28-35	Summary of his judgeship

ABBREVIATED PRESENTATION FORMAT

introduction   There will be characters for which you do not have enough data to fill out all the categories of the presentation format. You should feel free to do as many as you can and simply respond with no data on this to the ones that are unanswerable. That is, an abbreviated format is highly likely when studying critical incident sources, mini-sources, and midi-source material. It is highly unlikely that a maxi-source study would not have information on all the categories. In the following presentation format the items underlined are items that could be missing in some abbreviated studies.

1. *Biblical Name(s)*
2. *Biblical Data*:
3. *Abbreviated Time-Line:*
4. *Giftedness Indications:*
5. *Sphere of Influence:*
6. *Major Contributions*
7. *Biblical Context*
8. *Capsule*
9. *Major Lessons*
   - A. Pivotal Points
   - B. Major Processing
   - C. Barriers to finishing Well
   - D. Here include lessons learned from leadership acts--Give actual analysis in an attached Appendix.
   - E. General/ Other
   - F. Major Lessons Stated
10. *Ultimate Contribution Set*
11. *Appendices:*

example   A typical example of a mini-study like Habakkuk would have the following missing:

       3. Abbreviated Time-Line:
       4. Giftedness Indications:
       5. Sphere of Influence
       8. Capsule
       9. *Major Lessons*
            B. Major Processing
            C. Barriers to finishing Well
       10. Ultimate Contribution Set

LEADERSHIP ACT synonym: group influence

introduction	A leadership act occurs when a given person influences a group, in terms of behavioral acts or perception, so that the group acts or thinks differently as a group than before the instance of influence. Such an act can be evaluated in terms of the three major leadership categories: 1) leadership basal elements, 2) leadership influence means and 3) leadership value bases. It should be noted that any given act of leadership may have several persons of the group involved in bringing about the influence. While the process may be complex and difficult to assess, nevertheless, leadership can be seen to happen and be composed essentially of **influencer, group, influence means,** and **resulting change of direction** by the group--the four major parts of a leadership act.
definition	A <u>leadership act</u> is the specific instance at a given point in time of the leadership influence process between a given influencer (person said to be influencing) and follower(s) (person or persons being influenced) in which the followers are influenced toward some goal.
example	Barnabas, Acts 9:26-30; Acts 11:22-24; Acts 11:25-26
example	Agabus, Acts 11:27-28
example	leaders, whole church: Acts 11:29-30
example	Paul, Barnabas, apostles and elders in Jerusalem, Peter, James: Acts 15:1-21
comment	One can differentiate between a momentary instance of leadership which I call a leadership act, as defined above, and leadership as an ongoing process which I call leadership. The momentary leadership act recognizes the reciprocal nature of leadership (that is, the impact of gifts that all have) for any group in a given situation. The repeated persistence of leadership acts by a given person indicates the permanence of a leader in and specifies leadership.
comment	A major difference in one who influences momentarily in a group and one who persistently influences over time is the emergence of vision and sense of responsibility for seeing that vision fulfilled.

HOW TO STUDY A LEADERSHIP ACT

introduction   A leadership act is a vignette, usually some historical narrative, which contains a leader or leaders, followers, and some situation which demands leadership. The narrative gives enough information for one to analyze what the leader did and how he/she did it. Usually there is indications of leadership styles used, power bases used, problems being faced, solved or not, etc. Leadership lessons can usually be very readily derived. The overall tree diagram of leadership basal elements, leadership influence means, and leadership value bases provides categories which can be used to screen the data for ideas.

Steps	Procedure
1	Study the passage using normal hermeneutics to get the meaning of the passage in terms of its use in the chapter, section, or book.
2	Use the leadership basal elements. Describe what you see using those as stimulants for discovery. See if there is any individual processing or corporate processing that is going on. See if any of the followership laws are present or absent and if so are significant. Describe the macro context and local context in order to understand the situation. See if you can identify the reason why the act is included.
3	Use the leadership influence means to help you discover other leadership ideas. Identify if the leader is basically task, relational, or inspirational or some combination. See if you can identify leadership styles that are going on. See if you can identify power bases being used or needed.
4	Are there leadership values that are in view. What other lessons are suggested in the act.
5	At this point summarize in the form of principles. Try to raise the level of specific principles for wider application.
6	For each statement of truth, determine where on the certainty continuum it is located.
7	Comment on the broader application of your findings.

OLD TESTAMENT EXAMPLE: SAMUEL

introduction The following is an example of an Old Testament leadership act analyzed by Dr. J. Robert Clinton.

Samuel's Final Leadership Act

A Leadership Theological Reflection on I Samuel 12:1-25

I. The Leadership Act Examined

    A. Influencer--Samuel

Samuel is performing the last formal act of his leadership.[1] He is in convergence in his ministry development and moving into afterglow.[2] He is at the height of his power to discern God's direction and to be a channel through whom God works. He has been a judge, deciding on issues, throughout all of Israel. This has been a major step in God's plan to unite the commonwealth tribes into a nation. He has given spiritual leadership through his traveling judgeship in all the tribes. He has also introduced a leadership role of the era to come through which God will often give spiritual leadership--that of the prophet. So Samuel, as is often the case of a leader in a transition period reveals leadership patterns of the old era and the new.

But Samuel, in his own mind has been rejected as the leader of the people. He has given advice about the problems of kings ruling. And yet he has had this advice rejected. And he has taken it personally. But God steps in and points out a great spiritual authority lesson. (ULTIMATE REJECTION Observation seen here.) When we have spiritual authority and speak for God, rejections of what we say is ultimately rejection of God. Our response to this rejection shows our maturity. Samuel's is outstanding.[3]

---

[1] Samuel continues to bring influence to bear as seen in the patience vignette (I Sam 13:1-14), the Amalek vignette (I Sam 15:1-9), Saul's rejection (I Sam 15:10), David's anointing (I Sam 16:1-13) etc. However, it was not as the formal leader.

[2] See **The Making of a Leader** for a description of a generalized pattern of development in a leader's life. The six generalized phases include: Sovereign Foundations, Inner-life Growth, Ministry Maturing, Life Maturing, Convergence, and Afterglow.

[3] Samuel was at first distraught at this rejection and did take it personally (see I Sam 8:1-6). But see also God's answer to him in I Sam 8:7-9. Samuel rebounded as seen in this passage. Like in the Moses authority incidents (see Numbers 12:1ff and Numbers 16:1ff) and in the question of Aaron's authority (Numbers 17:1ff) Samuel knew that it was God's place to defend his spiritual authority. And in fact in this final leadership act God did vindicate Samuel.

Samuel's Final Leadership Act continued

B. Followers

The tribes in Israel are moving from commonwealth status, each little tribe acting as it thinks best, into a united Israel. It is difficult for separate acting entities to come under a centralized authority. The people have gone through the cycles of the Judges and have been delivered numerous times over 400 years. Now they want a better security. A unified group of people with a bigger force.[4] Spiritually the people are at a low level of maturity. They learn their lessons the hard way--do something wrong, punished for it, repent and try again.[5]

C. Relationship between Leader and Followers At this Point in Time.

In chapter 10 Samuel has just seen Saul acclaimed as king. His own traveling about judging all of Israel as come to an end as the only formal leadership pattern. And so an old leader, who has seen failure[6] in his own family, he can not pass the traces on to his boys because they are so ungodly and no one sees any spiritual authority in them at all. So God is gently transitioning out an old war horse who has done well but hasn't prepared for the future very well. The old war horse has been rejected by the people. God is going to give him a last triumphal retirement party. (LEADERSHIP TRANSITION Observation seen here.) Leaders must learn how to transition out of leadership which means both when it is best to do so and preparation of leadership for future.[7]

---

[4] I do not personally think the desire for a king was in itself wrong. God had promised to make Israel into a nation which would eventually require a centralized form of government. But in their act of asking for a king and a centralized army they were in fact trusting not in God but in the king and the army. They were rejecting the unseen God for what they could see. See passages in Deuteronomy pointing forward to kingdom. See Hannah's prayer in 1 Samuel 2 which mentions the king.

[5] We should note that while this repeated cycle seems rather a low level of maturity it should be recognized that at least they recognized sin finally and did repent. Today's nations and people are not even that mature--for there is not recognition of national sin nor repentance nor a returning to God.

[6] Notice that this is one of those six barriers. Samuel's model Eli had failed in this respect. The failure seems to be in the need for discipline and the inability to do it. The rejection of Samuel's plans for continuing the present form of decentralized ad hoc government was due in a large part to his nepotistic assumptions. However, in the final leadership act in 1 Samuel 12 when Samuel asks if their are any matters of integrity in which he is lacking they do not accuse him of this. Perhaps the context of the question limits it to the judging he has done.

[7] Part of the problem of the people wanting a king lies in the fact that Samuel had done such a poor job in providing an ongoing leadership like his own. His sons were evil and the people had no confidence in them. Part of the people's failure in wanting a king can be laid at Samuel's feet in his lack of providing ongoing leadership. His inability to bring his sons up in the nurture and obedience of the Lord (like Eli

Samuel's Final Leadership Act continued

D. The Influence Means (MULTI-STYLE/CONVERGENCE Observation seen here.

1. Integrity Base--Maturity Appeal (verses 1-3)

In verses 1-3 Samuel uses a leadership style of maturity appeal and obligation persuasion. [8] He has served the people faithfully for a long period. And he has done so with honesty and integrity. And he forces them to commit themselves openly to admit that what he says is true.[9] For a leader to have credibility with followers he/she must have integrity.

2. Power Form--Information Power (verses 6-12)

In verses 6-12 he using information power[10] as a form from which he will admonish with great power. He points out the hand of God in Israel's past history and how God has raised up and ordained leadership. And then he will transition into the present leadership and show that God will use it also if that leadership will listen and obey God. This is a frequently seen power base in the Bible. Leaders will review a period of history and give perspective on it from God's viewpoint. The lessons from this information are then applied to the present situation with great effect.

3. Power Praying (verses 13-17)

In verses 13-17 Samuel gives a word concerning the new leadership. He says that God will be with this new leadership and governmental form if

---

his predecessor) was costly for all concerned. Most leaders do not think ahead to leadership transition. Many have nepotistic inclinations without evaluating the true needs of the future work, the followers and the true abilities of the future leader.

[8] See Handbook I, Chapter 2, for a discussion of leadership style theory including the ten Pauline styles of which these two are part.

[9] Personal integrity is highlighted here. This is a must for a leader whom God would use greatly. Integrity is highlighted throughout the Old Testament. The whole concepts of oaths and covenants and the keeping of them is a major manifestation of integrity. In 1 Timothy 3 and Titus 1 the qualifications for leaders is focused in integrity and its manifestations in the various cultures. The central thrust of these qualifications is integrity. The list of qualifiers all manifest integrity in the cultures.

[10] See Hersey and Blanchard (1977: 178,179) for a simplified taxonomy of power forms: coercive power, legitimate power, expert power, reward power, referent power, information power, connection power. See also Handbook I, chapter 3 where power praying and power forms are defined in leadership emergence theory.

Samuel's Final Leadership Act continued

the leadership will obey God and the people follow the God-given direction. In order to authenticate that his word is from God and that God will honor this new leadership he demonstrates power from on high in answer to power praying. Notice verse 7. Samuel is going to demonstrate that the people were wrong in rejecting his leadership and asking for a king.[11] Samuel is using an apostolic leadership style coupled with a confrontation leadership style in this power praying.[12] (LEADERSHIP PUBLIC CONFIRMATION observation seen here.)

    4. Spiritual Authority (verses 18-19)

It is clear in verses 18-19 that God vindicates Samuel's spiritual authority[13] by answering the prayer in a way that clearly shows the answer is from God.

    5. Nurse Style (verses 20-25)[14]

In an amazing way Samuel shows greatness in this act here. He could have berated them and said I told you so. I was right and you were wrong. You rejected me and now I am going to turn my back on you. You deserve my rejection. But he doesn't. Here he is relatively gentle and shows the heart of all leadership--a burden and responsibility for the welfare of the people. He uses his spiritual authority in order to exhort toward the future.

    a. verse 20: Don't be afraid--God will accept you if you follow him with all your heart.

    b. verse 21: Don't go after false gods. The great temptation to go somewhere else for help rather than to the unseen God.

    c. verse 22: Samuel reassures the people of God's great promise is continue making them His people.
(EXPECTATION/HOPE Observation seen here.)

---

[11] See footnote 3. Let me clarify further that note. My personal feeling is that the timing was wrong, that the motivation was wrong, but the form was proper--a king.

[12] These are also part of the ten Pauline leadership styles.

[13] Spiritual authority is the right to lead conferred upon a leader by followers because of their perceived spirituality in the leader. The leader gains this right by deep experiences with God and knowledge of God and His ways, demonstration of Godly character, and use of gifted power which authenticates God-given backing.

[14] This is also a Pauline leadership style.

Samuel's Final Leadership Act continued

- d. verse 23: (LEADERSHIP MINISTRY PRAYER Observation seen here.) Here Samuel shows that leader definition of God-given responsibility to the fullest. When these people deserve his rejection, instead he will hold them up in prayer. Notice who the sin is against if Samuel neglects to take up the tremendous prayer burden that will be needed to keep these people for the Lord.

- e. verse 24: This is the closure act. Samuel gives his last formal leadership words. It is an admonition to Obey the Lord, to remember the great things God has done in the past (faith is always strengthened by remembering what God has already done), And then closes with a final admonition warning what will happen if they do not follow his warning.

II. The Lessons Seen in this Leadership Act

A. Observations Listed

Major Observation: **The Leadership Ministry Prayer Observation.**

Observation in Form of Principle
1. IF GOD HAS CALLED YOU TO A MINISTRY, THEN HE HAS CALLED YOU TO PRAY FOR THAT MINISTRY.

Other Observations:

Ultimate Rejection Observation.

Observations:
2a. WHEN WE HAVE SPIRITUAL AUTHORITY AND SPEAK FOR GOD, REJECTION OF WHAT WE SAY AND ARE SHOULD NOT BE TAKEN PERSONALLY OR HELD AGAINST THE PEOPLE FOR THEY ARE IN THE ULTIMATE SENSE REJECTING GOD.
2b. IT IS THEREFORE GOD'S RESPONSIBILITY TO DEFEND THE LEADER'S SPIRITUAL AUTHORITY.
2c. OUR RESPONSE TO REJECTION SHOWS OUR MATURITY.

Samuel's Final Leadership Act continued

Leadership Transition Observation.

Observations:

3a. LEADERS SHOULD BE FOREWARNED THAT LEADERSHIP TRANSITION IS A DIFFICULT PROBLEM FOR LEADERS AND FOLLOWERS.
3b. LEADERS MUST LEARN HOW AND WHEN TO PERSONALLY TRANSITION OUT OF A LEADERSHIP ROLE OR FUNCTION.
3c. LEADERS SHOULD BE RESPONSIBLE FOR AFFIRMING CONTINUITY OF LEADERSHIP.

Convergence/Multi-style Observation

Observation:
4. IN CONVERGENCE A LEADER BRINGS TO BEAR POWERFUL PERSONAL RESOURCES SUCH AS MULTI-STYLED LEADERSHIP STYLES, DEMONSTRATED POWER WHICH RESULT IN SPIRITUAL AUTHORITY AS THE PRIME POWER BASE.

Leadership Public Confirmation Observation

Observation:
5. NEW LEADERSHIP MUST BE PUBLICLY CONFIRMED AND BACKED BY THE OLD LEADERSHIP IN ORDER TO POINT OUT GOD'S CONTINUITY.

Expectation/Hope Observation

Observation:
6. A MAJOR LEADERSHIP GENERIC FUNCTION IS TO CREATE A SENSE OF EXPECTATION AND HOPE FOR FOLLOWERS IN TERMS OF GOD'S FUTURE ACTIONS FOR THEM.

B. Applying the Certainty Continuum Screen--Reordering Observations [15]

I am using the following continuum to determine level of application.

---

[15] See Handbook I, chapter 5 for the certainty screen, its definition, and guidelines for use.

Samuel's Final Leadership Act continued

The Certainty Continuum

| Suggestions   Guidelines   Requirements |
| TENTATIVE OBSERVATIONS   ABSOLUTES |
                                              Certain   Very Certain

More certain of truth   -->
Very Little Authority <--> Great Authority

Requirement--Very certain

The Leadership Ministry Prayer Observation

1. IF GOD HAS CALLED YOU TO A MINISTRY, THEN HE HAS CALLED YOU TO PRAY FOR THAT MINISTRY.

Expectation/Hope Observation

3. A MAJOR LEADERSHIP GENERIC FUNCTION IS TO CREATE A SENSE OF EXPECTATION AND HOPE FOR FOLLOWERS IN TERMS OF GOD'S FUTURE ACTIONS FOR THEM.

Ultimate Rejection Observation

2a. WHEN WE HAVE SPIRITUAL AUTHORITY AND SPEAK FOR GOD, REJECTION OF WHAT WE SAY AND ARE SHOULD NOT BE TAKEN PERSONALLY OR HELD AGAINST THE PEOPLE FOR THEY ARE IN THE ULTIMATE SENSE REJECTING GOD.
2b. IT IS THEREFORE GOD'S RESPONSIBILITY TO DEFEND THE LEADER'S SPIRITUAL AUTHORITY.
2c. OUR RESPONSE TO REJECTION SHOWS OUR MATURITY.

Guideline

Convergence/Multi-style Observation

4. IN CONVERGENCE A LEADER BRINGS TO BEAR POWERFUL PERSONAL RESOURCES SUCH AS MULTI-STYLED LEADERSHIP STYLES, DEMONSTRATED POWER WHICH RESULT IN SPIRITUAL AUTHORITY AS THE PRIME POWER BASE.

Samuel's Final Leadership Act continued

Leadership Public Confirmation Observation

5. IN A TIME OF LEADERSHIP TRANSITION NEW LEADERSHIP MUST BE PUBLICLY CONFIRMED AND BACKED BY THE OLD LEADERSHIP IN ORDER TO POINT OUT GOD'S CONTINUITY.

<u>Suggestion</u>

Leadership Transition Observation.

3a. LEADERS SHOULD BE FOREWARNED THAT LEADERSHIP TRANSITION IS A DIFFICULT PROBLEM FOR LEADERS AND FOLLOWERS.
3b. LEADERS MUST LEARN HOW AND WHEN TO PERSONALLY TRANSITION OUT OF A LEADERSHIP ROLE OR FUNCTION.
3c. LEADERS SHOULD BE RESPONSIBLE FOR AFFIRMING CONTINUITY OF LEADERSHIP.

Bibliography

Clinton, J. Robert
    1989   **Leadership Emergence Theory**. Altadena: Barnabas Publishers.

    1993   **HANDBOOK I. Leaders, Leadership and the Bible: An Overview**. Altadena: Barnabas Publishers.

Hersey, P., and Blanchard, K.H.
    1977   **Management of Organizational Behavior**. Englewood Cliffs, N.J.: Prentice-Hall.

CONTEXTUAL LEADERSHIP PASSAGE

introduction	A few passages in the Scripture are actually dealing contextually with some sort of leadership issue. For those rare situations you simply have to use standard hermeneutical and exegesis to arrive at the meaning of the passage. The meaning itself will be the basis for leadership findings.
definition	A <u>contextual passage</u> is a scriptural unit of context which deals directly with some leadership issue such as teaching or admonition to leaders, a description of a leadership situation, a mandate from the Lord to some leader, or a meeting of leaders to deal with a problem or the like.
example	1 Peter 5:1-4
example	Ezekiel 3:16-27
example	Ezekiel 11:1-15
example	Ezekiel 13:1-16
example	Acts 20:17-38
example	Micah 3:1-12
example	Malachi 2:1-9

NEW TESTAMENT EXAMPLE--ACTS 20:17-38

introduction The following analysis, *Paul's Final Encounter with the Ephesian Elders*, was done by Dr. Eddie Elliston. This is a direct contextual passage dealing with leadership. However, it is in historical narrative format so that the basic guidelines for examining historical material for principles applies.

Paul's Final Encounter with the Ephesian Elders
Some Leadership Reflections from Acts 20:18-38

I. Narrative Overview

Paul was in a hurry traveling to Jerusalem from Assos via Nitylene, Kios, Samos and Miletus. Arriving at Miletus, Paul sent for the church elders to come from Ephesus which was about 30 miles from the port. These elders were *Type B* leaders who had assumed responsibility for the church in Ephesus. At this time there was no distinction between *elder*, *pastor*, *shepherd* or bishop.

His purpose was a leadership transition of disengagement from Paul's accountability to the Ephesian elders' responsibility for the Ephesian church. He knew this visit was to be his last opportunity to personally encourage and bring about the transition of a sense of responsibility for the Ephesian Church. He had demonstrated the power of ?Christ in Ephesus in exorcism and healings. It was through Paul that the people had come to know the power of the Holy Spirit. In this transition he certainly wanted to encourage these church leaders and to re-enforce their sense of accountability for the church in Ephesus. He used his won example to emphasize his message. He warned the leaders of forthcoming dangers, but re-emphasized that the source of power and blessing is from God.

II. Paul's Message to the Ephesian Elders

His message may be observed in three stages. He reviewed his past leadership and ministry experience with these men. He went on to describe his present activities. He then went into his final message which focused on the leadership transition.

A. Review of His Past Leadership

Paul's review of his past leadership with the Ephesian brought his leadership style, modeling, *process items*, and his message into focus for

NEW TESTAMENT EXAMPLE--ACTS 20:17-38 continued

these men. He re-emphasized some key values both in what he said and by his own example. He called their attention to the integrity he had modeled for them. He had spent about three years among them so he could by simple references focus their attention on their shared experiences.

When one looks at Paul's leadership behaviors, both elements of *consideration* and *initiation of structure* appear. He showed *consideration* for these church leaders by calling them to meet him for greetings, encouragement, instruction, a blessing and for praying together. He recognized and affirmed these men as leaders--shepherds. He recognized them as being capable with God's grace. He produced a significant blessing on them and then prayed with them.

He also *initiated structure* among these leaders. He defined both their status relationships--shepherds and overseers--and the roles they were to have within these status relationships. They were to keep watch over themselves and the whole flock. They were to protect the flock by preserving the truth.

He focused on his own leadership style by his simply calling their attention to remember "how I lived the whole time I was with you...I served the Lord with great humility and with tears...You know how I have not hesitated to preach..., but have taught you publicly and from house to house."

He reminded these elders of how he responded with tears to times of difficulty and crisis with the Jews. What were *process items* in his own personal growth and ministry now served as an example for these Ephesian elders. He repeatedly called attention to his own example.

In turning their attention back to remember what he had done with them he also drew their attention again to the message he had proclaimed while he lived in Ephesus. The message was simple: that both Jews and Greeks must turn to God in repentance and have faith in Jesus as Lord.

B. Future Direction

Paul's present course was taking him permanently out of a leadership role with the Ephesian church. He noted that he was "compelled by the Spirit" to go to Jerusalem where he faced uncertainty. He related that he had been warned by the Holy Spirit that prison and hardship were facing him in the future.

NEW TESTAMENT EXAMPLE--ACTS 20:17-38 continued

Paul affirmed his commitment to follow the leading of the Spirit in the context of his sense of destiny. His calling was sure. He was determined to complete the ministry which he had been given. In seeking to be obedient he recognized that he would not visit Ephesus again and would not see these church leaders again. Even in his declaration that he was not to return to Ephesus he was modeling a firm commitment to obedience to God's call.

Paul recognized this encounter as being his last with these men and underscored its importance to these men by recalling the past and his present course which was taking him permanently away from direct influence among them.

C. Focus--Leadership Transition

Paul's final message focused on the leadership transition to these Ephesian elders. Again, he refers to his own example that he has been obedient and can not be held accountable for the blood of anyone. He had declared the "whole will of God." In his message for these men he focused their attention on themselves ("keep watch over yourselves"). He recognized the importance of the personal and interpersonal accountability among the leaders. He also focused the attention of these men on the church they served ("keep watch over...all the flock of which the Holy Spirit has made you overseers. Be shepherds of the church of God...of the church (God bought it with his own blood). He warned of the danger of distorting the message from within the church which would draw disciples away from the church.

He pronounced a blessing and benediction on these elders committing them to God's care.

Again, he reminded them of his personal example perhaps suggesting that the motivation for their leadership should not be material or financial gain. He demonstrated the importance of self-support and of caring for the poor.

Before leaving Paul prayed with them.

NEW TESTAMENT EXAMPLE--ACTS 20:17-38 continued

III. Some Leadership Lessons

I have identified several leadership lessons in this historical event. Table 1 contains my statements of these lessons. I am using the certainty continuum to judge the level at which this truth can be presented.

description	The <u>certainty continuum</u> is a horizontal line moving from suggestions on one extreme to requirements on the other extreme which attempts to provide a grid for locating a given statement of truth in terms of its potential use with others and the degree of authority with which it can be asserted.
basic ideas:	1. Principles are observations along a continuum. 2. We can teach and use with increasing authority those principles further to the right on the continuum.

The Certainty Continuum

```
| Suggestions              Guidelines                Requirements |
| TENTATIVE OBSERVATIONS                             ABSOLUTES    |
                                            Certain    Very Certain
More certain of truth      ----------------------------------->
Very Little Authority  <-----------------------------> Great Authority
```

TABLE 1. LESSONS IN PAUL'S FINAL ENCOUNTER--ACTS 20:17-38

Certainty	Summary of Lesson
Requirement Certain	Spiritual leaders are accountable for the people whom they directly influence. Paul said, "Keep watch," "Be shepherds," "Be on guard," "help the weak." Even as he sought to be accountable, he was calling these men to be accountable in their leadership.
Requirement Certain	Spiritual leaders can and often should reflect on their own leadership with the people whom they influence to encourage and model. Followers will model their own lives after their leaders. When the modeling is brought into direct focus the impact is increased.

NEW TESTAMENT EXAMPLE--ACTS 20:17-38 continued

TABLE 1. LESSONS IN PAUL'S FINAL ENCOUNTER continued

Certainty	Summary of Lesson
Guideline	Leadership transitions frequently occur and leaders should not only expect them, but work with their followers to insure that the transition goes well. Leaders are responsible for reproducing leaders. A time comes when the newly emerging leaders must be left on their own.
Requirement Certain	Progressive disengagement is another leadership development principle. A leader by this principle encourages/ facilitates the maximal use of the emerging leaders' gifts and abilities until they are mature in their application and have fully assumed responsibility. At this time the leader-developer can move on with confidence counting on the ones left in the former situation to continue as colleagues in the faith. (In this case Paul had spent three years at Ephesus during which elders had been appointed. They still looked to Paul as their leader and came when he sent for them. Now, however, he was giving them a final commission and disengaging further from them. The process of disengagement necessarily implies a corresponding engagement. However, disengagement does not necessarily mean termination. See 1,2 Timothy on this).
Requirement Very Certain	Continuing progress in the basics of personal commitment and growth in the "word of His grace" is required even of recognized leaders. Paul said, "Keep watch over yourselves..."

PARABOLIC LEADERSHIP LITERATURE

introduction	Parables proper and other parabolic literature provide a rich source for leadership principles. About 50% of the synoptic Gospel literature are parables or at least follow the parabolic format of instruction. Many of these deal with character values which are at the heart of Christianity. Others actually deal with leadership responsibility. Jesus often taught parables to his disciples privately for their edification. Remembering that Jesus is instilling a movement. These are the leaders who will bring that movement to fruition and institutionalize it in a structure. So a number of the parables are given to them as part of their leadership training--giving them perspective and values. The central truths can almost be applied directly to leadership situations today.
definition	A parable is a true-to-life narrative which teaches a central truth by means of a series of comparisons.
definition	Parabolic teaching is the use of a narrative, pictorial illustration, or figure of speech to teach a central truth by one or more comparisons.
comment	Parabolic teaching is the broader concept. A parable is a special form of parabolic teaching.
elements	Both parables and parabolic teaching have three observable elements: setting, story, sequel. The *setting* is the material which comes before the narrative, pictorial illustration, or figure of speech and relates to it. The story element is the narrative, pictorial illustration, or figure of speech. The *sequel* is the material that follows the story and applies it or explains it in some way in order to bring closure to the teaching.
elements	Both parables and parabolic teaching have three interpretive elements: comparisons, details not compared, the central truth. The narrative, pictorial illustration, or figure of speech will have one or more items compared to something in the real life setting. Not all details will be compared. The central truth is a concise statement in real life language (not the story language) which weaves together the Why of the Setting, the Emphasis of the Story, and the Application of the Sequel, and the comparisons so as to emphatically state the teaching being illustrated.

HOW TO STUDY PARABOLIC LITERATURE FOR LEADERSHIP

introduction	The parables are a rich source, qualitatively and quantitatively, for leadership principles. Your first step in studying them for leadership lessons is to realize just how much is available and how valuable it is. The second step is to discipline yourself to study them. The third step is to make sure you have the hermeneutical skills to do them. After these three steps just follow the general ones given below.
Step	Explanation
1	Study the parable or parabolic literature using standard hermeneutical principles. See the Study Sheets which follow which lead you into hermeneutical analysis.
2	Find the Main Principle by abstracting the specific central truth. That is, reduce the specific language into general language.
3	Does the main principle deal with an important leadership value or leadership perspective. If so, word it generally to apply to leaders.
4	Study the Main Principle and the parable as a whole to see if there are related implications or applications that are helpful for leadership.
5	Study the Whole Parabolic teaching in light of the bigger context of the book or leadership era to see if it suggests one or more macro-lessons.

PARABOLIC STUDY SHEET[16]

Title of Parable: _____ Setting _____

Scripture Reference for: _____ Story _____

                                                                         Sequel _____

1. From your analysis of the *Setting* write a concluding statement which clearly sets forth *Why* the parabolic teaching was given. That is, what provoked the parable? Is there a question being answered? Is there a problem being dealt with? Is there a special teaching given (like a proverb)? Is it giving general information? Is there no significant information? If so, can the setting be implied from the totality of the observable elements? Or can the setting be implied from the remote context preceding the parable?

2. Be sure you *understand* the Story as the original listeners did. Write down any hindrances to your understanding the Story. This means you should study the story in its own background and live with the story until you sense its punch. List any items in the story which need clarification in order for you to grasp the story as a story? Give the results of your analysis to clear up these hindrances.

3. Recognize the *most important point* in the Story element which is emphasized to the listener. Give a concise statement which summarizes this important point and give a reason for your choice of this important point. Six common hints for discovering the punch of the story include: (1) Follow the action of the main character. (2) Note carefully the beginning and ending. (3) Observe a climactic event. (4) Look for bold contrasts. (5) Watch out for the surprise element. (6) Look for a problem posed by the story and solved by it.

4.   Give here in concise statement what the story teller *emphasized* to the listeners in the Sequel. That is, did the author give a scriptural comment concerning the spiritual application? If so, state the application in your own words. Be sure you have identified and concisely stated the application given. If none is given is there one implied? State it concisely. Three common things observed in the Sequel include: (1) A direct command to obey or warning to follow. (2) A direct word of explanation which sheds light upon the meaning of the story. (3) A searching question which forces the hearers to agree with Jesus or at least to focus on an inescapable

---

[16] This study sheet is based on teaching given in **Parables--Puzzles With A Purpose**, available from Barnabas Publishers. That manual gives an in-depth treatment on how to answer all of these study questions. These study questions are each based on a major parables hermeneutical principle.

PARABOLIC STUDY SHEET continued

conclusion. Write also a statement indicating what response the story teller expected as a result of this emphasis.

5. Study the parable to identify the points of Comparison. List the possible points of comparison. Notice, all point will not be compared. Which of these can be clearly identified? Which of these can be only tentatively identified? Which of these can not be identified? List here any comparisons which you feel are *reliable comparisons*. List also any comments from others which tend to confirm your comparisons.

6. Remember that a parable is given to communicate one specific Central Truth. Every detail of the parable (the setting or occasion, the story itself, the sequel and its application) will *fall into place* in relationship to a correctly identified central truth. State concisely your final statement of the *central truth*. Add any comments concerning the central truth made more vivid by Details Not Compared. give also any comments from others which confirm your concepts of the central truth.

7. List here your main principle drawn from the central truth. Remember, the main principle is a generic statement of the specific wording of the central truth which allows the specific truth given in Jesus day to be applied by today's hearers. List also other principles discovered from your analysis of the main principle or other parts of the parabolic teaching.

8. See if one of your principles given in question 7 is a leadership principal or suggests a leadership principle. Reword or scan again the parable with a leadership focus to derive one or more leadership principles. Are there any macro-lessons taken from viewing the whole parabolic communication?

EXAMPLE PARABLE--MATTHEW 25:14-30

Title of Parable: Kingdom Accountability--Talents

Scripture Reference for: Total Scripture for Parabolic Teaching Matthew 24- 25:14-30, whole larger context dealing with second coming
Setting: <u>No immediate</u>
Story: <u>Matthew 25:14-30</u>
Sequel: <u>Matthew 25: (29)</u>

1. From your analysis of the **Setting** write a concluding statement which clearly sets forth *Why* the parabolic teaching was given. That is, what provoked the parable? Is there a question being answered? Is there a problem being dealt with? Is there a special teaching given (like a proverb)? Is it giving general information? Is there no significant information? If so, can the setting be implied from the totality of the observable elements? Or can the setting be implied from the remote context preceding the parable?

Christ answers this question, "What signs?" with a series of parables, then switches to answer his own rhetorical question, "who then is that wise and faithful servant (Matthew 24:45)?" The previous teaching concluded with, verse 13, "Watch out, then, because you do not know the day or the hour. All the previous teaching has been dealing with Christ's 2nd coming. This parable is given to motivate the disciples to minister during the time before the 2nd coming. So then this parable is given along with 4 others to show us the characteristics of a wise and faithful kingdom servant.

2. Be sure you *understand* the **Story** as the original listeners did. Write down any hindrances to your understanding the **Story**. This means you should study the story in its own background and live with the story until you sense its punch. List any items in the story which need clarification in order for you to grasp the story as a story? Give the results of your analysis to clear up these hindrances.

Hindrances to understanding:
- the general notion of a steward and accountability
- a talent = money ($1000?)/ not small like the pound

3. Recognize the *most important point* in the Story element which is emphasized to the listener. Give a concise statement which summarizes this important point and give a reason for your choice of this important point. Six common hints for discovering the punch of the story include: (1) Follow the action of the main character. (2) Note carefully the

EXAMPLE PARABLE--MATTHEW 25:14-30 continued

beginning and ending. (3) Observe a climactic event. (4) Look for bold contrasts. (5) Watch out for the surprise element. (6) Look for a problem posed by the story and solved by it.

The climax of the story has to do with the dealing with each servant after coming back. There is an emphasized contrast--2 used their money, 1 did not; 2 were rewarded equally (event though they had different amounts), the other was stripped of what he had.

4. Give here in concise statement what the story teller *emphasized* to the listeners in the **Sequel**. That is, did the author give a scriptural comment concerning the spiritual application? If so, state the application in your own words. Be sure you have identified and concisely stated the application given. If none is given is there one implied? State it concisely. Three common things observed in the **Sequel** include: (1) A direct command to obey or warning to follow. (2) A direct word of explanation which sheds light upon the meaning of the story. (3) A searching question which forces the hearers to agree with Jesus or at least to focus on an inescapable conclusion. Write also a statement indicating what response the story teller expected as a result of this emphasis.

The sequel is contained as an aside in the story. Verse 29 for to every person who has something, even more will be given, and he will have more than enough; but the person who has nothing, even the little that he has will be taken away. The idea being emphasized is that "you are accountable and will be rewarded according to your faithfulness to that for which you are accountable. Or to paraphrase it, "You are accountable to me for utilizing your resources for my kingdom; you will be rewarded positively or negatively according to your performance." Or another way of saying it, "My friend, I grant privileges to my kingdom followers. But every privilege carries with it responsibility.

5. Study the parable to identify the points of *Comparison*. List the possible points of comparison. Notice, all point will not be compared. Which of these can be clearly identified? Which of these can be only tentatively identified? Which of these can not be identified? List here any comparisons which you feel are *reliable comparisons*. List also any comments from others which tend to confirm your comparisons.

lord= Christ
leaving home of a trip = Jesus to go away to heaven
3 servants = kingdom followers (2 proved to be the wise and faithful servant)
5000 /talent servant = person with large resources
2000 Talent servant = person with less resources

EXAMPLE PARABLE--MATTHEW 25:14-30 continued

1000 Talent servant = person with relatively small resources
another country = heaven or eternity
talents = total resources: opportunity, abilities, gifts, influence, power, time, etc.
    That is, anything that a person has which can be used for the Kingdom.
coming back = 2nd coming
settling accounts = time of judgment/ time of accountability

6. Remember that a parable is given to communicate one specific **Central Truth.** Every detail of the parable (the setting or occasion, the story itself, the sequel and its application) will *fall into place* in relationship to a correctly identified central truth. State concisely your final statement of the **central truth.** Add any comments concerning the **central truth** made more vivid by Details Not Compared. give also any comments from others which confirm your concepts of the central truth.

You wise kingdom followers must recognize your accountability for I will reward you at my second coming on the basis of service rendered according to your faithfulness to your gifts, abilities, and opportunities and in terms of equal rewards for equal faithfulness, so be faithful and produce to your potential.

7. List here your **main principle** drawn from the central truth. Remember, the main principle is a generic statement of the specific wording of the central truth which allows the specific truth given in Jesus day to be applied by today's hearers. List also other principles discovered from your analysis of the main principle or other parts of the parabolic teaching.

Christ's followers must be utilizing their unique God-given resources to further the kingdom, while anticipating Christ's 2nd coming; for Jesus will hold them accountable and reward them at that time on the basis of equal rewards for equal faithfulness.

Note the reward basis--Where there are differing abilities etc. I do not have to compare myself with others but simply remember that equal rewards for equal faithfulness and tremendous loss for unfaithfulness in service. I do not necessarily have control over the gifts and abilities and privileges and opportunities given me but I do have control over my faithfulness to use them.

8. See if one of your principles given in question 7 is a leadership principal or suggests a leadership principle. Reword or scan again the parable with a leadership focus to derive one or more leadership principles. Are there any macro-lessons taken from viewing the whole parabolic communication?

EXAMPLE PARABLE--MATTHEW 25:14-30 continued

Christ is giving these parables to leaders; those who will institute the movement. They are leaders. And he is telling them the kind of values they must have as they work and wait for him.

a. A leader will be held accountable not for how much better or worse he/she did than someone else but how he/she did in respect of their own God-given resources (see also 2 Corinthians 5:10).

b. Every believer should be conscious that there is a ministry for him or her to do for God. All have some abilities, resources, etc. Hence, a leader must seek to help followers identify, build on, and use their resources for God's kingdom.

c. Kingdom privileges also carry Kingdom responsibility.

d. The Second Coming should be a motivating factor for leaders.

e. Leaders should reward faithful followers because it is right, because it is a means of motivating, and to encourage other believers to be faithful.

MACRO-LESSONS

key words: **PERSPECTIVE, ACCOUNTABILITY, MOTIVATION**

A. **PERSPECTIVE**--Leaders need the big picture in mind so that they can operate with today's pressures in perspective.

B. **MOTIVATION, Second Coming**--Wise leaders do what they do but are always mindful of the Second Coming. Doing what they should be doing in terms of giftedness and calling is the best way to be ready for the Second Coming.

C. **ACCOUNTABILITY**--Accountability is a necessary value for a leader. Christ holds his followers accountable. So too should Christian leaders. Leaders must challenge followers to grow and produce and hold them accountable.

INDIRECT

indirect	Much of the Bible is written not about leadership but in terms of God dealing with His people in general. Much of the teaching, admonitions, or commands when given to the people of God can be applied also to leaders. Particularly is this true of information which is primarily dealing with spiritual formation issues. The proper procedure then is to study the passages and interpret them for whom they are given. Then ask if any of these apply in a special way for leaders. Simply move the level of application up till it fits leaders.
indirect	The most general source of information in the Scriptures is the <u>indirect</u>, meaning information not given directly for leaders, but which may apply especially where dealing with character issues and standards of Christians life.
example	The Sermon on the Mount--replete with potential leadership lessons
example	The whole book of James deals with teaching and exhortation on Christian living which has a lot of potential for leadership lessons
example	The book of Proverbs is almost totally an indirect source that is filled with potential leadership lessons

<u>Some Typical Lessons from Indirect--Proverbs</u>

1. **FOUNDATIONAL RELATIONSHIP.** It is a vertical relationship that is given as foundational for understanding wisdom. Leaders first need to have a proper respect for God as the giver of wisdom before they can truly learn from life. Leaders need the wisdom of God in their ministries. The Proverbs assert that a proper relationship with God is the foundational access to that wisdom from God (Prov 1:7, 1:29, 3:7, 2:5, 8:13, 9:10, 10:27, 14:26, 14:27, 15:16, 15:33, 16:6, 19:23, 22:4, 23:17, 24:21)
2. **LEARNING POSTURE.** One of the findings concerning effective leaders states that Effective Leaders maintain a learning posture all their lives. The Proverbs certainly assert the validity of this finding. Wisdom does not come automatically. There must be proactive learning posture if a leader is to learn from God via life. (1:20-33, 2:1ff, 19:8 and many others).

INDIRECT SOURCE OF LEADERSHIP LESSONS continued

Lessons from Proverbs continued

3. **RESPONSE TO CORRECTION.** One way a learning posture is expressed is by a person who can learn from criticism. (9:8, 10:8, 10:17, 11:3, 12:1 and many others).
4. **DISCIPLINE.** Another way a learning posture is expressed is by a proper response to the discipline of the Lord. Processing in life is ultimately from the Lord and is meant to teach lessons of life. Particularly is this so where it is clear that the Lord is bringing discipline upon our lives. (3:11,12, 17:3, 17:10, 27:21 and others).
5. **CRISES.** It is the crises experiences in life which are particularly instructive. These tend to test us and shape us like no other experiences. A person with a learning posture will respond to crises expecting to go deep with God and to learn much about personality and character (24:10,11).
6. **USE OF WORDS.** A leader must be extremely careful in the use of the tongue even more than is indicated in the Proverbs which treats this as a major topic. This is so because people in influential positions are listened to with much more emphasis. That is, their words carry added weight (even if not intended) with followers who look to them (6:2, 6:16-19, 10:11, 10:19, 12:14, 12:19, 15:1, 15:4, 15:23, 15:28, 12:19, 16:24, 16:27, 28, 17:9, 17:27, 28, 18:13, 25:11, 26:18,19, 27:2, and many others).
7. **PRIDE.** Pride can lead to failure. It is one of the six major barriers which hinder leaders from finishing well. Proverbs warns against it and its dangers (13:10, 16:18, 18:12, 27:2).

BOOKS AS A WHOLE

introduction Books as a whole can be studied for macro lessons. These are large scale implications which be based on what is included, what not, what the book is doing in the canon, critical issues in the book, and perhaps critical incidents. There is no scientific way of getting at macro-lessons. Usually the more familiar you are with leadership issues in general the more you can see of macro-lessons. Whether macro-lessons are valuable or not is a whole another issue in itself. A given macro-lesson is valid if it meets the normal criteria given for any principle of truth across the Certainty Continuum. Usually macro-lessons which can be validated across books or are taught rather directly in some other book are legitimate.

Step	Explanation
1	Study the book hermeneutically as you would do normally to make sure you have the interpretation of the book as a whole.[17]
2	Exegete the small contexts that make up the major parts of the book to make certain you have interpretation for each.
3	Look for leadership kinds of topics in the book such as: process incidents, direct exhortations or teachings about leadership or to leaders.
4	Reflect on the book in terms of its larger purposes in the redemptive drama and the leadership era of which it is a part. What large leadership lessons are suggested. Make abstract high level generic statements about these lessons.
5	Consider other high level leadership lessons already identified in other books. Examine them to see if they are affirmed or not in the book.
example	See the book of Jude which illustrates the above steps. See also Handbook III which does this for every book in the Bible.

---

[17]Handbook III gives my basic hermeneutical approach. Laws 1, 2, and 3 are macro laws and deal with the book as a whole. Laws 4, 5, and 6 deal with smaller portions within the book. Law 7 deals with the book as it relates to other books and the Bible as a whole.

BOOK	**JUDE**	**AUTHOR:** Jude, Jesus' brother

Characters — none in focus, though many are used in conjunction with Old Testament events to punctuate the author's message

Who To/For — uncertain; possibly to the same kind of audience as the books of James and Peter

Literature Type — This is an exhortive letter.

Story Line — Certain believers were in danger of being led astray by false teachers. Jude writes to warn them of these dangers and to describe the false teachers so that they could be identified and avoided. He alludes to the Old Testament several times in giving his warning. Jude uses faith as a figure of speech standing for basic Christian truth.

Structure
I. (1-16) The Negative--Warnings From History About Departing From the Faith
II. (17-25) The Positive--Exhortations To Go On In the Faith

Theme — **CONTENDING FOR THE FAITH** (basic Christian truth)
- involves not only recognition and rejection of ungodly influence to depart from truth, but
- also positive efforts to live in and learn of this truth.

Key Words — ungodly (6); faith (2); these men (3)

Key Events — The author alludes to several Old Testament events and others occurring in that time but not in Scripture.

Purposes
- to warn against apostasy (being led astray from the true faith),
- to give several illustrations of apostasy so as to expose its nature and warn against its results,
- to show the importance of knowing thoroughly basic Christian truth and acting upon it.

Why Important — This book exposes the danger of apostasy. It gives illustrations of it which suggest its nature and causes:

JUDE continued

	unbelief leading to rebellion, not submitting to proper God-appointed situation; giving over to perversion; self-righteousness; greed; presumption. We are in danger of always being led astray. The process is implied: willful moral declension--some compromise of our convictions, justification of it in terms of Christian freedom, denial of Christ.
Where It Fits	Jude was probably written earlier than John's books but toward the end of the first century of the Church. Christianity has spread to the Gentiles. As it crosses cultural barriers there is always the danger that it will be misinterpreted or become syncretistic (mixed with local religion in a compromising way). Further there is the danger of leaders who are not genuine in their faith leading followers astray. Jude writes to counteract these leadership issues. He does so not in detail but in terms of basic issues that have wide application.

Leadership Lessons

1. **CONFRONTATION LEADERSHIP STYLE**: Confrontation (urge you) is one of ten Pauline leadership styles identified. Here Jude uses that style in confronting a problem of orthodoxic (beliefs) as well as orthopraxic (Christian practice) heresy.
2. **INDIRECT LEADERSHIP STYLE.** Another leadership style is indirect--one which attempts to do battle in the spiritual realm via intercession--rather than a direct confrontation at the human level. The word contend (vs 3, epagonizomai) is often used in terms of intercession (spiritual warfare)--see Colossians 2:1.
3. **RESPONSIBILITY TO DEFEND CHRISTIAN TRUTH.** There is a corporate responsibility (vs 3, entrusted to the Saints) for keeping Christianity pure.
4. **BALANCE OF TRUTH AND BEHAVIOR.** Orthopraxy (license for immorality) and orthodoxy (deny Jesus Christ) are twin dangers equally destructive to the purity of Christianity.
5. **ATTACKS FROM WITHIN/ SUBTLE.** Attacks from within the church are more subtle and hence sometimes more dangerous (secretly slipped, vs 4).

JUDE continued

6. **ATTACKS FROM WITHIN/ SYMPTOMS.** Symptoms of those who can destroy Christianity from within include:
   a. endorse sexual perversion (vs 4, 7, 8)
   b. reject authority (vs 8, 11)
   c. slander cosmic level warfare (vs 8, 9)
   d. use Christianity as a means of money making (vs 11).
   e. hypocritical practice of Christianity/ leadership (vs 12, 13)
   f. faultfinding (vs 16)
   g. boast about themselves (16)
   h. flatter others for their own advantage (16)
   i. cause splits (vs 19)

For Further Leadership Study

1. See **Conclusions on Leadership styles** for the 10 Pauline styles. Here confrontation and indirect styles are used. Normally the sequence is indirect first then confrontation next.
2. Through the ages the Church has required leadership to sign belief creeds in order to guard against heresy. They have sought to maintain orthodoxy by explicitly defining core tenets which leaders should *believe*. The Church has not been as stringent on Christian practice. Many times its leaders have not demonstrated their Christianity in their relationships with others or in the solving of church problems. One can be orthodox in belief and yet be heretical in practice. The blend, the balance, should be noted. See particularly the Pauline epistles where his practice in solving problems is just as important as what he says about the problems.

Special Comments
This book ends with a special word of encouragement--a doxology often given from the pulpit to close a Sunday morning service. As we attempt to make it our business to live out the Christian faith and grow in it we can rest assured that it is God who will establish us and keep us from apostasy.

HOW TO STUDY ACROSS BOOKS IN THE BIBLE

introduction	My hermeneutical law 7 states, In the Spirit, prayerfully study the book as a whole in terms of its relationship to other books in the Bible (the Bible as a whole) to include: a. its place in the progress of revelation, b. its overall contribution to the whole of Bible literature, and c. its abiding contribution to present time. It is the application of this law with a special emphasis on leadership lessons that is in view when studying across Bible books.

Step	Procedure
1	As you study each book in the Bible for its emphasis, identify all the leadership lessons for each book.
2	Compare lessons between several of the more important leadership books. From this comparison identify common macro-lessons that may likely occur in other books. Keep this list as you go.
3	Whenever you study a new book, check it for confirmation of previous macros and to see if it may add something new to the list.
4	See Handbook III for my own initial list of macro-lessons across the books of the Bible.[18]
examples	Note these macro-lessons from the Patriarchal Leadership Era.

Lesson Name	Statement Of Lesson
Blessing	God mediates His blessing to His followers through leaders.
Shaping	God shapes leader's lives and ministry through critical incidents
Timing	God's timing is crucial to accomplishment of God's purposes.
Destiny	Leaders must have a sense of destiny.
Character	Integrity is the essential character trait of a spiritual leader.

---

[18] I have identified 39 at the time of my writing of this manual. I continue to add to this list. Usually each new leadership era because of the change in leaders, followers, situations will add new macro-lessons while affirming most of the previous ones. See Appendix C for a listing.

LISTING OF SOURCE MATERIALS IDENTIFIED THUS FAR

introduction The following is a tentative listing of passages that deal with various topics. I am still in the process of identifying leadership acts and direct contextual passages. I will update this list regularly as I discover new information. See Chapter 3 for process items and abbreviations used here.

Biblical Information Sources for Leadership Study

Old Testament Passages

Book/Passage	Leadership Topic
Genesis	Biographical insights; character studies: Abraham, Isaac, Jacob, Joseph (probably most significant); many examples of processing
Exodus	Biographical insights (Moses); many process items illustrated
Leviticus	Biographical insights (less than Exodus or Numbers);
Numbers	Biographical insights; leadership transition insights
Deuteronomy	Biographical insights; leadership transition insights
Joshua	Biographical insights; Joshua is a leader worth studying in depth
Judges	Numerous biographical insights; usually minimum data but important in terms of intentional selection
I Samuel	Biographical insights; Samuel, one of three leaders in Bible that is affirmed as an intercessor; poor leadership transition in general but good recovery by Samuel; biographical insights into David's early development
II Samuel	Biographical insights into David's life; poor leadership transition
I, II Kings	Biographical insights in civil leaders; general pattern as the civil leader goes, so goes the tone of the country
I, II Chronicles	Biographical insights into David's development and other kings
Ezra	Biographical insights (whole book)
Nehemiah	Biographical insights (whole book); many leadership acts
Proverbs	Whole book-learning posture from all of life; many individual verses on character--especially use of words--emerging leaders need to learn these tongue lessons early; much indirect
Proverbs 1:20-33	Learning posture in life

Biblical Information Sources for Leadership Study continued

Old Testament Passages

Book/Passage	Leadership Topic
Proverbs 9:8	In leadership you will have to confront and be confronted; confrontation times are key times for growth
Proverbs 11:13	Confidentiality
Proverbs 11:14	Consensus in leadership decision making
Proverbs 13:20	Power of peer group pressure
Proverbs 21:1	Providential control of leadership
Ecclesiastes	Warning; as you grow older as a leader there is a tendency to become cynical--antidote: learn from the young and hope with them concerning ideals;
Isaiah 6	P (DR)/P (LCO) for Isaiah (destiny revelation, leadership committal)
Isaiah 7	P (FC), faith challenge, refused
Isaiah 9:13ff	Judgment on leaders; quasi-direct context
Isaiah 26:9,10	Key idea of processing immediate lessons
Isaiah 30	Corporate flesh act
Isaiah 36-39	Biographical insights
Isaiah 36	Power encounter
Isaiah 37	Faith challenge P(FC)
Isaiah 39	Flesh act
Jeremiah	Whole book is filled with deep processing of leader; conflict processing throughout the book; personal processing, value in ministry which is not success oriented
Jeremiah 1	P (LCO) leadership committal
Jeremiah 2	Four kinds of leaders: kings, officials (elders, administrators), priests (standard religious leaders), prophets (special religious leaders)
Jeremiah 5:30	Lack of spiritual authority--yet religious leaders
Jeremiah 6:9-30	No integrity in leadership
Jeremiah 14:11	Divine initiative in praying; crucial concept for a leader
Jeremiah 15:1	Summary passage, leaders/intercessors
Jeremiah 20:1-18	The prophet urge--sense of responsibility; ultimate vindication of leadership is the Lord's responsibility
Jeremiah 22:1-30	Leadership responsibility; watch over those who cannot take care of selves

Biblical Information Sources for Leadership Study continued

Old Testament Passages

Book/Passage	Leadership Topic
Jeremiah 23:1-40	Judgment of leadership/religious leadership
Jeremiah 32:1-16	Double confirmation (classic biblical example)
Jeremiah 32:17-29	Great classical illustration of a faith challenge
Lamentations	Personal processing of leader; inner attitudes in a massive failure situation; rejection
Lamentations 4:16	Lack of respect for religious leadership; a compassionate leader who could have said I told you so; but instead says I wish I didn't have to tell you so
Ezekiel 1-3	Importance of destiny processing; whole book will repeat this throughout; illustrations of experiential power base for spiritual authority
Ezekiel 33	Leadership responsibility
Ezekiel 37:1-14	Word gifting, one purpose of leadership -> give hope for future
Daniel	Leadership insights, development of leader (foundations of vision); theme of Daniel; civil leader formally, religious leader informally, lay leader; note summary passages on Daniel: righteousness
Hosea	In general--biographical leadership insights; shows danger of not perceiving God in the events of life
Hosea 1:1-11	P (LCO), modeling; God's processing of a leader as a model through which to reflect His character
Hosea 4:1-19	A major function of religious leadership
Hosea 6:1-10	Prophetical role
Hosea 9:1-17	Special religious leaders will be demeaned
Joel	Economic crisis, leadership insights
Amos	Special religious leader, lay leader --> prophet (1st generation); Biographical insights; role of prophet
Amos 7:14	Call; P(LCO), power of a lay person going full time or bi-vocational; instance of special religious prophet for renewal
Jonah	Processing of a leader toward God's purposes
Micah 3:1-12	Direct context; whole book dealing with leadership found wanting
Habakkuk	Divine affirmation for a leader (special religious) in the midst of discouraging and perplexing circumstances which reflect it; biographical insights

Biblical Information Sources for Leadership Study continued

Old Testament Passages

Book/Passage	Leadership Topic
Haggai	Leadership insight, civil, formal religion, special religious leader role
Malachi	This is a book about religious leadership in need of renewal.

New Testament Leadership Passages

Book/Passage	Leadership Topic
Matthew 10:1-4	Selection
Matthew 10:5-15	Training in Authority
Matthew 17:1-13	Leader-follower relations
Matthew 20:1-16	Workers in Vineyard followers
Matthew 20:20-28	Servant Leadership
Matthew 21:23-27	Authority
Matthew 22:15-22	Relationship to Civil Authority
Matthew 24:45-51	Faithful Servant--Trait
Matthew 25:1-13	Ten Virgins--Trait
Matthew 25:14-30	Talents, Accountability Capacity
Matthew 28:16-20	Authority/Task Oriented
Mark 3:13-19	Selection
Mark 9:33ff	Test of Greatness/Acquired Trait
Mark 10:35-45	Greatness/Acquired Trait
Mark 11:27-33	Authority
Mark 12:13-17	Relationship to Civil Authority
Mark 16:14-18	Task Mandate
Luke 5:1-11	Selection
Luke 5:27-32	Selection
Luke 9:28-36	Leader-follower relations
Luke 10:1-12	Selection/training
Luke 10:17-20	Ministry Success/Leader Evaluation/Foundational Lesson
Luke 12:35-40	Watchful Servant; acquired trait
Luke 12:41-48	Faithful Servant; Implications--Capacity
Luke 16:1-12	Unfaithful Servant, Leadership Emergence Pattern
Luke 17:7-10	Unprofitable Servant--base trait
Luke 19:11-27	Pounds--capacity

Biblical Information Sources for Leadership Study continued

New Testament Leadership Passages

Book/Passage	Leadership Topic
Luke 22:24-30	Leader--Servanthood, personality bent
John	Almost the entire book of John can be examined very profitably since there are so many leadership acts of Jesus given in intimate detail. Leadership style in terms of functions, follower, maturity, leader personality, and leader-follower relationship will reveal so much.
Acts	Many passages contain leadership acts which can be analyzed with great profit. See also Acts 20:17-38, Direct Context.
Romans 12:3-8	Gifts
Romans 14,15	Problem Solving
I Corinthians	Whole book illustrates confrontation, can see several leadership styles
II Corinthians	Many, many insights into Paul's leadership
Galatians	Forceful confrontation, unity--> purity continuum several leadership styles
Ephesians 4:7ff	Foundational passage on biblical leadership gifts
Philippians 4:9	modeling, book as a whole gives valuable leadership insights
Colossians	Illustration of how leader confronts problem, insights on powers see 2:15
I Thessalonians	Valuable from leadership styles viewpoint, follower-maturity
II Thessalonians	Deals with major function of leadership--creating hope, solving problems
I Timothy	Entire book is advice of mature leader to young leader
II Timothy	More of the same
Titus	One of most valuable books since it so clearly shows what a Type D leader must do and lays out so clearly God's purposes for level A, B, and C leaders.
Philemon	A major leadership act filled with leadership lessons
Hebrews	Application sections offer leadership warnings
James	Applicational leadership insights
I,II Peter	Filled with leadership insights, see especially I Peter 5:1-4, Direct Context
I,II,III John	Has implicit leadership information
Revelation	Difficult to assess from leadership vantage

FURTHER STUDY

Chapter 5 will tell more about deriving the principles some of which I gave as examples in this chapter along with the illustrations of analyzing the kinds of sources. Creating principles requires experience. The more you do the easier it gets. Chapter 5 will suggest analytical approaches but on top of that there is an intuitive leap to see them. The more you see the better you will be at seeing new ones. The other two Handbooks, II dealing with study of leaders and III dealing with books of the Bible will list many principles. As you continue to study these you will soon be able to see principles and derive them yourself.

Handbook II is devoted entirely to illustrating biographical studies. It will have examples of all but maxi-studies. Many, specific leadership principles as well as quite a few macro-lessons will be given.

Handbook III studies each book of the Bible for individual specific leadership lessons, for Macro-lessons from the Book, and for Macro-lessons across the Bible.

You should study Handbooks II and III. Keep Handbook I close by for reference.

Chapter 5   Principles of Truth--How To Get Them

Review

In Chapter 1, I introduced you to basic leadership definitions such as leaders, leadership styles, leadership acts, and leadership functions. These perspectives open our eyes as we view much of the leadership information in the Bible. We see things that are there because we have these labels and because we are looking for them.

In Chapter 2, I gave more specialized definitions. The ethnotheological models give cultural/ theological/ philosophical underpinnings for viewing the Bible in its progressive revelation across time and cultures. There were many miscellaneous concepts and models which helped us see leadership issues in various unique situations and ways. The philosophical leadership models from the New Testament (Steward, Servant Leader, Intercessor, Harvest, Shepherd) help us understand roles, giftedness, and values and how they interrelate. There were many concepts that specifically dealt with leaders--how they finish, why they finish well or poorly, how they transition into or out of ministry, how they view ministry, etc. These many models and concepts again open our eyes to see things in the Scriptures, that were always there but now are apparent.

Chapter 3, gives us many perspectives for viewing the individual development of a leader by God. We see the value of looking at the whole life through a time-line, of identifying processes in the life, and of generalizing patterns from this total display. Whereas chapters 1 and 2 help us in general in approaching any kind of leadership source material, this chapter especially helps us as we approach the biographical source of leadership information.

Chapter 4, takes a hard look at each of the 7 kinds of leadership source material and tells what to look for and how to study it.

Chapter 5, our present chapter now gives details of how to draw out truth from that source material as you study it. It suggests levels of truth, conceptual screens for generating and evaluating those truths. It finally gives some examples of truth derived from the various kinds of leadership source material.

some pre-suppositions — I should be clear with you about my own assumptions in approaching the Bible to get truth for my own life and for others. There are three guidelines I want to suggest for theologizing on leadership Bible data. Let me get all three of them before us and then I shall discuss each.

1. FEW PASSAGES WERE GIVEN TO DIRECTLY TEACH ON LEADERSHIP HENCE WE MUST EXERCISE CAUTION IN DRAWING LEADERSHIP TRUTH FROM THEM.

2. WE MUST RECOGNIZE THAT WE DO NOT VIEW THESE LEADERSHIP PASSAGES UNBIASED.

3. WE WILL DIFFER WITH OTHERS BOTH ON OUR IDENTITY OF TRUTH AND ON HOW HARD WE ASSERT IT FOR OTHERS, HENCE WE MUST HONOR DIFFERING CONVICTIONS.

Caution 1. — Few passages were given to directly teach on leadership hence we must exercise caution in drawing leadership truth from them. Since few of the sources we are looking at were given to directly teach us on leadership, we as leaders, must identify with the divine case book approach and recognize that truth is interwoven with life story in most of those genres and must be elicited. We rarely will have explicit leadership information handed to us on a platter. This being the case we must exercise caution as we seek to identify truth. To draw out truth that is not there is in the long run to weaken our credibility with our followers. Our basic rule is simple: what the Bible has to say, nothing more, nothing less, nothing else. But its application is complex. For that reason this chapter shall give several screens[1] that we apply to the passage and our potential truth statements. We need to recognize that there are differing levels of dogmatism. The certainty continuum helps us assess that. Our leadership observations/ results/ findings will fall along the certainty continuum. Probably few will fall on the very authoritative (requirement level). The applicability screen will help us to judge where along the continuum it falls and how hard we can assert the truth for ourselves or others. Hence we must screen data using criteria applicability screen.

Acknowledgment
My original thoughts on these issues, how to get at truth from various kinds of Bible passages, were prompted by Dr. Robertson C. McQuilkin of Columbia Bible College, I was his teaching assistant for two years. I wrote up a booklet called **Disputed Practices**,[2] published by the Learning Resource Center of Worldteam which put these ideas into written form for application to missionaries overseas who needed help on how to determine stands on issues of Christian living where there were so many denominational backgrounds and differing views on Christian practice. I have simplified what I had in those notes and sought to apply it to leadership data. This is a first attempt and will certainly be revised, clarified, and expanded as we get more and more theologizing on the leadership genre from the Scriptures.

caution 2
Recognize that you do not view these leadership passages unbiased. Tradition, movements, personal experience, your leadership perspectives all influence how you draw out your suggestions, principles, guidelines, requirements. Be aware that your findings must continually be challenged in terms of your various biases. We all perform isogesis, that is, we read into the situation things that may or may not have been there. We see them there because of our own experiences and perspectives. Sometimes this is not all bad because the truth we see may be valid somewhere else in the Bible. It is always best to use the strongest passages on a truth. The screens again force us to recognize our

---

[1] I am using the term screen metaphorically like a sieve. You strain something through a sieve and it helps weed out the impurities. So too, you use these screens I give to probe, question, evaluate, and guide you as you seek to word the leadership lessons you see.

[2] This has now been reprinted and is available from Barnabas Publishers.

tendencies because of our backgrounds to interpret differently from others. They help us assess our findings beyond our own biases.

caution 3   Honor differing convictions. We should not violate our consciences. That is a basic truth that is, in my opinion, a very broad absolute. God has given that safeguard to all of us. There is that inner sense of conviction that prompts us. We must not violate that and go against conscience. But we must recognize that same right for others. Even if something is an absolute for us we must recognize that others might not see it that way. And vice versa. But we must also recognize that consciences are not always right. We can be educated concerning those basics that form our presuppositions and assumptions making up our conscience. It is a Spirit-led conscience that we are constantly seeking to have.

conclusion   This chapter gets at all these issues of drawing out leadership truth for application to our leadership situations. At this point the actual process of deriving the truth is more of an art than a science. Intuition, general comparative understanding of leadership in the Bible, analytical skills, and other factors less well known are part of the process. We are becoming more scientific as we identify how to do it.

APPLICATIONAL CONTINUUM

introduction — Applicational distance refers to the problem of a modern reader seeking to understand material from the Bible and apply truth to a present situation. 4 Distance barriers hinder the application of truth from the Bible: Cultural distance, language distance, geographical distance, and historical distance. Assuming that one is working consciously to overcome these barriers (we do so by applying our anthropological models and our hermeneutical models) we then need to recognize the applicational continuum which helps us assess the truth in applicational terms. Some of the applications of truth in source materials in the Bible are much closer to us in terms of these distances than others. The applicational distance continuum helps us assess how near or far source materials are to us.

APPLICATIONAL CONTINUUM

CLOSE <--------	Applicational Distance -------->	FAR
	a complex function of:	
	• Cultural Distance	
	• Language Distance	
	• Geographical Distance	
	• Historical Distance	

• applies almost directly	• does not apply directly
• lower levels of truth	• higher levels of truth
• more specific transfer	• more generic transfer
• almost direct transfer	• very indirect transfer
example: various qualities applying truth to our lives and relationships from 1 Corinthians 13	example: command: Don't muzzle the ox, Deuteronomy Deuteronomy 25:4, 1 Corinthian 9

acknowledgment — I was stimulated to draw the above diagram by Jack Kuhatschek's narrative explanation of these ideas in his book, **Taking the guesswork Out of Applying the Bible.**[3]

---

[3] I highly recommend Kuhatschek's book for all students of this chapter.

APPLICATIONAL LEVELS OF TRUTH

introduction
: Kuhatschek's book spends several chapters explaining the process of moving up or down the Applicational Pyramid in order to apply truth. When you are to the right of the Application Continuum (far) you must move up to higher levels to apply the truth. You don't actually muzzle an ox, but you go to the next higher generic level of the principle which fits your situation. When you are to the left (near) you can use the truth almost directly. Or if the truth starts at a high level generically you must lower it more specifically and appropriately to fit your situation.

definitions
: <u>Applicational levels</u> refers to the fact that truth drawn from the Bible exists at several levels of application with fewer very generic statements of truths existing at the highest level and many more specific truths applied at the lowest level.

THE APPLICATIONAL PYRAMID

LEVEL 1
HIGH LEVEL GENERIC STATEMENTS

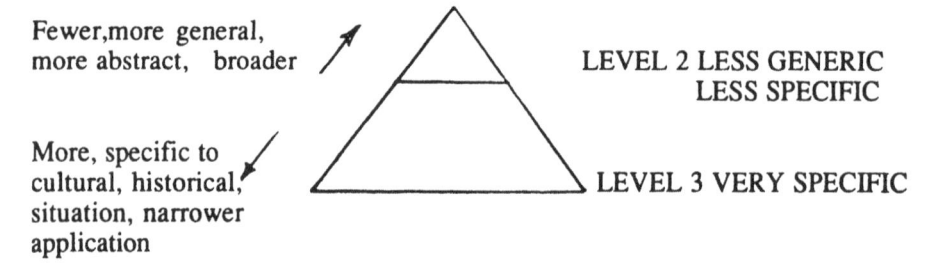

Fewer, more general, more abstract, broader

LEVEL 2 LESS GENERIC LESS SPECIFIC

More, specific to cultural, historical, situation, narrower application

LEVEL 3 VERY SPECIFIC

Basic Principle 1: The higher the level, the broader it applies across time, culture, language geography and history.

Basic Principle 2: The higher the level the fewer are the principles in the Bible but the easier they transfer across the applicational distance.

Basic Principle 3: The lower the level the more are the principles in the Bible but the harder they are to transfer.

Basic Principle 4: Principles that are applicationally far must be moved to different levels that bring them nearer in order to move across applicational distance.

COMMENTARY ON APPLICATION OF TRUTH

steps
: Kuhatschek gives 3 steps in his approach to getting at application of truth:
Step 1. Understand the Original Situation
Step 2. Find General Principles
Step 3. Apply the Principles Today
Step 1 is equivalent to our use of hermeneutics and ethnotheological models to get the truth (crossing the applicational distance barriers). The second step means to use the Applicational Pyramid to move to proper levels of application. In the third step, he suggest that principles can be applied to an identical situation, a comparable situation, or an entirely different situation.

identical
: An identical situation is one that is applicationally near. The principle applies as it did in the original situation.

comparable
: A situation today is comparable to a situation in the past if the key elements in the past situation also exist in the present situation and they relate to the principle being applied in the same way.

different
: Truth applied in a different situation can be applied today if the key elements in both situations are the same in terms of the general principle being applied.

comment
: Kuhatschek goes on to show how to apply commands, examples, and promises. He gives very helpful guidelines. Our next series of maps roughly is functional to what he says.

7 KINDS OF SOURCES OF TRUTH

introduction The kind of specific source from which we draw a given principle can actually help us to tentatively identify the certainty of the idea. These types of sources can occur in each of the genre. And several of them may occur in a single source passage. All of these categories have a presumed basis underlying them. God's character is the basis for drawing out truth. If God has revealed something about Himself, His desires, His truth in some context, then there is something in that revelation that will be consistent later with other revelation.

7 KINDS OF SOURCES FOR TRUTH

Label	Explanation
1. GENCOM	The passage contains a command(s) which is addressed or applied generally to all of God's people, no matter what culture, or whether in Old Testament or New. And the command has no cultural resrtictions attached to it. And finally it has not been modified or abrogated by other Scripture.
2. GENTEACH	The passage contains a teaching which is directed generally to all people of God, no matter what culture, or whether in Old Testament or New. Or it is abstract teaching on the nature or essence of some truth and is not limited to a specific situation.
3. CULCOM	The passage contains a command given to a specific cultural situation but it is applied in several differing cultural situations. And the commands are not qualified or modified by other Scriptures.
4. SPECCOM	A command which was specific to a historical/ cultural/ temporal situation and directed to that situation . Such a command can be assumed to have reflected the will of God in some given context and hence the purpose or reason

7 KINDS OF SOURCES TRUTH continued

Label	Explanation
	underlying why it was given if explicitly given is a source of principle.
5. SPECTEACH	A teaching which was specific to a historical/ cultural/ temporal situation and directed to that situation . Such a teaching can be assumed to have reflected the will of God in some given context and hence the prupose or reason underlying why it was given if explicitly given is a source of principle.
6. HISPRIN	A given historical incident whether a bio-sketch or slice of life vignette or simply historical narrative which is commended or condemned explicitly in Scripture.
7. GENPRESUP	A presumed truth which is used by God's people of all time as a basis for other truth.
comment	There can be variations or combinations of the basic categories given above. Any specific passage may reflect more than 1 category. For example a passage could have GENCOM, GENTEACH, and perhaps HISPRIN materials. See Acts 20:17-38 Paul's message to the Ephesian elders.

PRINCIPLES

introduction
One useful result of leadership studies is the observations of truth. These truths help us understand other leadership situations and predict what ought to be. They also help us in the selection and training of leaders since they give guidelines that have successfully been applied in past leadership situations. These truths are usually seen first as specific statments concerning one leader in his/ her situation. They are then generalized to cover other leaders and like situations. The question of how generally they can be applied to others is a genuine one. The certainty continuum and screening questions provide cautions about this.

definition
<u>Principles</u> refer to generalized statements of truth which reflect observations drawn from specific instances of leadership acts or other leadership sources.

comment
God's processing of leaders including shaping of the three formations, spiritual, ministerial, or strategic, serves as an important stimulus for principles.

example
Analysis of God's use of the integrity check, word check, and obedience check to develop spiritual formation in numerous young leader's lives led to these 3 principles.

INTEGRITY IS FOUNDATIONAL FOR LEADERSHIP; IT MUST BE INSTILLED EARLY IN A LEADER'S CHARACTER.

OBEDIENCE IS FIRST LEARNED BY A LEADER AND THEN TAUGHT TO OTHERS.

LEADERSHIP GIFTS PRIMARILY INVOLVE WORD GIFTS WHICH INITIALLY EMERGE THROUGH WORD CHECKS

example
Analysis of Samuel's final public leadership act in 1 Samuel 12 (see especially verse 23) led to the following truth.

WHEN GOD CALLS A LEADER TO A LEADERSHIP SITUATION HE CALLS HIM/ HER TO PRAY FOR FOLLOWERS IN THAT SITUATION.

THE CERTAINTY CONTINUUM

introduction — Attempts to derive statements of truth from leadership studies meet with varied success. Some people seem to intuitively have a sense of generalizing from a specific situation a statement which apparently fits other situations. Others are not so good at this skill. This part of leadership theory is in is infancy stage. In the future we hope to delineate more structured approaches for deriving statements and for validating them. But for now we need to recognize that these statements often can not be proved as truth (in the sense that physical science can prove truth) hence we, as researchers, need to be careful of what we say is truth. Below is given the certainty continuum and the major generalization concerning the derivation of *truth* statements. These are an attempt to make us as researchers cautious about applying our findings.

MAJOR GUIDELINE — Principles of truth are attempts to generalize specific truths for wider applicability and will vary in their usefulness with others and the authoritative degree to which they can be asserted for others.

description — The <u>certainty continuum</u> is a horizontal line moving from suggestions on one extreme to requirements on the other extreme which attempts to provide a grid for locating a given statement of truth in terms of its potential use with others and the degree of authority with which it can be asserted.

basic ideas:
1. Principles are observations along a continuum.
2. We can teach and use with increasing authority those principles further to the right on the continuum.

The Certainty Continuum

Suggestions	Guidelines	Requirements
TENTATIVE OBSERVATIONS		ABSOLUTES
	Certain	Very Certain

More certain of truth -->
Very Little Authority <----------------------------------> Great Authority

comment — I am identifying principles as a broad category of statements of truth which were true at some instant of history and may have relevance for others at other times.

CERTAINTY CONTINUITY DEFINITIONS

introduction	There is little difference between Suggestions and Guidelines on the continuum. In fact, there is probably overlap between the two. Some Guidelines approach Requirements. But there is a major difference from going from Suggestions to Requirements--the difference being Suggestions are optional but Requirements are not. They must be adhered to.
definition	<u>Suggestions</u> refers to truth observed in some situations and which may be helpful to others but they are optional and can be used or not with no loss of conscience.
definition	<u>Guidelines</u> are truths that are replicated in most leadership situations and should only be rejected for good reasons though their will be no loss of conscience.
definition	<u>Absolutes</u> refer to replicated truth in leadership situations across cultures without restrictions. Failure to follow or use will normally result in some stirrings of conscience.
comment	Absolutes are principles which evince God's authoritative backing for all leaders everywhere.
comment	Suggestions are the most tentative. They are not enjoined upon people. They may be very helpful though.
comment	Remember that a Suggestion or Guideline may move to the right or left if more evidence is found in the Bible to support such a move. If a suggestion or guideline identified in one place in the Scriptures is found to be abrogated, modified or somehow restricted at a later time in the progressive flow of revelation then it will move most likely to the left. However, if later revelation gives evidence of its more widespread usage or identifies it more certainly for everyone then it will move to the right.

6 ASSUMPTIONS UNDERLYING DERIVATION OF PRINCIPLES

introduction Principles are derived from Biblical leadership situations as well as from life situations. Several assumptions underlie my approach to deriving principles of truth.

6 ASSUMPTIONS ON DERIVING PRINCIPLES OF TRUTH.

1. **Truth Assumption**: All truth has its source in God.

explanation I need not fear the study of secular material (social science materials, leadership theory, present day situations, etc.). If there is any truth in it I can be certain it is of God. For there is no truth apart from God. I don't have to limit truth to the Bible. The Bible itself shows how God has revealed truth by many different means. These means were certainly not just limited to ancient written revelation. The problem then lies in how to discern if something is truth.

2. **Source Assumption.** All of life can be a source of truth for those who are discerning.

explanation The central thrust of Proverbs 1:20-33 and in fact the whole book of Proverbs is that God reveals wisdom in life situations. The book of Proverbs is more than just content for us to use; it is a modeling of how that content was derived over time and in a given society. We can trust God to reveal wisdom in the life situations we study (whether from the Bible or today). Truth that evolved in Israeli history came to take on at least guideline status and much of it became absolutes.

3. **Applicability Assumption.** Just because a statement of truth was true for a specific given situation does not mean the statement has applicability for other leaders at other times. Wider application must be determined via comparative means.

explanation A statement of truth is an assertion of fact drawn from a specific situation. The dynamics of the situation may well condition the statement. That is, the truth itself may apply only in situations which contain the same dynamics. The fact that the truth did happen means it is at least worthy of study for potential wider use. Because of the consistency of God's character we know that the truth can not violate His nature. But its happening is not sufficient justification for its use anywhere at anytime by any leader.

6 ASSUMPTIONS ... DERIVATION OF PRINCIPLES continued

4. DOGMATIC ASSUMPTION. We must exercise caution in asserting all truth statements as if they were absolutes.

explanation	Fewer truths will be seen as absolutes if screened with applicability criteria. The use of applicability criteria, especially that of comparative study, will force one to identify a higher level function behind a given principle. Thus a statement of truth at some lower level when compared with other situations and similar statements of truth might lead to a higher order generic statement of truth. These higher level statements of truth, though more general in nature, preserve the function intended rather than the form of the truth. Such statements will allow more freedom of application. Statements which do not carry wide applicability or have attached to them dynamics of situations which can not be fully assessed will most likely have to be asserted with less dogmatism.

5. DEPENDENCE ASSUMPTION. We are forced more than ever to depend upon the Holy Spirit's present ministry to confirm truth we are deriving.

explanation	Because of the sources (life as well as Biblical) from which we are drawing truth we will need more dependence upon the ministry of the Holy Spirit. That is, we will be forced to situationally rely on and become more sensitive to the Holy Spirit's leading and voice. We will need to recognize giftedness in the body and learn to trust those who have spiritual gifts which expose, clarify, and confirm truth (discernings of spirits, word of knowledge, word of wisdom, teaching, exhortation, etc.).

6. TRUST ASSUMPTION. Because we are following Biblical admonitions (Hebrews 13:7,8; 1 Corinthians 10:6,11, Romans 15:4) in our attempts to derive truth we can expect God to enable us to see much truth.

explanation	God does not command us to do things that are impossible. God's commands contain the promise of enablement. Because there are great needs for more and better leadership and because we need leadership truth to develop that leadership and because God has told us to study leaders to learn from their lives we can expect God to lead us to truth that will greatly affect our lives. By faith we can trust Him to do this.

BACKGROUND FOR APPLICABILITY SCREEN

introduction	Much of the Bible comes to us in the form of historical narrative, examples, or truth already applied to people in a specific historical / cultural situation. From this historically progressive revelation of God with His people we must draw forth truth which we can use in our own historical / cultural situations. Using the best hermeneutics and exegesis and mindful of our worldview limitations, we will theoretically arrive at that which the author meant for those to whom the writing was directed. In some cases the writings are inclusive of all mankind in which case the interpreted truth can be applied to all; sometimes the truth was given to special groups--how it applies to others is a question which must be determined. Sometimes there are eternal truths underlying the specific application to given groups. It is these kinds of truths that we will define as principles of truth. It is because of these difficulties that two screens are suggested.
Guideline	When attempting to draw principles of truth from a Biblical passage first apply the Certainty Factors Screen to the passage, then use the Applicability Screen.
comment	In addition to the difficulty of working with source data which is applied truth we need to bear in mind that few passages were given to directly teach on leadership. We are usually deriving principles from situations whose context is for a purpose other than leadership truth.
comment	We view these leadership passages with bias. Our worldviews include theological presuppositions arising from our personal church experience. This affects what we see. Comparative study among others who differ adds a corrective. We may thus see ideas that we have not or could not see previously. These uncertainty factors should make us tolerant of those with whom we differ. We do have the indwelling Holy Spirit to lead us into truth if we will acknowledge our dependence and be willing to obey what is shown. And we do have the basic conscience guideline. So be warned and do use the Applicability Screen and Certainty Continuum as you study Biblical leadership.

CERTAINTY SCREEN FOR BIBLE PASSAGES

introduction   Below are listed some factors which affect our eliciting a principle from a passage in Scripture. Following this list of factors is a question check-list which reflects these factors and can be used to screen a passage. Assuming good certainty factors then next use the applicability screen.

8 Factors Bearing on Certainty of Principles Taken from a Biblical Source

1. Assurance that the text is correct (textual criticism).
2. Clarity of the passage.
3. Consensus interpretation of the major thrust of the passage.
4. Consensus concerning to whom the passage applies.
5. Consensus concerning under what circumstances the passage applies.
6. Other passages which contradict, modify, restrict, clarify, or otherwise limit the passage.
7. Assurance that progressive revelation has not abrogated or in some way modified the thrust of the passage.
8. Intentional selection--the principle is repeated in a number of was through various passages.

Questionnaire Checklist To Use in Screening For Certainty

Concerning the Actual Principle seen in the passage,
Yes No

1. Are there textual problems involved that affect the principle?
2. Do these problems bear directly on the principle?
3. Is the passage obscure?
4. Is there a consensus interpretation on the passage?
5. Is there consensus that the passage is limited,
   a. as to whom applied?
   b. as to when it applies?
   c. as to circumstances under which it applies?
6. Do other passages seem to contradict, modify, restrict, clarify, or limit the passage?
7. Would the principle be affected by the progressive revelation of truth in the Scriptures?
8. Is the principle seen in other passages and other ways in the Scriptures?

APPLICABILITY SCREEN: FACTORS/ APPROPRIATE LEVELS

introduction — Assuming strong certainty factors as assessed by the Certainty Factors Screen, use the level indicated on the Certain Continuum according to the following screen.

Apply At Level	Source	Criteria for Screening Leadership Data
1. Absolute	1. commands	Where commanded, generically, and applied cross-culturally, non-uniquely, unlimited.
2. Toward Absolutes	2. teaching	Where teaching is given to all and not qualified in any way.
3. Toward Guidelines	3. commands teaching	Where commands or teaching is qualified in Scripture as to whom and/ or under what circumstances they apply.
4. Toward Guidelines	4. historical other genre	Where observed in historical or other non-didactic genre and confirmed in varied contextual/ cultural situations.
5. Toward Suggestions	5. historical other genre	Where seen in one cultural situation and/ or specific situation or group.

comment — If you arrive at a truth and are uncertain of exact placement along the continuum tend toward the left rather than the right. As you continue your life long grasp of the Scriptures you will probably get confirmation of your position or new evidence which will allow you to move the truth to a more certain position.

4 SUGGESTIONS ON GETTING THE ACTUAL PRINCIPLE

introduction Assuming you have screened to identify the source and level, then simply follow the steps below to get at the principle.

Level	Source	How to Get At Principle
1. Absolute	1. commands	Principle is the interpretive statement of the command.
2. Toward Absolutes	2. teaching	Principle is found by using hermeneutical principles for the language form in which the teaching is given. Generalized wording of such statements forms the principle.
3. Toward Guidelines	3. commands teaching	These sources reflect the will of God in some given context and hence will be compatible with the nature of God. The reasons for specific limitations are most likely cultural or due to progressive revelation of truth. Since the teaching or command was the will of God in a given context the *purpose* or *reason* underlying why the teaching or command was given will always be compatible with God's nature. Where such a purpose or reason is explicitly given in Scripture a principle of universal application can usually be derived. IF the reason or purpose is explicitly given AND an interpretive statement of reason or purpose which is compatible with God's nature can be stated THEN the interpretive statement of the purpose or reason reduced to a generalized statement of the purpose or reason reduced to a generalized statement becomes the principle.
4. Toward Guidelines	4. historical other genre	Unclear. Intuitive, analytical approach. Attempt to get some consensus.
5. Toward Suggestions	5. historical other genre	Unclear. Intuitive, analytical approach. Attempt to get some consensus.

EXAMPLE: USING APPLICABILITY SCREEN--LEADERSHIP ACT

introduction   I have studied a 1 Samuel 12, Samuel's last public leadership act and identified several possible statements of truth. I give these as an unscreened list. Then I screen them on the Applicability Screen. Finally, I list them after screening. This passage has strong certainty factors.

PASSAGE: 1 Samuel 12, Samuel's Last Public Leadership Act

<u>Unscreened Attempts at Identifying Potential Principles</u>

1. <u>The Leadership Ministry Prayer Principle</u>
Observation: If God has called you to a ministry, then He has called you to pray for that ministry.

2. <u>Ultimate Rejection</u>
Observation:
a. When we have spiritual authority and speak for God, rejection of what we say and are should not be taken personally or held against the people for they are in the ultimate sense rejecting God.
b. Hence, it is God's responsibility to defend the leader's spiritual authority.
c. Our response to rejection shows our maturity.

3. <u>Expectation/ Hope</u>
Observation: A major leadership generic function is to create a sense of expectation and hope for followers in terms of God's future actions for them.

4. <u>Convergence/ Multi-style</u>
Observation: In convergence a leader brings to bear powerful personal resources such as multi-styled leadership styles and demonstrated power which result in spiritual authority as the prime power base.

5. <u>Leadership Public Confirmation</u>
Observation: In a time of leadership transition new leadership must be publicly confirmed and backed by the old leadership in order to point out God's continuity.

6. <u>Leadership Public Confirmation</u>
Observation:
a. Leaders should be forewarned that leadership transition is a difficult problem for leaders and followers.
b. Leaders must learn how and when to personally transition out of a leadership role or function.
c. Leaders should be responsible for affirming continuity of leadership.

EXAMPLE: USING APPLICABILITY SCREEN continued

After Screening--First Attempts At Locating on Certainty Continuum

Absolutes--Very Certain
1. If God has called you to a ministry, then He has called you to pray for that ministry.

Absolutes--Certain
2. Spiritual Authority Principles
   a. When we have spiritual authority and speak for God, rejection of what we say and are should not be taken personally or held against the people for they are in the ultimate sense rejecting God.
   b. Hence, it is God's responsibility to defend the leader's spiritual authority.
   c. Our response to rejection shows our maturity.

3. A major leadership generic function is to create a sense of expectation and hope for followers in terms of God's future actions for them.

Guideline
4. In convergence a leader brings to bear powerful personal resources such as multi-styled leadership styles and demonstrated power which result in spiritual authority as the prime power base.
6. Leadership Public Confirmation Principles
   a. Leaders should be forewarned that leadership transition is a difficult problem for leaders and followers.
   b. Leaders must learn how and when to personally transition out of a leadership role or function.
   c. Leaders should be responsible for affirming continuity of leadership.

Suggestion
5. In a time of leadership transition new leadership must be publicly confirmed and backed by the old leadership in order to point out God's continuity.

APPLICABILITY SCREEN: NON-BIBLICAL SOURCES OF TRUTH

introduction — One must always use what is known of truth in the Scriptures as a reliable source of comparison. This assumes that God is consistent and revealed truth in Scriptures will never be inconsistent with revealed truth elsewhere. Two ethnotheological models helpful in this regard include Model 1 The-Bible-As-Yardstick and Model 3 The-Bible-As-Tether. We can expect to use the Bible as a yardstick to measure truth being identified via other sources. However, not all truth we see elsewhere will be spoken to directly or indirectly in the Scriptures. And we can use the Bible as a tether to gives us the range of truth. It will help us to see the kinds of truth that can be expected from God which will be consistent with His character, nature, and expectations from people.

Five Factors For Discerning Truth From Non-Biblical Sources

Screening Question	Result on Certainty Continuum
1. Does it violate your conscience?	If so, don't use personally even at suggestion level. But permit others their view on it if they differ simply on the basis of conscience. This screen assumes no Biblical source of comparison is known. Two things should be remembered. Your conscience is not an absolute standard. It may be warped by worldview and other factors. It may be changed as truth comes to light. However, regardless of this non-absolutistic nature of your conscience, you should not violate it. But do permit freedom for others who may not have been shaped the same way as you. You can trust God to bring freedom and clarify truth that is needed to reeducate yours or others' consciences.
2. Does it violate known moral tenets in the Bible?	A truth seen in leadership which might be pragmatically acceptable in terms of effectiveness or efficiency may be invalidated on the basic of ethical considerations determined in the application of moral truth from the Scriptures. If so, again do not use personally even at suggestion level and do not allow others whom you influence to use that truth. There is that category of truth which is real but unacceptable on moral grounds.

APPLICABILITY SCREEN: NON-BIBLICAL SOURCES OF TRUTH
continued

Five Factors For Discerning Truth From Non-Biblical Sources

Screening Question	Result on Certainty Continuum
3. Is it harmonious with the tenor of Scripture concerning leadership issues?	Perhaps the Bible does not speak directly to the truth seen but it is in line with the kind of things revealed in Scripture. SUGGESTION level is apropos.
4. Is it demonstrated via example and affirmed in Scripture? or taught but limited?	Frequently, a truth seen in a non-Biblical source can prompt one to see the same truth in the Scriptures. If the source in Scriptures is historical, that is, example, but not explained via teaching then repeated example in differing cultures and situations is a safe guideline. Such a truth can be asserted at least at GUIDELINE level within the given limitations.
5. Is it explicitly taught in Scripture and not limited in application by any limiting factors of culture or dynamics of situation? or if commanded in the Bible and not limited?	If explicitly taught or commanded in Bible--and limited, use at GUIDELINE level within the limitations. If not limited, then use at ABSOLUTE level. What we shall most likely find is that there will be truth in secular theory which is indeed of absolute nature and we shall see it confirmed in Scripture but the discovery process would be difficult with our first having seen it articulated in secular theory.
comment	From the nature of the screening questions given above, it is clear that a researcher needs an excellent working knowledge of the Scriptures. An inadequate working knowledge of the Scriptures may keep one from screening out a principle or force one to assert at a lesser level of authority than might otherwise be the case.

EXAMPLES FROM BIOGRAPHICAL STUDIES

introduction   The following were identified in a biographical study on the life of **Barnabas**.

<u>Absolutes--Very Certain</u>
Early Testing. Leaders are often tested early-on with regards to obedience and finances. Positive responses to these will lead to expanded personal growth and ministry.

<u>Absolutes--Certain</u>
Gifted Power. One who exhorts (Barnabas on giving) does so best out of personal life-changing experiences.

<u>Guidelines</u>
Relational Empowerment. A mentor (Barnabas) may accomplish more in the indirect sphere of influence through the potential leader (Paul) than ever by direct ministry.

Destiny/ Selection. Early details (island upbringing) in a life often have long term significance on major selection decisions (apostolic task to Antioch).

New Movement. When establishing a new movement, fundamental error on the part of the main leadership needs to be confronted openly (Paul/ Barnabas/ Galatian error).

New Movement. When establishing a new movement, disagreements on peripheral truth should be viewed flexibly (Paul and Barnabas on John Mark).

Information Distribution Principle. When the workings of God are shared they often bring fresh outbreaks of like results in the new setting in which they are shared.

<u>Suggestions</u>
Warning/ Mentor Sponsor. Championing a potential leader (John Mark) can create dissension in other relationships (Paul).

EXAMPLES FROM CONTEXTUAL LEADERSHIP PASSAGE

introduction   The following are seen in the leadership contextual passage in which Peter in his old age exhorts fellow elders in 1 Peter 5:1-4.

<u>Absolutes--Very Certain</u>

1. **Shepherd Model.** Pastors must care for their followers.

2. **Servant Model.** Pastors must not use overly authoritative influence but exercise servant leadership.

<u>Absolutes--Certain</u>

3. **Attitude Toward Ministry.** Pastors should willingly and eagerly serve in ministry.

4. **Motivation.** Finances should not be a dominant motivating factor for a shepherd leader.

5. **Modeling.** Effective leaders strongly influence their followers by modeling in their own lives.

<u>Guidelines</u>

6. **Leadership Style.** Maturity appeal is an effective style for a leader with long experience.

<u>Suggestions</u>

7. **Motivation.** Rewards at the return of Christ should be a motivating factor for pastors.

EXAMPLES FROM PARABOLIC

introduction — Parables are true-to-life stories which teach a central truth by a series of comparisons. The central truths are concise statements of the specific truth taught to the hearers. When these are abstracted into general statements of truth and applied to a leadership situation they become excellent sources of truth for leaders. Some of the parables, the stewardship, are especially directed toward leaders. Below is given some generalized truths drawn from parables. All generalized statements usually operate at Guideline level or above.

Parable: Matthew 25:14-30, The Talents--key word faithfulness
Central Truth: You wise kingdom followers must recognize your accountability for I will reward you at my second coming on the basis of service rendered according to your **faithfulness** to your gifts, abilities, and opportunities, and in terms of **equal rewards for equal faithfulness.**

Abstracted Leadership Truth: Wise leaders must develop their potential for they will be accountable to Jesus at the second coming for their use of gifts, abilities, and opportunities.

Parable: Luke 19:1-27, The Pounds--key words zealous, results
Central Truth: My kingdom is not coming right away hence **do not lose heart in your service** for I expect you with **utmost zeal** to take advantage of opportunities to serve with **tangible results** until I return at which time I will reward according to your **zealous efforts and results.**

Abstracted Leadership Truth: Leaders with a proper perspective on the 2nd coming of Christ will take advantage of opportunities to work patiently without losing heart over the long run, work zealously, and work with tangible results because they will answer to Jesus at the second coming.

Parable: Matthew 20:1-16, The Workers in the Vineyard
Central Truth: You should serve God not demanding rewards for your service but thankfully **because** you know that God will not give you what you deserve only but will reward exceedingly above all you expect.

Abstracted Leadership Truth: Leaders recognize that rewards are not the major motivation for leadership but that God can be trusted to reward for service.

EXAMPLES FROM INDIRECT--PROVERBS

introduction   The Proverbs are typically indirect truth from which leaders can profit greatly. Their thrust on horizontal relationships with others and their emphasis on character make them especially applicable to leaders who must develop relational skills and must have character as foundational to their leadership. This is an example of the leadership genre, Indirect --passages dealing with Christian character or behavior which also applies to Christian leadership as well.

Absolutes--Very Certain

1. **FOUNDATIONAL RELATIONSHIP.** *It is a vertical relationship that is given as foundational for understanding wisdom.* Leaders first need to have a proper respect for God as the giver of wisdom before they can truly learn from life. Leaders need the wisdom of God in their ministries. The Proverbs assert that a proper relationship with God is the foundational access to that wisdom from God (Prov 1:7, 1:29, 3:7, 2:5, 8:13, 9:10, 10:27, 14:26, 14:27, 15:16, 15:33, 16:6, 19:23, 22:4, 23:17, 24:21)
2. **LEARNING POSTURE.** One of the findings concerning effective leaders states that *Effective Leaders maintain a learning posture all their lives.* The Proverbs certainly assert the validity of this finding. Wisdom does not come automatically. There must be proactive learning posture if a leader is to learn from God via life. (1:20-33, 2:1ff, 19:8 and many others).
3. **CRISES.** *Leaders are shaped by the crises experiences in life.* These tend to test us and shape us like no other experiences. A person with a learning posture will respond to crises expecting to go deep with God and to learn much about personality and character (24:10,11).
4. **INTEGRITY.** *In leadership, character, and especially integrity and honesty, are necessary if followers are to trust leaders* (4:23, 10:9, 11:1, 11:3, 16:11, 17:15, 20:10)

Absolutes--Certain

5. **RESPONSE TO CORRECTION.** *One way a learning posture is expressed is by a person who can learn from criticism.* (9:8, 10:8, 10:17, 11:3, 12:1 and many others).
6. **DISCIPLINE.** *Leaders express a learning posture by a positive responce to discipline in their lives.* Another way a learning posture is expressed is by a proper response to the discipline of the Lord. Processing in life is ultimately from the Lord and is meant to teach lessons of life.

EXAMPLES FROM INDIRECT--PROVERBS continued

Absolutes--Certain continued

Particularly is this so where it is clear that the Lord is bringing discipline upon our lives. (3:11,12, 17:3, 17:10, 27:21 and others)...
7. **USE OF WORDS.** *A leader must be extremely careful in the use of the tongue.* Proverbs treats this as a major topic. This is so because people in influential positions are listened to with much more emphasis. That is, their words carry added weight (even if not intended) with followers who look to them (6:2, 6:16-19, 10:11, 10:19, 12:14, 12:19, 15:1, 15:4, 15:23, 15:28, 12:19, 16:24, 16:27, 28, 17:9, 17:27, 28, 18:13, 25:11, 26:18,19, 27:2, and many others).
8. **PRIDE.** *Pride can lead to failure.* It is one of the six major barriers which hinder leaders from finishing well. Proverbs warns against it and its dangers (13:10, 16:18, 18:12, 27:2).

Guidelines
8. **CORPORATE WISDOM.** *Wise leaders need counsel from peers and upward mentors in their decision making.* Major leadership decisions should never be made just unilaterally (11:14, 15:22, 20:18, 24:6, and others)

Suggestions
9. **ULTIMATE CONTRIBUTION.** *A leader's good reputation, both in character and achievement should be a major determining factor in living out life, since it will be a major legacy left behind* (10:7, 11:3, 19:1, 19:22, 20:17, 22:1).
10. **GENEROSITY.** *Generosity is especially esteemed as a characteristic of a wise person.* Even more so, does it stand out in leadership (11:24, 25, 26, 14:21, 19:17, 21:13, 22:9,)
11. **OPPORTUNITIES.** *One of the positive signs of growing leadership is its ability to recognize and exploit opportunities.* Proverbs exhorts to make the most of opportunities. One of the signs of plateauing is the inability to sense opportunity or the inability to follow up on it (12:27, 14:4, 28:19, 31:1ff)
12. **STRATEGIC PLANNING.** *Leaders must give foresight to their leadership.* Planning is good but it must always be held in perspective of God's sovereignty (14:15, 16:1, 16:4, 16:9, 16:33, 19:21, 21:1, 21:30, 21:31, 22:13, 27:12).

EXAMPLES FROM BOOK AS A WHOLE--2 TIMOTHY

introduction The following principles were elicited from 2 Timothy, one of the major leadership books in the New Testament Church.

Absolutes--Very Certain
1. **MINISTRY PRAYER PRINCIPLE.** *If God has called you to a ministry then He has called you to pray for that ministry.* See 2 Timothy 1:3. Paul illustrates the ministry prayer principle first seen in Moses and highlighted in Samuel's ministry.
2. **ULTIMATE ACCOUNTABILITY.** *Christian leaders minister always with a conscious view to ultimate accountability to God for their ministry.* Paul was conscious of a future day in which God would hold him and others accountable for their actions (see 1:16, 4:8, 4:14). This is more fully developed in 2 Corinthians, and 1, 2 Thessalonians but is affirmed in many epistles.
3. **BIBLE CENTERED MINISTRY.** *An effective leader who finishes well must have a bible centered ministry.* 2 Timothy 2:15 and 3:16,17 give the keynotes on a Bible centered ministry. It is a God ordained requirement. It brings confident ministry (litotes = not ashamed). It is a matter of integrity (correctly handling). It will change life and ministry (3:16,17).
4. **LEARNING POSTURE.** Effective leaders maintain a learning posture all during their lives. *"And the books, Timothy, don't forget the books!"* speaks reams about Paul. 2 Timothy 4:13.

Absolutes--Certain
5. **GIFTEDNESS DEVELOPMENT.** *Christian leaders must constantly keep in balance doing and being.* Giftedness development is highlighted in this book. Christian leaders must constantly keep in balance doing and being. We must produce in our ministry. But we must also develop the production capability. We must develop ourselves. Both our production and our production capability must be tended to. Giftedness can be and must be developed or atrophy sets in (1:6). Gifts can be imparted (1:14) by those having spiritual authority. They should be used with gifted power (1:7). Self-discipline is needed both to develop and use giftedness (1:7 and 4:1-5).
6. **FINANCIAL PRINCIPLE.** *A leader's ministry is worthy of remuneration.* This is not a big thing with Paul. But a leader who is effective should not be ashamed of reward for having done effective ministry. (2:6,7)

EXAMPLES FROM BOOK AS A WHOLE--2 TIMOTHY continued

7. **ADVENT OF CHRIST.** *The return of Christ should be a major motivating factor for a person's leadership.* The return of Christ was a major motivating factor of Paul's leadership. He advocates this for all leader's (all those who love his appearing). See 2 Timothy 4:7,8

Guidelines
8. **LEADERSHIP SELECTION.** *Effective leaders see leadership selection and development as a priority function in their life.* Paul here (2:2, 2:14ff) advocates top down recruitment of potential leaders. The selection criteria focuses on three major qualities: a. faithfulness, b. teachableness, and c. ability to pass on to others that which has been life changing for them.
9. **OPPOSITION.** *Effective leaders should expect opposition to their ministry--especially on issues of truth they teach.* Forewarned is forearmed. However, major on the majors. See 2:22-26 and 3:8.
10. **MODELING/TRANSPARENCY.** *Transparency in modeling god's enabling grace in a life and ministry provides an effective base for influencing followers toward maturity.* Paul was conscious of his own life as being a model for others and used it deliberately as such. He shared the ups and downs and always the need for the grace of God to enable one in the midst of them. See 2 Timothy 3:10-14.

Suggestions
11. **FOCUS.** *To persevere in ministry a leader must have a single minded focus.* 2:1-4, 10, 21. Life and its many problems can encumber and entangle so as to side track one from a disciplined life that counts for Christ.
12. **GENTLENESS.** Gentleness rather than argument is a major influence means for a leader to affect change. There are few gentle leaders. Such a one stands out. Gentle persuasion is a major tool for a change agent. See 2 Timothy 2:22-26.

EXAMPLES FROM ACROSS BOOKS, THE BIBLE AS A WHOLE-- MACRO-LESSONS

introduction It is much more difficult to assess macro-lessons along the certainty continuum since they are level 1 kind of statements on the application pyramid. Usually they are at least guidelines and move from guidelines to certain and very certain absolutes. If they are reduced to level 2 or level 3 in order to apply then they can more readily be assessed along the continuum. The very fact that they are macro, statements identified as sweeping across Scriptures tends to make them requirements. I'll share one or two from each of the major leadership eras

Lesson Name	Era First Seen	Statement Of Lesson
Blessing	Patriarchal	God mediates His blessing to His followers through leaders.
Character	Patriarchal	Integrity is the essential character trait of a spiritual leader.
Presence	Pre-Kingdom	The essential ingredient of leadership is the powerful presence of God in the leader's life and ministry.
Unity	Kingdom	Unity of the people of God is a value that leader's must preserve.
Spiritual Leadership	Kingdom	Spiritual leadership can make a difference even in the midst of difficult times.
Recrudescence	Kingdom	God will attempt to bring renewal to His people until they no longer respond to Him.
Future Perfect	Post-Kingdom	A primary function of all leadership is to walk by faith with a future perfect paradigm so as to inspire followers with certainty of God's accomplishment of ultimate purposes.

EXAMPLES FROM ACROSS BOOKS, THE BIBLE AS A WHOLE-- MACRO-LESSONS continued

Lesson Name	Era First Seen	Statement Of Lesson
Perspective	Post-Kingdom	Leaders must know the value of perspective and interpret present happenings in terms of God's broader purposes.
Modeling	Post-Kingdom	Leaders can most powerfully influence by modeling godly lives, the sufficiency and sovereignty of God at all times, and gifted power.
Selection	Pre-Church	The key to good leadership is the selection of good potential leaders which should be a priority of all leaders.
Movement	Pre-Church	Leaders recognize that movements are the way to penetrate society though they must be preserved via appropriate on-going institutional structures.
Universal	Church	The church structure is inherently universal and can be made to fit various cultural situations if functions and not forms are in view.
Word Centered	Church	God's Word is the primary source for equipping leaders and must be a vital part of any leaders ministry.
Complexity	All eras	Leadership is complex, problematic, difficult and fraught with risk which is why leadership is needed.

FOR FURTHER STUDY

Study the **Disputed Practices** booklet for guidelines on arriving at truth for questionable practices over which Christians differ.

I highly recommend that you study Jack Kuhatschek's book, **Taking the Guesswork Out of Applying the Bible**, a 1990 printing from InterVarsity Press. This book is focused on getting and applying truth.

Study my book, **Parables--Puzzles With A Purpose** available from Barnabas Publishers for learning skills for identifying central truths and abstracted applicational truths.

Study my book, **Hebrew Poetry**, available from Barnabas Publishers for learning skills for studying Hebrew Poetry in the English Bible. This booklet focuses on identifying concisely statements of truth.

Chapter 6 Where To Now?

Review

In Chapter 1, I introduced you to basic leadership definitions such as leaders, leadership styles, leadership acts, and leadership functions. These perspectives open our eyes as we view much of the leadership information in the Bible. We see things that are there because we have these labels and because we are looking for them. The more familiar you are with these leadership concepts the more you will see them whenever you open the Bible.

In Chapter 2, I gave more specialized definitions. The ethnotheological models give cultural/ theological/ philosophical underpinnings for viewing the Bible in its progressive revelation across time and cultures. There were many miscellaneous concepts and models which helped us see leadership issues in various unique situations and ways. The philosophical leadership models from the New Testament (Steward, Servant Leader, Intercessor, Harvest, Shepherd) help us understand roles, giftedness, and values and how they interrelate. There were many concepts that specifically dealt with leaders--how they finish, why they finish well or poorly, how they transition into or out of ministry, how they view ministry, etc. These many models and concepts again open our eyes to see things in the Scriptures, that were always there but now are apparent.

Chapter 3, gives us many perspectives for viewing the individual development of a leader by God. We see the value of looking at the whole life through a time-line, of identifying processes in the life, and of generalizing patterns from this total display. Whereas chapters 1 and 2 help us in general in approaching any kind of leadership source material, this chapter especially helps us as we approach the biographical source of leadership information. This was a very brief treatment. You should really go on to study the major reference works for life long development. But this chapter gets you off to a good start. You will notice processing all throughout the Scriptures. And you'll see those testing patterns both negative and positive.

Chapter 4, takes a hard look at each of the 7 kinds of leadership source material and tells what to look for and how to study it. You ought to do detailed studies on each of the kinds of sources both to learn the skills and to get leadership findings to use and teach in your own ministry.

Chapter 5, gave details of how to draw out truth from that source material as you study it. It suggests levels of truth and conceptual screens for generating and evaluating those truths. It finally gives some examples of truth derived from the various kinds of leadership source material. Its emphasis is on using the Scripture. We may have the highest view on Scripture there is but if we don't study it, don't apply it, and don't feel its impact in our lives and ministries it doesn't matter whether we have a low or high view. Chapter 5 is seeking to make James 1:22, 23 as practicable as possible. Leaders ought to be people who seek for and use lessons, values, and principles.

Chapter 6 will be brief. It will do three things. It will suggest that you need to know your Bible and use it so that its suggestions, guidelines, requirements, lessons, and macro-lessons are part of your thinking. It will suggest that you should assess your present understanding of the Scriptures so you will have a starting point to build from. It will then suggest that you set goals so that you will master the Scriptures over your lifetime.

Are The Scriptures Central In Your Life and Ministry

I'm going to ask you to read the following Scriptural passages and seek to identify the common thread that I think is there. I'm going to quote from the King James, not because I think it is the best translation but because that is the version in which I did most of my memory work.

1. And these words, which I command thee this day, shall be in thine heart: And thou shalt teach them diligently unto thy children, and shalt talk of them when thou sittest in thine house, and when thou walkest by the way, and when thou liest down, and when thou risest up. And thou shalt bind them for a sign upon thine hand, and they shall be as frontlets between thine eyes. And thou shall write them upon the posts of thy house, and on thy gates. **Deuteronomy 6:6-9**

2. And it shall be, when he (speaking of the king who they will have some day) sitteth upon the throne of his kingdom, that he shall write him a copy of this law in a book out of that which is before the priests the Levites: And it shall be with him, and he shall read therein all the days of his life: that he may learn to fear the Lord his God, to keep all the words of this law and these statutes, to do them: That his heart be not lifted up above his brethren, and that he turn not aside from the commandment, to the right hand, or to the left: to the end that he may prolong his days in his kingdom, he, and his children, in the midst of Israel. **Deuteronomy 17:18-20**

3. This book of the law shall not depart out of thy mouth; but thou shalt meditate therein day and night, that thou mayest observe to do according to all that is written therein: for then thou shalt make thy way prosperous, and then thou shalt have good success. **Joshua 1:8**

4. But his (a person who follows God) delight is in the law of the Lord; and in his law doth he meditate day and night. And he shall be like a tree planted by the rivers of water, that bringeth forth his fruit in his season; his leaf also shall not wither; and whatsoever he doeth shall prosper. **Psalm 1:1-3**

5. The law of the Lord is perfect, converting the soul: the testimony of the Lord is sure, making wise the simple. The statutes of the Lord are right, rejoicing the heart: the commandment of the Lord is pure, enlightening the eyes. The fear of the Lord is clean, enduring for ever: The judgments of the Lord are true and righteous altogether. More to be desired are they than gold, yea, than much fine gold: sweeter also than honey in the honeycomb. Moreover by them is thy servant warned: and in keeping of them there is great reward. **Psalm 19:7-11.**

6. Wherewithal shall a young man cleanse his way? by taking heed thereto according to thy word. With my whole heart have I sought thee: O let me not wander from thy commandments. Thy word have I hid in mine heart, that I might not sin against thee. **Psalm 119:9-11**

7. I have more understanding than all my teachers: for thy testimonies are my meditation. **Psalm 119:99**

8. I will worship toward thy holy temple, and praise thy name for thy lovingkindness and for thy truth: for thou hast magnified thy word above all thy name. **Psalm 138:2**

9. For Ezra had prepared his heart to seek the law of the Lord, and to do it, and to teach in Israel its statutes and judgments. **Ezra 7:10**

10. In the first year of his reign I, Daniel, understood by books the number of the years, whereof the word of the Lord came to Jeremiah the prophet, that he would accomplish seventy years in the desolations of Jerusalem. **Daniel 9:2**

11. But he answered and said, It is written, Man shall not live by bread alone, but by every word that proceedeth out of the mouth of God. **Matthew 4:4**

12. For whatsoever things were written aforetime were written for our learning, that we through patience and comfort of the Scriptures might have hope. **Romans 15:4**

13. Now these things (Old Testament recounting of the wilderness wanderings) were our examples, to the intent we should not lust after evil things, as they also lusted... Now all these things happened unto them for ensamples: and they are written for our admonition, upon whom the ends of the world are come. **1 Corinthians 10:6,11**

14. Study to shew thyself approved unto God, a workman that needeth not to be ashamed, rightly dividing the word of truth. **2 Timothy 2:15**

Are you getting the point? God has revealed himself in His word. And he will continued to reveal himself in His word. People of God of all ages--lay persons, politicians, military leaders, prophets, poets, lawyers, and church leaders--have testified to the importance of the word of God and its power in their lives and ministry.

The Scriptures not only provide the basal content for a leader's ministry, they will provide *know how* on leadership, the doing of that ministry. But you must study them with a leadership focus in mind if you want help in leadership. At this present time in your ministry what do you know about what the Bible teaches about leadership? Consider the following which are some important books that are a source of leadership findings. I have listed them in the order that they are important to me. I would not quibble if someone else ordered them differently or even took some off this list and added others. But at least these ought to be studied seriously with a leadership focus.

Book	Focus of Leadership Findings
1. 1 Timothy	Mentoring, local church leadership lessons, consulting ministry, developmental focus
2. 2 Timothy	Mentoring, finishing well, developmental focus
3. Titus	Apostolic ministry, local church leadership, use of spiritual authority
4. Deuteronomy	leadership values, leadership transition, biographical, processing, motivational techniques, finishing well
5. 2 Corinthians	leadership values, processing, spiritual authority
6. Daniel	perspective, leadership lessons, biographical, processing
7. Ezekiel	leadership lessons, processing

Book	Focus of Leadership Findings
8. Joshua	leadership transition, leadership lessons, spiritual authority, biographical, processing
9. Habakkuk	processing, perspective
10. Jonah	processing
11. Haggai	leadership lessons, task oriented leadership, motivational techniques
12. Luke	mentoring, leadership training, processing
13. Nehemiah	leadership lessons, task oriented leadership, motivational techniques
14. Malachi	leadership lessons, renewal issues
15. 1 Corinthians	leadership lessons, problem solving, spiritual gifts
16. Isaiah	perspective, processing, leadership lessons
17. 1, 2 Samuel	biographical, processing, leadership lessons
18. 1,2 Kings	biographical, processing, leadership lessons
19. Hebrews	renewal issues, inspirational leadership
20. Micah	leadership lessons, urban influence

Do you know these books? Do you know what they teach about leadership? Do the leadership lessons and values of these books form a part of your own value system for ministry? My suggestion is that you take a hard look at this list. Make a willful decision to study these books for their content--both hermeneutically, to use them in your ministry and from a leadership standpoint, to help shape your own leadership.

You want be able to do this in a day or so. You must set life long goals to master the Scriptures. Step 1, get the background you need to see the Bible with leadership eyes. That is what this Handbook I is all about. Get the knowledge and learn the skills to study the Bible with a leadership focus. Step 2, set a goal to master at least 1 or 2 books a year for use in ministry and for informing you on their contribution to leadership. Step 3, get a mentor to hold you accountable in your Bible goals. Write out your yearly Bible goals. Give a copy to your mentor. Give that mentor the right to hold you accountable and to check up on you. Step 4, use the Bible in your ministry. Share what you are learning about leadership from the Bible with others.

Now you may not be able or may not have the time to do all original study on the books of the Bible for leadership. You can get a jump start by studying the following two Handbooks and building on what I have done. Again you can use the advice I have just given--but you don't have to necessarily re-invent the wheel again.

HANDBOOK II. THEY LIVED BY FAITH--FINDINGS FROM BIBLE LEADER'S LIVES

This handbook studies a number of important Bible leaders for leadership findings. It applies the Biblical leadership mandate of Hebrews 13:7,8. You can profit greatly from its insights.

HANDBOOK III. THE BIG PICTURE--LEADERSHIP AND THE BIBLE AS A WHOLE, MACRO STUDIES

This handbook studies each book of the Bible first in terms of its contribution to the redemptive drama. That is, it studies the book to see what it is contributing to the message of the Bible as a whole. Then it also adds its contribution to leadership. It gives leadership lessons seen in each book. Now it is only a start. The lessons can be improved, added to, clarified, and even modified. But they are a start. You will be a better leader for grappling with these leadership lessons and having God make some of them real for you.

Let me close by paraphrasing a statement of truth from Paul, an old leader who is finishing well, and can speak from a lifetime of experience. He is giving his advice to a close companion, colleague, and friend--a young leader, Timothy. Would you believe this advice? Would you make some fundamental decisions based on your belief in this truth?

> All Scripture is given by inspiration of God and is profitable for reproof, for correction, for teaching, and for instruction in righteousness that a leader of God might be fully equipped to properly lead. 2 Timothy 3:16,17

My question to you is, what difference does 2 Timothy 3:16, 17 make in your life? This is the only guarantee we have of being equipped to serve God as leaders. Now let me repeat my question, if that is true, what difference does that verse make in your life? What are you doing to let this word of God penetrate your life and equip you to be the best leader you can?

(This page is deliberately left blank)

Appendix A. Table of Process Items

Below is given a more complete list of process items along with their central thrust or meaning. See **Leadership Emergence Theory** for an expanded definition of each of these with explanations, implications, and applications.

Name	Basic Idea
Authority Insights	The learning of important lessons about authority both being under it and using it
Basic Skills	Those skills and attitudes that are learned in the foundational phase which shape the early abilities of a leader
Conflict	Negative processing that may affect character, skills or values
Contextual	The impact of the local, regional, national, or international situation in the shaping process of a leader
Crises	Severe threats concerning ministry or life
Destiny	Intimations of God's ultimate purposes for a leader which can be preparatory, clarifying, and leading to fulfillment
Divine Affirmation	The sensing of God's approval through a variety of means for one's person
Divine Contact	The unusual arrival of a person into a situation in a timely and appropriate way so as to give importance guidance to a person
Double Confirmation	A sovereignly confirmed instance of guidance where the confirmation comes externally from an unexpected source
Entry Context	Usually a retrospective discovery of uniqueness by seeing how God has used and/or will use the setting into which the leader is born to not shape the leader but give future intimations of fit into ministry

Appendix A. Table of Process Items continued

Name	Basic Idea
Faith Check	An early challenge by God to trust God on some issue; focuses on learning to trust God
Faith Challenge	Later challenges by God to trust Him for ministry; focuses on guidance and stretching in ministry
Family Influence	A very high level concept which describes the various shaping factors that a family has on the foundational shaping of a leader
Flesh Act	Instances in guidance where the leader moves ahead of God either in what, when or how to do something and learns later through the process
Giftedness Discovery	Finding out one's natural abilities, acquired skills, and spiritual gifts and how these relate to ministry.
Gifted Power	The use of natural abilities, acquired skills, and spiritual gifts so as to see God's unusual enabling for ministry
Ideal Role	The discovery of adaptations that can be made to a role in order to make it more compatible with one's giftedness, calling, and experience
Influence Challenge	A move by God to stretch the leader to new capabilities in terms of people being influenced either in extent, intensiveness, or comprehensiveness of the ministry to those people
Integrity Check	Early test of character
Isolation	A process of being set aside for deepening
Leadership Backlash	A recognition that followers may rebel against some intended action after its success even when they initially approved it

Appendix A. Table of Process Items continued

Name	Basic Idea
Leadership Committal	a destiny item which culminates in a leader's willingness to be used by God in a ministry of God's choosing
Life Crisis	A special instance of crisis processing in which the threat extends even to loss of life
Literary	the use of writings or oral stories or the like to teach vicarious lessons from others experiences and knowledge
Mentoring	The use of individuals to empower and shape a leader via relationships
Ministry Affirmation	The sensing of God's approval through a variety of means for one's ministry efforts
Ministry Assignment	A retrospective discovery of ministry insights via a major ministry role
Ministry Challenge	A move by God to sovereignly place a leader in a new role or situation or type of ministry which will force development of the leader
Ministry Conflict	the special aspect of conflict processing which centers on ministry as opposed to personal conflict
Ministry Insights	A discovery of lessons on how to effectively impact in one's ministry
Ministry Skills	the definite acquisition of one or more identifiable skills which aids a leader in applying his/her leadership
Ministry Task	A short assignment from God which primarily tests a person's faithfulness and obedience but often allows use of ministry gifts in the context of a task which has closure, accountability, and evaluation

Appendix A. Table of Process Items continued

Name	Basic Idea
Negative Preparation	A guidance process item in which God uses negative situations not only to shape character but to move a leader on willingly to a new situation
Networking Power	The recognition of and use of God's sovereign arrangement of connections to people in order to further one's leadership and God's work
Obedience Check	Early test of volition and response to God
Paradigm Shift	A breakthrough of a new perspective which radically changes how one perceives something
Power	A learning experience of God's breakthrough of supernatural power in a situation
Power Encounter	A public confrontation of God with spirit powers in a situation so as to demonstrate God's superiority
Prayer Challenge	An intense time in which God seeks to drive a leader to meet a ministry situation by prayer; focuses on helpless dependence upon God
Prayer Power	The use of prayer in a specific situation which demonstrates that God breaks through to answer prayer in unmistakable ways
Relationship Insights	lessons about how to and the importance of relating to people so as to enhance ministry effectiveness
Social Base	Those insights about how God will meet our social needs: emotional, sexual, desire for family, a home base out of which to operate--this high level generic concept actually may have many other process items involved in the shaping
Sovereign Guidance	The general category of guidance which refers to special instances of direction that unmistakable have the marks of God's handiwork

Appendix A. Table of Process Items continued

Name	Basic Idea
Spiritual Authority	the discovery of insights about spiritual authority
Spiritual Warfare	A process of learning to discern supernatural issues in ministry and to combat them with spiritual power
Training Progress	A significant experience in some training which takes the leader to a new level of ministry effectiveness
Word Check	Early test of sensitivity to God's speaking
Word Processing	The continued activity of God to speak to a leader so as to shape the leader personally, give input for ministry, give guidance, and to give leadership ideas

(This page deliberately left blank.)

Appendix B. Table of Important Patterns

The following represent the major patterns with a brief explanation. I do not here give the actual stages in these patterns but simply describe the pattern so as to emphasize its usefulness. See <u>Leadership Emergence Theory</u> for detailed explanation and stages and implications. These are given not alphabetically but in the normal order in which they come as one develops in ministry.

Pattern	Brief Explanation
Heritage	The foundational pattern describing a leader who comes from a Christian heritage
Radical	The foundational pattern describing a leader who comes from a non-Christian background
Accelerated	A special Christian heritage pattern which describes a leader who goes into ministry early and develops rapidly
Delayed	A special Christian heritage pattern which describes a leader who initially chooses not to follow God's call into leadership but who later does so
Destiny Pattern	A three-fold pattern describing how God unfolds a destiny to a leader through destiny preparation, destiny revelation, and destiny fulfillment
Negative Testing	A three-fold pattern which tests a leader in response to God: test, response and failure, remedial processing to again teach the lessons
Positive Testing	A three-fold pattern which tests a leader in response to God: test, positive response, expansion of the leader
Transitional Training Pre-Service	The pattern of training which includes formal training in a Seminary or Bible School prior to actual full time ministry

Appendix B. Table of Important Patterns

Pattern	Brief Explanation
Transitional Training In-Service	The pattern of training which involves on-the-job experience which leads to full time ministry without any formal training--focuses on informal training
Transitional Training Modified In-Service	The pattern of training which highlights mid-career interrupted training a-periodically after a leader is already in ministry, no matter what the pattern of entry into it was; focuses on combinations of formal, non-formal and in-formal training
Foundational Ministry	A pattern of faithfulness which involves being faithful in ministry and being thus expanded to new levels of ministry
Like-Attracts- Like	Potential leaders are intuitively attracted to leaders who have like spiritual gifts.
Giftedness Drift	Potential leaders respond intuitively to ministry challenges and assignments that fit their spiritual gift even if not explicitly known.
Role/ Gift Enablement	A role assigned to a person can be the stimulus for discovery of a latent gift or acquisition of new gift needed to function in the role.
Authority Insights	A 5 stage pattern which describes a leader's learning about authority from beginning lessons right on up to use of spiritual authority.
Giftedness Development	A 9 stage pattern which describes how a leader normally discovers natural abilities, acquired skills, and spiritual gifts across time right on up to maturing in giftedness which involves mature use of a gift-cluster

Appendix B. Table of Important Patterns

Pattern	Brief Explanation
Spirituality Authority	An 8 stage pattern describing the learning experience of a person developing in spiritual authority.
Ministry Entry	A description of the ways that leaders are usually challenged into ministry. Includes 14 variations.
Reflective	A 5 stage pattern describing how God matures a person by focusing on processing which forces a deeper dependence upon God with a view toward reflecting on ministry, life, and ultimate reality.
Gift-Cluster Ripening	An advanced stage of the giftedness development pattern
Convergence Balance	A pattern assessing fit between giftedness, role, and influence-mix
Convergence Guidance	A pattern describing how God guides into balance in convergence including the five major factors of convergence (giftedness, role, influence-mix, upward dependence, ministry philosophy) and the 6 minor factors of convergence (experience, personality, geography, special opportunity, prophecy, destiny)

(This page deliberately left blank.)

Appendix C. Macro-Lessons Identified To Date

The following represent the major macro-lessons that have been identified to date. **The Bible and Leadership Values** is the source of these lessons. The earlier macro-lessons are usually repeated in succeeding leadership eras. Usually I show only the first time it is introduced or emphasized except where a later era really does emphasize the lesson. The are important concepts that must be studied for the possibility of universal application to all Christian leaders. Needed today are leadership values which can stabilize Christian leaders. These given, and their sub-concepts which flow from them in given situations. may provide some needed help for Christian leaders today.

BIBLICAL MACRO-LESSONS

LESSON	ERA	STATEMENT OF LESSON
1. Blessing	Patriarchal	God mediates His blessing to His followers through leaders.
2. Shaping	Patriarchal	God shapes leader's lives and ministry through critical incidents.
3. Timing	Patriarchal	God's timing is crucial to accomplishment of God's purposes.
4. Destiny	Patriarchal	Leaders must have a sense of destiny.
5. Character	Patriarchal	Integrity is the essential character trait of a spiritual leader.
6. Faith	Patriarchal	Biblical Leaders must learn to trust in the unseen God, sense His presence, sense His revelation, and follow Him by faith.
7. Purity	Patriarchal	Leaders must personally learn of and respond to the holiness of God in order to have effective ministry.
8. Intercession	Pre-Kingdom	Leaders called to a ministry are called to intercede for that ministry.
9. Presence	Pre-Kingdom	The essential ingredient of leadership is the powerful presence of God in the leader's life and ministry.
10. Intimacy	Pre-Kingdom	Leaders develop intimacy with God which in turn overflows into all their ministry since ministry flows out of being.
11. Burden	Pre-Kingdom	Leaders feel a responsiblility to God for their ministry.
12. Hope	Pre-Kingdom	A primary function of all leadership is to inspire followers with hope in God and in what God is doing.
13. Challenge	Pre-Kingdom	Leaders receive vision from God which sets before them challenges that inspire their leadership.

BIBLICAL MACRO-LESSONS continued

LESSON	ERA	STATEMENT OF LESSON
14. Spiritual Authority	Pre-Kingdom	Spiritual authority is the dominant power base of a spiritual leader and comes through experiences with God, knowledge of God, godly character and gifted power.
15. Transition	Pre-Kingdom	Leaders must transition other leaders into their work in order to maintain continuity and effectiveness.
16. Weakness	Pre-Kingdom	God can work through weak spiritual leaders if they are available to Him.
17. Continuity	Pre-Kingdom	Leaders must provide for continuity to new leadership in order to preserve their leadership legacy.
18. Unity	Kingdom	Unity of the people of God is a value that leader's must preserve.
19. Stability	Kingdom	Preserving a ministry of God with life and vigor over time is as much if not more of a challenge to leadership skills than creating one.
20. Spiritual Leadership	Kingdom	Spiritual leadership can make a difference even in the midst of difficult times.
21. Recrudescence	Kingdom	God will attempt to bring renewal to His people until they no longer respond to Him.
22. By-pass	Kingdom	God will by-pass leadership and structures that do not respond to Him and will institute new leadership and structures.
23. Future Perfect	Post-Kingdom	A primary function of all leadership is to walk by faith with a future perfect paradigm so as to inspire followers with certainty of God's accomplishment of ultimate purposes.
24. Perspective	Post-Kingdom	Leaders must know the value of perspective and interpret present happenings in terms of God's broader purposes.
25. Modeling	Post-Kingdom	Leaders can most powerfully influence by modeling godly lives, the sufficiency and sovereignty of God at all times, and gifted power.
26. Ultimate	Post-Kingdom	Leaders must remember that the ultimate goal of their lives and ministry is to manifest the glory of God.
27. Perseverance	Post-Kingdom	Once known leaders must persevere with the vision God has given.

BIBLICAL MACRO-LESSONS continued

LESSON	ERA	STATEMENT OF LESSON
28. Selection	Pre-Church	The key to good leadership is the selection of good potential leaders which should be a priority of all leaders.
29. Training	Pre-Church	Leaders should deliberately train potential leaders in their ministry by available and appropriate means.
30. Focus	Pre-Church	Leaders should increasingly move toward a focus in their ministry which moves toward fulfillment of their calling and their ultimate contribution to God's purposes for them.
31. Spirituality	Pre-Church	Leaders must develop interiority, spirit sensitivity, and fruitfulness in accord with their uniqueness since ministry flows out of being.
32. Servant	Pre-Church	Leaders must maintain a dynamic tension as they lead by serving and serve by leading.
33. Steward	Pre-Church	Leaders are endowed by God with natural abilities, acquired skills, spiritual gifts, opportunities, experiences, and privileges which must be developed and used for God.
34. Harvest	Pre-Church	Leaders must seek to bring people into relationship with God.
35. Shepherd	Pre-Church	Leaders must preserve, protect, and develop God's people.
36. Movement	Pre-Church	Leaders recognize that movements are the way to penetrate society though they must be preserved via appropriate on-going institutions.
37. Structure	Church	Leaders must vary structures to fit the needs of the times if they are to conserve gains and continue with renewed effort.
38. Universal	Church	The church structure is inherently universal and can be made to fit various cultural situations if functions and not forms are in view.
39. Giftedness	Church	Leaders are responsible to help God's people identify, develop, and use their resources for God.
40. Word Centered	Church	God's Word is the primary source for equipping leaders and must be a vital part of any leaders ministry.
41. Complexity	All eras	Leadership is complex, problematic, difficult and fraught with risk-- which is why leadership is needed.

(This page deliberately left blank.)

Bibliography

Clinton, Dr. J. Robert

1974   **Interpreting the Scriptures: Parables--Puzzles With A Purpose.** Altadena: Barnabas Publishers.

1977   **Interpreting the Scriptures: Figures and Idioms.** Altadena: Barnabas Publishers.

1983   **Interpreting the Scriptures: Hebrew Poetry.** Altadena: Barnabas Publishers.

1986   **Coming to Conclusions on Leadership Style.** Altadena: Barnabas Publishers.

1986   **A Short History of Leadership Theory.** Altadena: Barnabas Publishers.

1987   *Reading in the Illusive Field of Leadership.* Altadena: Barnabas Publishers.

1987   **Reading On The Run.** Altadena: Barnabas Publishers.

1988   **The Making of A Leader.** Colorado Springs: NavPress.

1989   **Leadership Emergence Theory.** Altadena: Barnabas Publishers.

1989   *The Way To Look At Ledership.* Altadena: Barnabas Publishers.

1989   *Listen Up, Leaders!* Altadena: Barnabas Publishers.

1989   *The Ultimate Contribution.* Altadena: Barnabas Publishers.

1992   **Connecting--The Mentoring Relationships You Need To Succeed in Life.** Colorado Springs: NavPress.

1993   *The Paradigm Shift.* Altadena: Barnabas Publishers.

1992   **Bridging Strategies--Leadership Perspectives for Introducing Change.** Altadena: Barnabas Publishers.

Bibliography continued

1993   **Handbook II. They Lived By Faith--Findings From Bible Leader's Lives.** Altadena: Barnabas Publishers.

1993   **Handbook III. The Big Picture--Leadership and the Bible as A Whole, Macro Studies.** Altadena: Barnabas Publishers.

1993   **Disputed Practices.** Reprint 1976. Altadena: Barnabas Publishers.

Clinton, Dr. J. Robert and Clinton, Dr. Richard W.
1991   **The Mentor Handbook--Detailed Guidelines and Helps for Christian Mentors and Mentorees.** Altadena: Barnabas Publishers.

Davis, Stanley
1982   *Transforming Organizations: The Key to Strategy Is Context* in **Organizational Dynamics,** Winter 1982.

1987   **Future Perfect: A Startling View of the Future We Should Be Managing Now.** New York: Addison-Wesley.

Fiedler, Fred
1967   **A Theory of Leadership Effectiveness.** New York: McGraw-Hill.

Fiedler, Fred with Chemers and Mahar,
1977   **Improving Leadership Effectiveness: The Leader Match Concept.** New York: McGraw-Hill.

Foster, Richard J.
1978   **Celebration of Discipline.** San Francisco: Harper and Row.

Harville, Sue
1974   **Reciprocal Living.** Coral Gables: Worldteam.

Hersey, Paul
1982   **The Situational Leader,** New York: Warner Books

Hersey, Paul and Blanchard, Ken
1977   **Management of Organizational Behavior--Utilizing Human Resources.** Englewood Cliffs, N.J.: Prentice-Hall.

Bibliography continued

Kraft, Charles H.
   1977   **Christianity in Culture.** New York: Orbis.

Kuhatschek, Jack
   1990   **Taking the Guesswork Out of Applying the Bible.** Downers Grove: InterVarsity Press.

Schaller, Lyle E.
   1972   **The Change Agent--The Strategy of Innovative Leadership.** Nashville: Abingdon Press.

Tippett, Alan
   1969   **Verdict Theology. Lincoln, Ill.:** Lincoln Christian College.

Wagner, C. Peter
   1984   **Leading Your Church To Growth.** Ventura: Regal Books.

   1981   **Church Growth and the Whole Gospel.** San Francisco: Harper and Row.

Warkentin, Marjorie
   1982   **Ordination--A Biblical Historical View.**

Willard, Dallas
   1989   **The Spirit of the Disciplines.** San Francisco: Harper and Row.

Wrong, Dennis
   1980   **Power--Its Forms, Bases, and Uses.** New Yourk: Harper and Row.